EVALUATION FOR CHILD CUSTODY

BEST PRACTICES IN FORENSIC MENTAL HEALTH ASSESSMENT

Series Editors

Thomas Grisso, Alan M. Goldstein, and Kirk Heilbrun

Series Advisory Board

Paul Appelbaum, Richard Bonnie, and John Monahan

Titles in the Series

Foundations of Forensic Mental Health Assessment, *Kirk Heilbrun, Thomas Grisso, and Alan M. Goldstein*

Criminal Titles

Evaluation of Competence to Stand Trial, *Patricia A. Zapf and Ronald Roesch*

Evaluation of Criminal Responsibility, *Ira K. Packer*

Evaluating Capacity to Waive Miranda Rights, *Alan M. Goldstein and Naomi E. Sevin Goldstein*

Evaluation of Sexually Violent Predators, *Philip H. Witt and Mary Alice Conroy*

Evaluation for Risk of Violence in Adults, *Kirk Heilbrun*

Jury Selection, *Margaret Bull Kovera and Brian L. Cutler*

Evaluation for Capital Sentencing, *Mark D. Cunningham*

Evaluating Eyewitness Identification, *Brian L. Cutler and Margaret Bull Kovera*

Civil Titles

Evaluation of Capacity to Consent to Treatment and Research, *Scott Y. H. Kim*

Evaluation for Guardianship, *Eric Y. Drogin and Curtis L. Barrett*

Evaluation for Personal Injury Claims, *Andrew W. Kane and Joel A. Dvoskin*

Evaluation for Civil Commitment, *Debra Pinals and Douglas Mossman*

Evaluation for Workplace Discrimination and Harassment, *Jane Goodman-Delahunty and William E. Foote*

Evaluation of Workplace Disability, *Lisa Drago Piechowski*

Juvenile and Family Titles

Evaluation for Child Custody, *Geri S. W. Fuhrmann and Robert A. Zibbell*

Evaluation of Juveniles' Competence to Stand Trial, *Ivan Kruh and Thomas Grisso*

Evaluation for Risk of Violence in Juveniles, *Robert D. Hoge and D. A. Andrews*

Evaluation of Parenting Capacity in Child Protection, *Karen S. Budd, Mary Connell, and Jennifer R. Clark*

Evaluation for Disposition and Transfer of Juvenile Offenders, *Randall T. Salekin*

EVALUATION FOR CHILD CUSTODY

GERI S. W. FUHRMANN

ROBERT A. ZIBBELL

OXFORD
UNIVERSITY PRESS

OXFORD
UNIVERSITY PRESS

Oxford University Press, Inc., publishes works that further
Oxford University's objective of excellence
in research, scholarship, and education.

Oxford New York

Auckland   Cape Town   Dar es Salaam   Hong Kong   Karachi
Kuala Lumpur   Madrid   Melbourne   Mexico City   Nairobi
New Delhi   Shanghai   Taipei   Toronto

With offices in
Argentina   Austria   Brazil   Chile   Czech Republic   France   Greece
Guatemala   Hungary   Italy   Japan   Poland   Portugal   Singapore
South Korea   Switzerland   Thailand   Turkey   Ukraine   Vietnam

Copyright © 2012 by Oxford University Press, Inc.

Published by Oxford University Press, Inc.
198 Madison Avenue, New York, New York 10016
www.oup.com

Oxford is a registered trademark of Oxford University Press

CIP on file with Library of Congress

ISBN: 978-0-19-532951-3

9 8 7 6 5 4 3 2 1

Printed in the United States of America
on acid-free paper

We would like to thank Chris and Ina for their unwavering love, patience, and support during the writing of this book.

G.F. and R.A.Z.

About Best Practices in Forensic Mental Health Assessment

The recent growth of the fields of forensic psychology and forensic psychiatry has created a need for this book series describing best practices in forensic mental health assessment (FMHA). Currently, forensic evaluations are conducted by mental health professionals for a variety of criminal, civil, and juvenile legal questions. The research foundation supporting these assessments has become broader and deeper in recent decades. Consensus has become clearer on the recognition of essential requirements for ethical and professional conduct. In the larger context of the current emphasis on "empirically supported" assessment and intervention in psychiatry and psychology, the specialization of FMHA has advanced sufficiently to justify a series devoted to best practices. Although this series focuses mainly on evaluations conducted by psychologists and psychiatrists, the fundamentals and principles offered also apply to evaluations conducted by clinical social workers, psychiatric nurses, and other mental health professionals.

This series describes "best practice" as empirically supported (when the relevant research is available), legally relevant, and consistent with applicable ethical and professional standards. Authors of the books in this series identify the approaches that seem best, while incorporating what is practical and acknowledging that best practice represents a goal to which the forensic clinician should aspire, rather than a standard that can always be met. The American Academy of Forensic Psychology assisted the editors in enlisting the consultation of board-certified forensic psychologists specialized in each topic area. Board-certified forensic psychiatrists were also consultants on many of the volumes. Their comments on the manuscripts helped to ensure that the methods described in these volumes represent a generally accepted view of best practice.

The series' authors were selected for their specific expertise in a particular area. At the broadest level, however, certain general principles apply to all types of forensic evaluations. Rather than repeat those fundamental principles in every volume, the series offers them in the first volume, *Foundations of Forensic Mental Health Assessment*. Reading the first book, followed by a specific topical book will provide the reader with both the general principles that the specific topic shares with all forensic evaluations and those that are particular to the specific assessment question.

The specific topics of the 19 books were selected by the series editors as the most important and oft-considered areas of forensic assessment conducted by mental health professionals and behavioral scientists. Each of the 19 topical books is organized according to a common template. The authors address the applicable legal context, forensic mental health concepts, and empirical foundations and limits in the "Foundation" part of the book. They then describe preparation for the evaluation, data collection, data interpretation, and report writing and testimony in the "Application" part of the book. This creates a fairly uniform approach to considering these areas across different topics. All authors in this series have attempted to be as concise as possible in addressing best practice in their area. In addition, topical volumes feature elements to make them user friendly in actual practice. These elements include boxes that highlight especially important information, relevant case law, best-practice guidelines, and cautions against common pitfalls. A glossary of key terms is also provided in each volume.

We hope the series will be useful for different groups of individuals. Practicing forensic clinicians will find succinct, current information relevant to their practice. Those who are in training to specialize in FMHA (whether in formal training or in the process of respecialization) should find helpful the combination of broadly applicable considerations presented in the first volume in combination with the more specific aspects of other volumes in the series. Those who teach and supervise trainees can offer these volumes as a guide for practices to which the trainee can aspire. Researchers and scholars interested in FMHA best practice may find researchable ideas, particularly on topics that have received insufficient research attention to date. Judges and attorneys with questions about FMHA best practice will find these books relevant and concise. Clinical and forensic administrators who run agencies, court clinics, and hospitals in which litigants are assessed may also use some of the books in this series to establish expectancies for evaluations performed by professionals in their agencies.

We also anticipate that the 19 specific books in this series will serve as reference works that help courts and attorneys evaluate the quality of forensic mental health professionals' evaluations. A word of caution is in order, however. These volumes focus on best practice, not on what is minimally acceptable legally or ethically. Courts involved in malpractice litigation, or ethics committees or licensure boards considering complaints, should not expect that materials describing best practice easily or necessarily translate into the minimally acceptable professional conduct that is typically at issue in such proceedings.

The present volume, *Evaluation for Child Custody*, is one of the most complex areas of FMHA. Child custody cases often arise when divorcing parents have reached an impasse when trying to resolve their differences regarding the custody of their children. The law's efforts to reach a conclusion that is in the best interests of the children creates an extraordinary burden on the clinician who is asked to assist the court in that determination. The search for relevant data requires a study of the personalities and behaviors of the parents, as well as the needs of the children, and requires the development of a dynamic picture of the family. All of this is used to infer likely outcomes for the children under various future hypothetical custody arrangements. Often none of those potential arrangements offers all of the circumstances that one would want ideally for the children's welfare. Moreover, the clinician's analysis often reveals that one arrangement is likely to be "better" for the children than another in some ways but not as good in others.

Meeting these challenges requires specialized knowledge. The courts that hear child custody cases, whether family courts or other types of civil courts, have their own set of laws and procedures that differ from courts in other areas of law. Evaluating parents and children in custody cases requires expertise in adult personality and psychopathology, in child development and child psychopathology, and in family dynamics. Specialized tools have been developed for use in child custody cases, some with promise and many with serious limitations. This volume, written by two child custody examiners with years of experience and an exceptional depth of understanding of the area, provides the foundation that any mental health professional needs when pursuing specialization in the evaluation of parents and children in child custody cases.

Thomas Grisso
Kirk Heilbrun
Alan M. Goldstein

Acknowledgments

This book represents current thinking about child custody evaluations
and the issues related to them. It is an effort to synthesize the
highest quality of work in the field and articulate best practices
based upon professional guidelines, law, and research. Historically,
child custody has had minimal overlap with other forensic
subspecialty areas. As part of a 20 volume series on best practices in
forensic mental health, child custody practice firmly aligns itself with,
is informed by, and informs other areas of forensic practice.

We would like to thank many colleagues and others whose
willingness to read and comment on sections of the book enriched it.
They include Stan Brodsky, Robin Deutsch, Dana Fuhrmann, Hon.
Arline Rotman (ret.), Richard Wolman, and Amanda Zelechoski. We
offer special thanks to James Bow for his willingness to review the
manuscript in its entirety and for his ideas and clarifying comments.
We are grateful to the series editors—Kirk Heilbrun, Thomas Grisso,
and Alan Goldstein—for creating this "Best Practice" series and for
giving us the opportunity to contribute to it. In particular, we are
grateful for the diligence and insights of our primary editor, Tom
Grisso, without whom this book could not have been written.

Geri S. W. Fuhrmann would like to express her gratitude to and
admiration for the faculty and staff of the Child and Family Forensic
Center at University of Massachusetts Medical School, particularly
Linda Cavallero, Jessica Griffin, and Joseph McGill. The lessons
I have learned from years of discussion, teaching, and evaluating
families together permeate this book. It has been a privilege to work
with colleagues who are passionate about the work and hold to the
highest standard. I would also like to thank Mary O'Connell for
convincing me that I should and could accept this challenge. My
sincerest thanks go to Bob Zibbell for saying yes when asked to write
this book with me. His erudition is evident throughout the work, and
I am indebted to him as a colleague and a friend.

Robert A. Zibbell would like to thank his colleagues in mental
health and law who have taught him that it is as important to *think*
about good practice, as it is to practice well. In particular, over the
years, the legal and mental health professionals at the Child and
Family Forensic Center at the University of Massachusetts Medical
School in Worcester, MA, have been instrumental in promoting this
value. In addition, I would like to thank Geri Fuhrmann, my co-author,
for giving me the opportunity to make such a contribution to this
area of forensic mental health and for helping me to push my limits
of thinking and writing.

Contents

FOUNDATION

Chapter 1   The Legal Context   3

Chapter 2   Forensic Mental Health Concepts   31

Chapter 3   Empirical Foundations and Limits   59

APPLICATION

Chapter 4   Preparation for the Evaluation   111

Chapter 5   Data Collection   129

Chapter 6   Interpretation   163

Chapter 7   Report Writing and Testimony   175

Appendices   209

References   233

Tests and Specialized Tools   259

Case Law and Statutes   262

Key Terms   263

Index   269

About the Authors   277

FOUNDATION

The Legal Context 1

Child custody evaluations are frequently described as the most difficult, complex, and challenging type of forensic assessment (e.g., Otto, Buffington-Vollum, & Edens, 2003). Whether or not this is actually so, there is no doubt that conducting child custody evaluations offers extraordinary challenges. Examining the unique aspects of each family's life is difficult enough; but child custody examiners also face the limitations of *empirical* studies to inform their work, ill-defined legal *standards* to define their work, and the increased risk of ethical complaints to add to the anxiety about doing the work.

We begin this chapter by examining how child custody determinations historically have reflected the social customs of their time and culture. Given the fluid state of family structure in America, laws relating to child custody continue to change, altering the focus of subsequent forensic assessments across time. A brief historical overview of the social and legal underpinnings of child custody law provides perspective for current evaluators. We follow this with an examination of the legal standards that currently guide child custody evaluations, as well as the legal process in which examiners participate when they perform child custody evaluations.

Sociolegal Purpose and History

Colonial America (17th–18th Centuries): Paternal Dominance

Imagine that in 1670, 10-year-old Thomas lives with his parents, Thaddeus and Elizabeth, in Hull in the Massachusetts Bay Colony. After learning of Elizabeth's infidelity, Thaddeus seeks a divorce which the Colonial Court grants, based on English Common Law. The divorce petition omits any mention of the child, as the assumption is that custody remains with the father. Let us further imagine that Thaddeus dies of pneumonia and the court has to determine who will have custody of Thomas. Because Thaddeus neglected to designate a guardian in his will, the court appoints a male guardian who assumes legal authority for the care of Thomas. The male guardian determines that Thomas will continue to live with his mother under the guardian's watchful eye until he turns 12, at which time he will be apprenticed to Joseph, a local blacksmith, with whom he will reside until he reaches adulthood.

In colonial America, this vignette would have been unusual from the start, because divorce rarely occurred. For example, in Massachusetts, a state with one of the highest colonial divorce rates, fewer than 150 divorce petitions were filed (much less granted) in the 17th and 18th centuries (Mason, 1994). But regardless of the parents' reasons for no longer living together, custody disputes between mothers and fathers were nonexistent, because colonial mothers had no legal rights to their children. Child custody disputes, when they occurred, were primarily between fathers and masters to whom children were apprenticed. Children were important economic assets for families, and fathers had absolute authority over the custody and care of their children (Mason, 1994).

INFO

In colonial America, fathers had absolute authority over their children. Custodial disputes were primarily between fathers and masters, rather than between fathers and mothers. Mothers had no legal rights to their own children.

This paternal dominance over children gave rise to the notion that children were property or chattel (Marafiote, 1985; Melton, Petrila, Poythress, & Slobogin, 2007). Unlike with other property (such as slaves), colonial fathers were legally required to provide their children with education, religion, and vocational training (Mason, 1994; Grossberg, 1985). The child's labor and monetary earnings were, in turn, viewed as compensation for such provisions. Fathers typically took this responsibility seriously, because their children's failure to learn to read and write, attend church, and develop vocational skills could result in fines, imprisonment, loss of custody, or loss of labor. In a predominantly agrarian society, fathers generally worked at or close to home and were central to child rearing. Paternal power over and responsibility for children were unquestioned. In contrast, women in colonial America had no claim to children either during marriage or after divorce. With few legal rights, women also had few obligations, and their husbands were held accountable if their children failed to be contributing members of their communities. Consideration of children's custody had little significance in divorce determinations until the 19th century.

The 19th Century: Emergence of Tender Years Doctrine

In 1845, 6-year-old Mary lived with her parents, Joseph and Katherine, in Ithaca, New York. Katherine filed for a divorce on the grounds of adultery after learning of Joseph's affair. The court awarded custody of Mary to her father, citing as paramount his rights and position as head of the household.

The same year, Frances Marks of Pennsylvania filed for divorce and custody of 6-year-old Ellsbeth after discovering that her husband, Frederick, was unfaithful. The court awarded custody to the mother, citing Ellsbeth's gender, the mother's natural attachment to her child, and the child's welfare.

These fictitious cases with similar fact patterns and markedly different outcomes and rationales illustrate the inconsistent and changing nature of 19th-century custody determinations in America. Divorce rates multiplied, nearly tripling from the mid- to latter part of the century, which is not surprising considering all states permitted divorce by this time (Mason, 1994). *Judicial discretion*, rather than statutory or *case law*, was paramount in deciding family law cases. Citing an 1843 case, Mason (1994) writes, "The tradition of judicial discretion became so firmly imbedded that many judges often gave no more than lip service to precedent, or even to legislation in their own state, but instead sought to probe tangled fact situations to discover the best interests of an individual child. Practical rather than legally correct results (i.e., father custody) were often the consequence" (pp. 59–60). Judge Robert Grant humorously captured the enormity of judicial power and the primacy of judicial discretion in family law cases in 1903 when he wrote the following:

> Concerning other things,
>
> His power outrivals that of kings,
>
> Your children, when you prove unfit,
>
> Are whisked away by sovereign writ.
>
> In short, it may truly be said,
>
> He has you living, he has you dead.
>
> The moral is, as on you trudge
>
> Propitiate the Probate Judge. (Grossberg, 1985, p. 285)

Emerging concerns for child welfare and the notion of maternal superiority in parenting conflicted with the traditional paternal-rights focus of colonial times and gave rise to an interesting dichotomy in 19th-century America. While a couple was married, paternal authority and rights were paramount and sacrosanct. When a family dissolved, however, postcolonial thinking about innate maternal abilities and child welfare increasingly influenced decision making about child custody. Judges began employing and expanding on the old English doctrine of *parens patriae*, which held that the state was responsible for taking care of its citizens, so that gradually they began to justify decisions that prioritized children's interests over paternal supremacy. Early in the century, a South Carolina case, *Prather v. Prather* (1809), became the first published case in which a court overrode paternal rights and awarded custody of a young child to her mother (Grossberg, 1985; Kohm, 2008; Mason, 1994). The facts in that case were particularly compelling in that the mother was described as "a prudent, discreet and virtuous woman," and the father, after forcing his wife from the marital home, was having an adulterous relationship. Recognizing that it was "treading on new and dangerous grounds" by not upholding the rights of fathers to custody of their children, the Prather Court gave custody of the youngest daughter to her mother. Custody of the older children, however, was granted to the father reflecting the standing laws supporting male authority.

The evolving view of women as innately more nurturing than and morally superior to men led to widespread acceptance of a maternal custody preference during children's "tender years," defined sometimes as below age 7 and sometimes as before puberty (Grossberg, 1985). Fathers were still typically awarded custody if women had violated the standards of moral behavior. However, in *Commonwealth v. Addicks* (1815), Pennsylvania Chief Justice William Tilghman justified his decision to grant an adulterous mother custody of her two young daughters by stating, "[O]ur anxiety is principally directed to the children. It appears to us, that considering their tender years, they stand in need of the kind of assistance which can be afforded by none so well as a mother." It was unusual for mothers to gain custody when their behavior was considered immoral. Three years later, as the girls neared puberty, the father prevailed when the court changed custody, noting that the children's needs had changed with maturity. The court reasoned that the mother's immoral behavior coupled with the children's diminishing need for maternal care suggested that the father was now the better custodial parent (Grossberg, 1985; Kohm, 2008). Of note, the Addicks Court did not base the change in custody on paternal right, but rather on the "girls' welfare" and, in particular, on the importance of teaching children the sanctity of vows (Kohm, 2008). Although *Prather v. Prather* heralded an upcoming change in societal attitude, *Addicks* is the first known case to use "best interest of the child" as the legal standard on which to base a child custody determination (Kohm, 2008).

CASE LAW

Prather v. Prather
(1809)

- First published case in which a court denied the custodial rights of the father and legally recognized the ability of the mother to nurture the child.

- The young girl's mother was awarded custody.

CASE LAW

Commonwealth v.
Addicks
(1815)

First known case to use
"best interest of the child" as
the legal standard on which
to base a child custody
determination.

In 1840, in *Mercein v. People,* a New York court highlighted the conflict between paternal authority and the emerging "*tender years doctrine.*" In that case, the trial court's award of custody to the mother was based on "maternal law" and the idea that the infant was "of tender age . . . peculiarly requiring a mother's care and attention" (Kohm, 2008; *Mercein v. People,* 1840). In 1842, however, the New York Supreme Court reversed the ruling and returned the child to her father, citing the common law rights of men (*People v. Mercein,* 1842).

By the latter part of the 19th century there had been a clear shift in American jurisprudence toward a focus on children's needs as a prominent, if not dominant, factor in custody disputes (Kohm, 2008). Children's best interests were increasingly viewed as being consistent with maternal preference, which, when coupled with the tender years doctrine, dominated thinking in child custody determinations (Melton et al., 2007). By the early part of the 20th century, maternal preference had taken a firm hold. Even immoral behavior on a woman's part, as judged by the prevailing conservative Christian society, did not necessarily mean that she would lose custody of her children.

The 20th Century: From Maternal Preference to Best Interests of the Child

Imagine that in 1910, in Topeka, Kansas, Mr. Harper sued for divorce on grounds of adultery and sought custody of his 10- and 12-year-old children. After chiding Mrs. Harper for her immoral and wrongful behavior, the court granted a divorce and awarded custody of the children to their mother, despite the mother's "immoral" behavior.

During the Progressive Era in America (i.e., 1890–1920), the double standard for sexual behavior diminished and was largely overridden by the tender years doctrine. Generally, in divorces, mothers were the preferred custodians of young children, especially female children. Although women's supposedly immoral behavior could be a factor, it no longer determined custody outcomes (Mason, 1994). Because judicial discretion continued to be significant in family law cases, it was possible that a particular judge could weigh the facts differently when determining an outcome, but, on most occasions, mothers retained custody. An increasing focus on the welfare of children dominated the nation as the 20th century progressed. This development was reflected in the establishment of the first juvenile court in Chicago in 1899 and the rise in social work and philanthropic agencies to help mistreated and poor children (Mason, 1994). By the end of the Progressive Era, women, unless deemed unfit, customarily retained custody of their children following divorce, regardless of the ages of the children. This change was based on the widely held belief that it was in children's best interests to be in their mothers' custody.

CHILD SUPPORT

Child support, however, was another matter. Under the older common law, a father was legally entitled to his children's earnings and custody. In return, he was obligated to support his children. In the early 20th century, however, when fathers frequently lost custody of their children, a debate arose regarding whether the noncustodial parent, typically the father, should be liable for the children's support and education. Poverty was no longer seen as a reason for the removal of children from families; biological mothers were viewed as children's optimal caretakers, even if they were poor. Accordingly, the state provided funds to impoverished mothers to support their children, and the legislature passed laws compelling child support payments from noncustodial fathers (Mason, 1994). The concept that parents were entitled to financial aid generalized to the divorce arena and the notion that noncustodial parents remained obligated to support their children, even if they were denied custodial rights, took hold. Noncustodial parents' financial obligation for their children, an issue raised over 100 years ago, continues to be a contentious issue in child custody today.

INFO

In the early 20th century, the idea developed that noncustodial parents were obligated to support their children, even if they were denied custody.

DECLINE OF MATERNAL PREFERENCE

The belief that maternal custody was synonymous with children's best interest remained paramount for several more decades. Then, during the social upheaval of the 1960s and 1970s, the idea that nature innately endowed women with parental superiority was increasingly challenged. At the same time, the divorce rate rose dramatically, further destabilizing decision making by parents and courts. Finally, in 1973, in *Watts v. Watts* (1973), a New York court strongly expressed a belief that was brewing in American homes and courts: "The simple fact of being a mother does not, by itself, indicate a capacity or willingness to render a quality of care different from that which the father can provide."

Numerous advocacy groups supported this revocation of gender bias in legal decision making. Feminist groups attacked the inherent sexism of a belief that tied women to home and children, fathers increasingly sought more time with their children, and social scientists entered the fray with new resources about fatherhood (e.g., Lamb, 1976). In popular culture, the movie *Kramer v. Kramer* (1979) heralded the notion that a father is competent to parent on his own, while *Mrs. Doubtfire* (1993) demonstrated the hurdles fathers face in taking care of their children. Most state legislatures and courts did not adopt the strong language of the *Watts* decision, but that ruling nonetheless heralded the defeat of the maternal preference that had so strongly dominated family law. Accordingly, the tender years doctrine, closely tied to maternal preference, fell out of favor. By 1990, most states had

CASE LAW

Watts v. Watts
(1973)

● Expressed the idea that women were not superior parents just because they were women.

● This de-emphasis of gender bias in legal decision making was supported by many social groups, including feminists, fathers, and social scientists.

legally abolished the tender years doctrine as a basis for determining child custody (Mason, 1994). Without the tender years doctrine, the judiciary had little to guide decision making beyond the vaguely defined "Best Interests" Standard (see discussion below).

MODERN DIVORCE

Imagine that in 1999, Geoffrey Miller, a dentist in private practice, and Beth Miller, a software engineer working for a large company in Aurora, Colorado, file for divorce on the basis that the marriage is irretrievably broken. There are no *allegations* of domestic violence, child maltreatment, parental psychiatric illness, or substance abuse. Their marriage, which has been distant but not conflictual, dissolves when Dr. Miller tells his wife that he is in love with another woman. On the advice of their attorneys, the Millers meet with a mediator/psychologist to help them resolve the custodial issues related to their children, Jessica (age 16), Nicole (age 13), and Andrew (age 7). The Millers agree that Ms. Miller will remain in the marital home and retain *physical custody* of the children, although the parties will share *legal custody*. In a detailed six-page *parenting plan*, they specify days/vacations/holidays that the children will spend with each parent, and they stipulate financial responsibility for post–high school education. Dr. Miller agrees to pay child support in accordance with Colorado child support *guidelines*. The Millers also agree to utilize mediation for future contested parenting decisions. The judge accepts the Millers' *stipulation*, as their decision reflects current thinking about the *"Best Interests of the Child" Standard*.

This hypothetical scenario reflects common aspects of modern divorce, for example, divorcing couples arriving at stipulated agreements. The Millers have self-selected the most frequently chosen

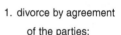

INFO

Common aspects of modern divorces include the following:

1. divorce by agreement of the parties;
2. shared decision making (legal custody);
3. the mother as the primary residential parent (physical custody);
4. a parenting plan with defined parenting time for the nonresidential parent (visitation); and
5. defined child support following state guidelines.

postdivorce custody arrangement. Although judges cannot consider gender in deciding custody, when parents decide on their own, mothers most often remain the parent with primary caretaking responsibility (Maccoby & Mnookin, 1992).

Had the Millers disagreed and both insisted on being the residential parent due to each one's perceived parenting superiority or the other parent's significant deficits, the Millers' divorce process could have been very different. For example, Dr. Miller might have alleged that Ms. Miller suffered from severe depression, and 16-year-old Jessica may have been so angry at her mother that it was in her best interests to live with him. Ms. Miller might have contended that she had always been the primary caretaker, that Dr. Miller was hardly home, and that his bid for physical custody was another example of his insensitivity to the children's needs and reflective of his poor parental judgment. Let us suppose in that case that the parents and their lawyers agree that a child custody evaluation would be helpful and further agree to the court appointment of Nathan Jones, PhD, a forensic psychologist. They stipulate that Dr. Jones's fee will be paid out of marital assets. Dr. Jones, following best practice standards, conducts a forensic evaluation guided by the questions of the court, Colorado law regarding the best interests of the child, and professional guidelines, and then he submits his report to the court. Dr. Jones is prepared to testify if the case goes to trial and if he is subpoenaed, but his role with the family ends when he submits his report. The Millers and their attorneys, informed by reading Dr. Jones's careful evaluation, have a four-way meeting and decide to settle their differences about the parenting plan without going to trial, a common occurrence. Had they gone to trial, the judge could not have considered gender or a parent's behavior that did not affect parenting; rather, the judge would have based any decision on the best interests of the children.

This abbreviated socio-legal history highlights several emerging themes that underlie custody decisions:

- Children were considered an economic asset.
  In colonial times, no thought was given to
  children's experience or needs; instead,
  their potential contribution to the labor force

was paramount. The law upheld men's absolute right to economic assets.

- As the United States became less agrarian and the pressing need for children to work diminished, so did their financial value. This change likely allowed the consideration of children's best interests to slowly emerge in custody decisions.

- In postrevolutionary America and through the 1800s, the *parens patriae* responsibility of the courts, child welfare concerns, and beliefs about mothers' innate parenting abilities took center stage as fathers' rights gave way to maternal preference in custody decisions, particularly with respect to young children.

- By 1900, over 55,000 divorce judgments were being made annually (Grossberg, 1985) by judges whose decisions were guided by their judicial discretion and personal beliefs about what was in the best interests of children.

- By the early part of the 20th century, the tender years doctrine was widely accepted, and mothers, unless clearly unfit, retained custody of children after divorce. Legislative mandates for paternal custody were removed, and societal condemnation of sexual misconduct by women diminished, thus removing additional previous barriers to maternal custody.

- The notion of child welfare, with its strong focus on children's needs, and the recognition that poverty did not preclude capable parenting paved the way for child support orders and enforcement.

- Until the 1960s, American society and its legal system did not question the belief that, in the event of a divorce, a mother was the superior parent to care for a child. But, like many of the conservative social standards of the post-WWII generation, the child custody assumptions were eventually challenged and overthrown by the revolutionary mindset of that decade.

- In the latter part of the 20th century, divorce laws and presumptions had changed dramatically, concurrent with women choosing to work over staying home, the fight for the Equal Rights Amendment, no-fault divorce, the rise in numbers of unwed parents, increasing numbers of nontraditional families, the rapid rise in divorce rates, and constitutional concerns over gender equality (Kohm, 2008).

- With the tender years doctrine and maternal preference overturned, the Best Interests of the Child became the standard to inform judicial decision making.

The Legal Standard: Best Interests of the Child

Much has been written on the variability and *indeterminacy* of the Best Interests of the Child (hereinafter the BIC) Standard and the resultant lack of guidance it provides for decision making in child custody determinations (Gould & Martindale, 2007; Melton et al., 2007; Mnookin, 1975; Rohman, Sales, & Lou, 1987; Schepard, 2004). The notion of basing custody decisions on what is best for children, as opposed to parental rights or *attributes*, appears consistent with current child-focused societal values, but specific guidance about how to apply this standard in individual cases has been elusive. Critics of the BIC Standard emphasize its vagueness, which can result in increased litigation and heavy reliance on judicial discretion. Judicial discretion remains substantial in family law cases, and it has been argued that relying on this discretion results in decisions that are too individualistic and dependent on the particular judge (Kohm, 2008). Whether broad judicial discretion is beneficial or detrimental is left to scholarly debate; it does, however, make the outcome of child custody cases difficult to predict, which sometimes inadvertently increases parental conflict and adversarial tactics.

To define more specifically the BIC Standard, many states have adopted the language of the Uniform Marriage and Divorce Act (UMDA; 1970):

The court shall determine custody in accordance with the best interest of the child. The court shall consider all relevant factors including:

1. The wishes of the child's parent or parents as to his custody;

2. The wishes of the child as to his custodian;

3. The interaction and interrelationship of the child with his parent or parents, his siblings, and any other person who may significantly affect the child's best interest;

4. The child's adjustment to his home, school, and community; and

5. The mental and physical health of all individuals involved.

The court shall not consider conduct of a proposed custodian that does not affect his relationship to the child.

Notably, the UMDA specifies that the court shall consider "all relevant factors," which underscores the indeterminacy of the standard and the importance of judicial discretion in making child custody determinations. In addition, critics of the BIC Standard frequently highlight the fact that neither *statutes* nor case law assign relative weights to these factors. Consequently, the decision about which factors should carry more weight in the decision-making process is again left to judicial discretion.

Some states have codified the BIC Standard, either by adopting the UMDA language or by crafting their own statutory language, thereby expanding or clarifying the criteria on which judges should base a best interests decision. Because of the well-recognized ambiguities inherent in the BIC Standard, many states have attempted to further define its components (see Appendix A for a listing of factors in the 50 states). One of the most well-known and often cited examples is Michigan's statute

(Michigan's Child Custody Act of 1970, M.C.L.A. §722.23, amended 1980, 1993), which states the following:

722.23 "Best interests of the child" defined.
Sec. 3.

As used in this act, "best interests of the child" means the sum total of the following factors to be considered, evaluated, and determined by the court:

(a) The love, affection, and other emotional ties existing between the parties involved and the child.

(b) The capacity and disposition of the parties involved to give the child love, affection, and guidance and to continue the education and raising of the child in his or her religion or creed, if any.

(c) The capacity and disposition of the parties involved to provide the child with food, clothing, medical care or other remedial care recognized and permitted under the laws of this state in place of medical care, and other material needs.

(d) The length of time the child has lived in a stable, satisfactory environment, and the desirability of maintaining continuity.

(e) The permanence, as a family unit, of the existing or proposed custodial home or homes.

(f) The moral fitness of the parties involved.

(g) The mental and physical health of the parties involved.

(h) The home, school, and community record of the child.

(i) The reasonable preference of the child, if the court considers the child to be of sufficient age to express preference.

(j) The willingness and ability of each of the parties to facilitate and encourage a close and continuing parent–child relationship between the child and the other parent or the child and the parents.

(k) Domestic violence, regardless of whether the violence was directed against or witnessed by the child.

(l) Any other factor considered by the court to be relevant to a particular child custody dispute.

1
chapter

What emerged in the late 1970s and 1980s were two seemingly opposite approaches to child custody determinations. One approach was the preference for joint custody and a shared parenting schedule, based on the belief that children benefit from maximizing time with each parent. The other approach favored the primary caretaker as the custodial parent for minor children and argued that *sole physical custody* was in children's best interests (Cochran, 1991). (See Table 1.1)

The rationales underlying the primary-caretaker-versus-joint-custody approaches to child custody determinations were contradictory. Joint custody proponents argued that the best interests of children were served by their having substantial contact with both parents, and that parenting roles were not gender based and were interchangeable (Elkin, 1991; Mason, 1994). Conversely, advocates of a primary parent cited literature touting the importance of stability, consistency, and predictability in a child's life, noting that one residence with a primary parent provides an established home base (e.g., Goldstein, Freud, & Solnit, 1973;).

In 1980, California's public policy decision to support a preference for joint custody influenced other jurisdictions to do the same (Mason, 1994; McIsaac, 1991). "The legislature finds and declares that it is the public policy of this state to assure minor children frequent and continuing contact with both parents...and to encourage parents to share the rights and responsibilities of child rearing in order to effect this policy" (Cal. Civil Code §4600 [Deering, 2010]). Currently, 42 states and the District of Columbia (D.C.) have approved joint parenting provisions, either through legislation (39 states and D.C.) or case law (3 states) (American Bar

INFO

Joint *legal* custody, rather than joint *physical* custody, is the rule in most states today.

Table 1.1 | Types of Custody

Legal Custody: The right and responsibility to make decisions relating to the health, education, and welfare of the child

A. Joint legal custody: Both parents have equal rights to make major decisions about their child

B. Sole legal custody: Only one parent has the right to make major decisions about the child

Physical Custody: The right and obligation of a parent to live with a child

A. Joint physical custody: The child spends a significant amount of time with both parents

B. Sole physical custody: The child lives primarily with one parent and may have parenting time with the other

N.B. One should be aware that courts are increasingly adopting more sensitive language to describe parenting arrangements that reflect a continuum of possibilities and to move away from the connotation of "winners" and "losers." Some judiciaries and many child custody evaluators refer to "residential parents," "parenting time," and "parenting schedules" rather than the more demeaning "custody and visitation."

Association, 2010). These legal arrangements typically presume joint custody is in the child's best interest when the parents agree to it.

While many states were adopting the joint custody (legal custody) preference, which purportedly follows the BIC Standard, some states (e.g., Minnesota, 1985; West Virginia, 1981, later repealed) adopted the *primary caretaker presumption*, interpreting it as being in a child's best interests when parents cannot agree to a custody arrangement (Mason, 1994). The primary caretaker presumption awards physical custody to the adult who has done the majority of the physical caretaking and parenting of the children. This has led to the use of questionnaires or surveys to quantify the amount of caretaking each parent has provided before the separation in order to help determine which parent is the primary caretaker. Although some tout this as a gender-neutral approach, others criticize this presumption for its inherent maternal bias.

As noted, the BIC Standard has been widely criticized, particularly for its lack of guidance for judges in making child custody determinations. In response to these criticisms, the American Law Institute (ALI) adopted the *approximation rule* to give judges more specific guidance (ALI, 2000). Essentially, the approximation rule recommends that the proportion of caretaking time postdivorce should be about the same as the proportion of caretaking for which each parent was responsible during the relationship (Clark & Estin, 2005; Kohm, 2008; Melton et al., 2007). Proponents of this rule argue (a) that reliance on past parenting choices is more dependable than attempts to predict future parenting and (b) that the rule is consistent with social science and *attachment theory* research. Furthermore, a quantifiable rule would help to lessen the substantial variability in decision making due to judicial discretion and an unclear BIC Standard. Although this rule has not yet been empirically tested, proponents hope that a clearer standard will simplify the child custody decision-making process and, thereby, decrease postseparation parental conflict and destructive, prolonged litigation (Emery, 2007; Kelly & Ward, 2002; O'Connell, 2009; Riggs, 2005).

Critics of ALI's approximation rule argue that it is an over-simplification to equate the quantity of parenting with either the quality of parenting or the strength of children's attachments and is, therefore, not in accordance with attachment theory. Additional criticisms highlight the static nature of the approximation rule in that the rule ignores the fact that families (and parenting roles) can, do, and should change during and after divorce. Some think that litigious parents will simply focus their dispute on the calculation of the proportion of former parenting (Warshak, 2007), as often happens when there is disagreement about who was the primary parent. A number of critics have expressed concern that the approximation rule is a return to gender bias, specifically

INFO

The ALI's "approximation rule" recommends that the proportion of caretaking time following a divorce should be about the same as it was for each parent during the marriage. Critics argue that quantity does not equal quality, parenting roles change over time, and the approximation rule could lead to gender bias.

maternal preference, because mothers more frequently provide the majority of parenting during the marriage (e.g. Riggs, 2005; Warshak, 2007). Scholarly debate forges on with respect to the merits of the approximation rule as a replacement for or a defining criterion of the BIC Standard. As of 2009, only West Virginia had adopted the approximation rule to guide disputed child custody decisions (WV Code §48-9-206).

The Legal Process in Child Custody Cases

Governed by state law, divorce and custody proceedings vary from state to state. Thus the following description of the legal process of child custody cases is general and should not be presumed to describe the legal process in any particular state. We conclude this section with a description of the role of mental health professionals in child custody proceedings, as well as the evolution of this forensic evaluation specialty.

The legal process begins when a divorce complaint or petition is filed with the court. Unless the parties file a joint petition, the one who files must notify the other party of the action. This typically occurs when either the other party voluntarily signs for the papers or the papers are served by a constable, sheriff, or other legally authorized person. After receiving the papers, that party must file a response in the court within a given number of days.

If the parties cannot agree to an interim arrangement regarding parenting time and child support, they can file a motion with the court for temporary orders. Many courts have professional staff to assist litigants in structuring their temporary arrangements. Some courts have mandatory mediation, requiring parties to attempt mediation prior to any court appearance. If the parties cannot reach an agreement, they would then appear before a judge.

At each step in the legal process, the court encourages parents to resolve their differences and come to an agreement. To this end, various types of resources are available for parents to educate themselves regarding their options. For example, parent education classes for separated families are available in all states, and in some *jurisdictions* they are required. Model parenting plans have been

Table 1.2 | Examples of Model Parenting Plans

Massachusetts, available at
http://www.mass.gov/courts/courtsandjudges/courts/probateandfamilycourt/
parentingplan.pdf
Oregon, available at
http://courts.oregon.gov/OJD/OSCA/cpsd/courtimprovement/familylaw/
parentingplan.page?
Arizona, available at
azcourts.gov/Portals/31/ParentingTime/PPWguidelines.pdf

developed as guidelines for creating parenting schedules, such as the examples in Table 1.2.

Mediation, which is geared toward empowering parents to make decisions outside of court, has increased in popularity. Collaborative law, in which each party and that party's attorney are committed to settling the case through legal advice and advocacy, without litigating, offers another alternative dispute resolution approach to divorce that is nonadversarial.

In cases where the parents are contesting custody, either party may file a motion to request a child custody evaluation, the parties may jointly agree to an evaluation, or the court may order an evaluation on its own. Some courts employ mental health professionals who work within the court itself; others contract with mental health professionals or agencies within the community. In many states, the court may appoint an attorney as guardian ad litem (GAL) to represent the child's best interests in the process. Attorney GALs may retain a forensic mental health evaluator to assess issues relevant to the child's best interests; this is a *child custody evaluation*. In a few states, GALs may be mental health professionals who perform evaluations and report in writing to the court. In some instances, the court might order a brief, focused assessment to provide information about limited issues.

Attorneys may use a child custody evaluation as a tool to help settle differences and avoid a trial. Four-way meetings with the parties and their attorneys may be held at this point in an effort to negotiate agreement on some or all of the disputed issues. Before a contested case goes to trial, the court may schedule a pretrial hearing in an effort to either settle the case or narrow the issues for trial.

General steps in the legal process of child custody cases:

- The legal process begins when a divorce complaint or petition is filed with the court.

- If the parties cannot agree to an interim arrangement regarding parenting time and child support, they can file a motion with the court for temporary orders.

- At each step in the legal process, the court encourages parents to resolve their differences and come to an agreement.

- Mediation has increased in popularity; so has collaborative law.

- In cases where the parents are contesting custody, either party may file a motion to request a child custody evaluation.

- Eventually, the court will issue an order granting a divorce. This order specifies factors related to child custody.

In an uncontested trial, the parties agree upon all matters and present a written agreement to the judge for review and approval. In contrast, in a contested trial, the parties present all issues to the court for judicial decision. In some instances, a judge may allow the parties to submit a partial agreement and have a trial limited to the issues in dispute. Whether the differences between the parties are resolved through trial or stipulation, ultimately the court issues an order granting a divorce. A divorce decree will specify the terms of the ending of the marriage, including the division of assets and debts (including property and rights of use and occupancy of the marital home, if relevant), financial responsibilities, the particulars of custody and visitation of the minor children, payment of child support, and such other relief as may be appropriate (Mercer & Pruett, 2001).

After a final judgment, the court order remains in effect unless either party successfully obtains a *modification*. A parent wishing to change the court-ordered parenting plan or seeking to change custody of a child postadjudication can file a motion requesting a modification of the original order. For a modification of a support- or child-related order, the plaintiff must demonstrate that there has been a substantial change in circumstances since the entry of the order. Typical changes of circumstances that lead to requests for custody modifications include parent repartnering, children's needs changing with development, a desire to relocate with a child, or a decline in a party's ability to parent. Modification requests regarding child custody and visitation might be a point of entry for forensic evaluators even when child custody evaluations were not obtained prior to the divorce.

Disputes between never-married parents over the care and custody of their child have increased substantially in recent years. For instance, in Massachusetts, filings involving never-married parents nearly equaled divorce filings in 2008 (Massachusetts Probate and Family Court, 2008), and in some states, filings of never-married parents outnumber divorce filings (O'Connell, 2009). Absent a court order or legal agreement to the contrary, mothers generally have *sole legal custody* of their children. If a father whose paternity has been established files for custody or increased contact, parenting disputes follow the same process as divorce proceedings.

In divorce and never-married cases, unlike in criminal or child protection cases, the law does not provide legal representation for the parties. Parties who represent themselves without legal counsel (*pro se*), an increasingly common occurrence, are likely to have trouble navigating the legal process. Many courts across the country have initiated procedures and disseminated information in order to make the process easier and less mysterious. Family courts in many states provide information to litigants on state court websites. Some bar associations have volunteer "lawyers for the day" available to pro se litigants in the local courthouses. Unrepresented parties add another layer of complexity to the already complicated legal process of family courts.

Role of the Child Custody Examiner

Mental health evaluators are most often involved in cases of divorcing or never-married parents, but child custody issues also arise in guardianship and child welfare cases. The focus of child custody evaluations can vary widely, but they typically include the following:

- assessing the strengths/weaknesses of parents as custodians/caretakers of their child(ren);

- assessing children's needs, including any special needs;

- assessing the sources of, impact of, and interventions for decreasing conflict between feuding parents;

- evaluating the quality of relationships between children and parents;

- assessing allegations of parental alienation, in which one parent engages in behaviors that undermine and/or destroy the relationship between a child and the other parent;

- assessing aligned children, meaning those who resist contact with one parent;

- assessing allegations of child maltreatment, including exposure to domestic violence, in the context of parental separation; and

- evaluating the impact of a variety of factors on parents' ability to provide adequate care for their child(ren). Such factors can include psychiatric illness, cognitive impairment, or substance use disorder; however, anything can be raised as a factor if there is concern that such a factor would diminish a party's capacity to parent the child(ren). Courts may ask the evaluator to address each parent's ability to meet a child's medical, psychological, educational, or other special needs.

Not all "child custody evaluations" focus on the issue of custody per se; a more accurate term would be "forensic evaluations in the context of child custody cases." For example, an evaluation might be requested to assess the ability of a parent to provide adequate supervision for a young child during that parent's parenting time. More specifically, a court might ask whether supervised visitation is necessary in light of a parent's history of medication noncompliance for her bipolar disorder leading to recent psychiatric hospitalizations and suspended contact with her 5-year-old child. In this example, the court is asking not who the better custodial parent is, but under what conditions would the child be safe in the mother's care. Another example might involve a 12-year-old who reportedly refuses to participate in court-ordered parenting time with his father. The primary issue is not physical or legal custody. The court requests an evaluation of the factors that contribute to this disrupted relationship. For the sake of brevity, however, as well as consistency in the field, the term "child custody evaluation" is commonly used and understood in reference to the assessment of a wide range of issues that may impact the care of children.

Mental health professionals may be engaged in a contested custody dispute through different mechanisms and at different stages of a legal case. Unlike in criminal law, a custody determination cannot be considered final until a child is 18 and no longer a minor. Therefore, a psychological evaluation can be sought at multiple points to assist the court in determining what is in the best interests of the child. Also, courts may request updates after initial evaluations are completed for families who return to court for subsequent modifications to the custody order.

Although states differ in their terminology and procedural details, forensic mental health professionals generally become involved in child custody cases in one of four ways: as a court-appointed evaluator; hired by one attorney as an

INFO

Many child custody evaluations could more accurately be described as forensic evaluations in the context of child custody cases. In other words, the legal dispute may not be about who should have custody of the child. Evaluations assess diverse factors that influence parent–child relationships.

evaluator; hired by one attorney as a science expert; or hired by one attorney as consultant.

Court-Appointed Evaluator

A *court-appointed evaluator* is either a mental health professional whom the court appoints directly or a professional whom the court's neutral appointee (e.g., GAL) hires to conduct an assessment. The benefits to the evaluator of being court appointed (or hired by the GAL/*special master* or other neutral court appointee) are many. In particular, typically, the court order defines the role of the evaluator and the scope of the assessment. In the event that the order is unclear, the evaluator can seek clarification from the court. When an evaluator is court appointed, the court is the evaluator's client; this minimizes the appearance of bias and maximizes the neutrality of the evaluator. The evaluator's role is to assess the family with respect to the specific questions posed by the court and the forensic mental health *constructs* relevant to those questions. One important advantage of a court appointment as a neutral evaluator is that it provides the evaluator with quasi-judicial immunity, or protection from liability for work performed under the court order (Kirkland, Kirkland, King, & Renfro, 2006).

Hired by One Attorney as an Evaluator

An attorney or one party to the dispute can retain a mental health professional to conduct an evaluation. However, a forensic mental health professional cannot conduct a child custody evaluation without involving both parents and children. Because a child custody evaluation typically involves the comparative assessment of the relative strengths and weaknesses of parents, a forensic evaluator cannot do an adequate evaluation without access to all of the involved parties. Occasionally, attorneys ask forensic evaluators to assess their client's parenting ability and relationship with the child. It is clinically and ethically ill advised to evaluate a child without both parents' knowledge and permission absent an emergency or court order. Conducting such an evaluation puts the child in the position of keeping a secret (i.e., the evaluation) from one parent, and the evaluator becomes an accomplice in creating an untenable situation and, potentially, further conflict. Even if both parents and the court give permission to evaluate the child, the issue of the appearance of bias remains if one side has retained the evaluator. The children might be influenced by knowledge of which parent hired the evaluator and alter their answers accordingly. In addition, children might have to endure two separate evaluations if the court permits each side to hire an independent evaluator, raising ethical concerns and clinical dilemmas for the evaluator.

There might be situations where this is unavoidable. For example, some jurisdictions might rely on independent assessments obtained by each party. It is important to note that these concerns do not extend to a psychological evaluation of the attorney's client, as opposed to an evaluation examining what is in the best interests of the child. For example, an attorney might hire an evaluator to assess his client's mental illness, substance abuse, or other questions about the individual's psychological or emotional functioning. The evaluator can conduct such an evaluation without the concerns previously noted, but she must be careful not to extend an opinion regarding comparative parenting or about the parent or children she did not assess.

Hired by One Attorney as a Science Expert

A forensic mental health professional may be hired by an attorney as an expert regarding an issue in the field about which he has specialized knowledge and experience. Also known as a "state of the science" or "state of the practice"

BEWARE Unless there is an emergency or a court order, do not agree to evaluate a child without both parents' knowledge and permission.

expert, the mental health professional remains neutral and states what is known in the field about the specific issue being addressed. Here are two examples:

1. An expert might be hired to testify about what research has found with respect to the credibility of children's disclosures of sexual abuse.

2. An expert might be hired to present the latest findings on the criteria that must be met for a diagnosis of Asperger's disorder and how that might be considered in parenting plans.

A key aspect of this role is that the expert neither evaluates nor expresses opinions about individuals involved in the litigation.

Hired by One Attorney as a Consultant

A forensic mental health professional may be hired by an attorney as a consultant. The consultant typically helps the attorney prepare for trial by explaining psychological evidence with which that attorney might be faced or assisting in the preparation of questions for a witness. This is an advocacy role, the goal of which is to assist the attorney in winning her case. A dilemma emerges when a forensic evaluator serves in more than one role on the same case. For example, it is not ethically possible to serve both as a "state of the science" expert and as a consultant, because one would be in the dual role of presenting psychological truth while simultaneously working for one party's interests (Hess, 1988; Weissman & Debow, 2003).

Each of the roles described above is valid for mental health professionals with expertise in custody evaluations. However, each role is mutually exclusive with respect to the others in any given case (Weissman & Debow, 2003).

BEWARE
It is not *ethically* possible to serve both as a "state of the science" expert and as a consultant, because you would be in the dual role of presenting psychological truth while simultaneously working for your party's interests.

Conclusion

The most important concept that has been reviewed in this chapter is the prevailing legal standard for child custody cases today—the Best Interests of the Child (BIC) Standard. The most helpful and informative evaluations assess psychological factors that are relevant to this standard. Each state has constructed a definition of "best interests"; these vary in their degree of specificity, but each has overarching commonalities with those of other jurisdictions (see Appendix A). The forensic evaluator must be familiar with the specific factors and nuances of the best interests definition that is unique to his state. Generally, the relative weights assigned to the variables that determine best interests are left to judicial discretion. In the next chapter, we examine how issues typically considered under the BIC Standard can be translated into *psycho-legal* constructs that are within the purview of the mental health professional's assessment. We then further delineate factors that form these constructs and lay the bases for child custody evaluations.

1
chapter

Forensic Mental Health Concepts

2

Chapter 1 identified the Best Interests of the Child (BIC) Standard as the legal standard for child custody determinations across the United States. The task of the forensic evaluator in child custody evaluations is to provide information to the court relevant to the court's decision about the best interests of the child. The primary purpose of the present chapter is to use the law—and forensic commentary on child custody evaluations—to define what types of psychological information are relevant to the legal questions in child custody cases. We address five questions related to this objective:

1. What does the law tell us about *general classes (or categories) of information* that are relevant in child custody cases?

2. What does the mental health field tell us about *psychological constructs* that are relevant to those classes of information?

3. How can *the psychological constructs be translated into factors to be assessed*?

4. What is the proper role of psychological information in child custody evaluations?

5. What are the differences between child custody and other types of evaluations?

What Does the Law Tell Us About General Classes (or Categories) of Information that Are Relevant to the BIC Standard?

At the outset, we should recognize that everyone who has attempted to clarify what the BIC Standard means has complained about its elusive quality. As noted in Chapter 1, the law itself defines the standard only vaguely, which "invites endless interpretation and application" (Schutz, Dixon, Lindenberger, & Ruther, 1989, p. 1) and allows for broad judicial discretion in child custody determinations. This is because the standard itself says nothing, and implies nothing, about *what* an examiner should assess. The standard simply describes a desired outcome: the child's best welfare. Were this approach to a legal standard applied in some other area of law, such as civil commitment, it would be as though the standard for civil commitment were "welfare of the patient," instead of "in need of treatment and a danger to self or others." The BIC Standard by itself does not tell the evaluator what things need to be addressed in making the decision. It says only that the outcome must be of benefit to the child. Some courts, in turn, have delineated factors to be assessed, essentially defining the BIC Standard in its orders for child custody evaluators.

As noted above and in Chapter 1, the indeterminacy of the BIC Standard has prompted many states, through statute or case law, to devise a list of factors for courts to consider when making custody decisions (see Appendix A, Custodial Best Interest Factors in 50 States). In general, these factors fall into four broad categories, as shown in Table 2.1.

These four basic areas of information, along with specific questions that may arise in the individual case, usually form the foundation for custody decisions. They also correspond to the mental health constructs essential for providing psychological information that speaks to best interest.

INFO

The goal of the BIC Standard is to achieve the best possible outcome for the child, but the standard does not say anything about *what* should be assessed.

Table 2.1 | Main Factors that Courts Consider in Making Child Custody Determinations

1. Information about parents and their parenting
2. Information about children and their development
3. Information about the relationship between parents and their children
4. Information about the relationship between the parents

What Does the Mental Health Field Tell Us About Relevant Psychological Constructs When Evaluators Seek to Provide Those Classes (or Categories) of Information?

These general categories make it possible to translate the otherwise vague BIC Standard into "psycho-legal constructs." What do we mean by this term? Grisso (2003) defined constructs as "hypothetical conditions or states that cannot be observed directly; only their behavioral signs can be observed. We use constructs to summarize our observations about individuals . . ." (p. 22). Psycho-legal constructs are the conceptual links between the legal standard and behavior, or, in this case, the related general classes of information (as above) and behavior. Using those psycho-legal concepts, one can then develop a picture of the specific areas that an examiner would need to assess in order to provide information about them to the court. For example, parenting style is a psycho-legal construct relevant to the BIC Standard. Although as a concept it is not wholly observable or measurable, behavioral indices of the construct are. The challenge, of course, is identifying what

INFO

Psycho-legal constructs are the links between observed behaviors and legal standards. In other words, these constructs allow the forensic mental health professional to determine what areas to assess in order to move forward with an evaluation.

psycho-legal constructs are important to courts when considering the BIC Standard and then defining what observable behaviors to use to assess the identified construct.

Fortunately, child custody experts and our national professional organizations have addressed this problem. Some national organizations have promulgated codes of ethics and practice guidelines that summarize the current consensus relevant to the interpretation of the BIC Standard for custody evaluators. Table 2.2 presents a list of these guidelines and standards, along with the types of professionals for whom they are intended. This volume will reference three of these guidelines in subsequent chapters:

1. American Psychological Association's (APA, 2009) *Guidelines for Child Custody Evaluations in Family Law Proceedings.* This document, whose goal is to "promote proficiency in the conduct of these particular evaluations" (p. 2), offers guidance for many aspects of child custody assessments, including the relation of the examiner to the parent and other parties, and general requirements for the quality of methods and interpretations. These aspects of the *APA* custody guidelines will be referenced at various points throughout the present volume. Of greatest importance for our interpretation of the BIC Standard in this chapter, however, is the document's identification of the essential purpose of child custody evaluations—to "assist in determining the psychological best interests of the child"—which the guidelines translate into broad objectives and psychological constructs that should form the basis of child custody evaluations.

2. *The Association of Family and Conciliation Courts' (AFCC)* "Model Standards of Practice for Child Custody Evaluations" (AFCC, 2007): This document is intended for multiple audiences, one of which is child custody evaluators. For both forensic

evaluators and consumers of their work (i.e., parents, attorneys, and courts), the goal of the AFCC model standards is to "promote good practice" (p. 5). The document encompasses recommendations about the nature of the role of the forensic examiner, his credentials, and the process of the evaluation itself. It highlights that a comprehensive assessment includes all relevant parties and the relationships among them.

3. The third document is the *Practice Parameters for Child Custody Evaluations,* promulgated by the American Academy of Child and Adolescent Psychiatry (AACAP, 1997a). The AACAP practice parameters' recommendations are "basic principles" concerning the role of the evaluator and the areas of assessment in the evaluation, as well as the process of performing an assessment.

Currently, the leading definition of what courts need to know from child custody examiners is presented in two documents. One is the APA (2009) custody guidelines, which replaced the 1994 guidelines (APA, 1994). The document was developed as a consensus among APA-identified experts in child custody law and child custody evaluations, in a process that took account of extensive prior reviews of child custody law and literature. In this document, the APA identified three types of information, which might be called "psycho-legal constructs," that form the bases of child custody evaluations relevant to the BIC Standard. Those constructs, along with a fourth one derived from the research on divorce, are the "things needed to be assessed" that correspond to the four general categories of information the court needs to know about, as shown in Table 2.3. The second document, the 2007 AFCC model standards replaced the

> **INFO**
>
> The APA's *Guidelines for Child Custody Evaluations in Family Law Proceedings* provide broad objectives and psychological constructs that form the basis of child custody evaluations.

Table 2.2 | Professional Guidelines for Child Custody Evaluations

Intended Audience	Title	Author	Year Published	Authoritative Weight
Qualified mental health professionals	*Model Standards of Practice for Child Custody Evaluation*	Association of Family and Conciliation Courts	2007	Aspirational
All psychologists	*Ethical Principles of Psychologists and Code of Conduct*	American Psychological Association	2002	Mandatory (Code of Conduct)
Forensic psychologists	*Specialty Guidelines for Forensic Psychologists*	Committee on Ethical Guidelines for Forensic Psychologists	1991	Aspirational
	Guidelines for Child Custody Evaluations in Family Law Proceedings	American Psychological Association	2009	Aspirational
All psychiatrists	*The Principles of Medical Ethics with Annotations Especially Applicable to Psychiatry*	American Psychiatric Association	2010	Mandatory (Code of Conduct)
Forensic psychiatrists	*Practice Parameters for Child Custody Evaluation*	American Academy of Child and Adolescent Psychiatry	1997	Aspirational
	Child Custody Consultation: Report of the Task Force on Clinical Assessment in Child Custody	American Psychiatric Association	1988	Aspirational
	Ethics Guidelines for the Practice of Forensic Psychiatry	American Academy of Psychiatry and the Law	2005	Aspirational

Adapted from Zelechoski, A. (2009). The content of child custody evaluation reports: A forensic assessment principles-based analysis. Unpublished doctoral dissertation, Drexel University, Philadelphia, PA.

Table 2.3 | Legal Factors and Corresponding Psycho-Legal Constructs

Factors based on statute/case law psycho-legal construct:
• Information about parents and their parenting (parent attributes)
• Information about children and their development (child needs)
• Information about the relationship between parents and their children (resulting "fit")
• Information about the relationship between the parents (co-parenting relationship)

2
chapter

"Model Standards of Practice for Child Custody Evaluations" (AFCC, 1994). A task force of mental health and legal professionals created this professional directive, which they revised and changed subsequent to feedback from the AFCC membership. It focuses on a *forensic mental health process of assessment* and prioritizes the assessment of parents, children, and the parent–child relationship, consistent with the three mental health constructs recommended by the APA custody guidelines.

Parent Attributes

The first of these constructs, corresponding to the court's need for information about parents and parenting, is *parent attributes*, referring to the functional abilities or deficits of both parents. The original APA document referred to them as "the adults' capacities for parenting, including whatever knowledge, attributes, skills, and abilities, or lack thereof" (APA, 1994, p. 678). The APA's interpretation of parent attributes does not focus on the mental status, personality, or morals of the parent, but on *abilities* or *capacities*. Weissman and DeBow (2003) referred to these as "functional abilities in parental competencies" (p. 43). Similarly, Grisso's (2003) model for evaluating legal competencies emphasizes the primacy of assessing individuals' functional abilities—not merely their mental illness or personality—when performing competency evaluations for courts. For example, parent attributes would include their understanding of and ability to meet the child's needs and any aspect of functioning that would inhibit those capacities (Otto & Edens, 2003). The focus is not on psychological status, but on what the parent actually can or cannot do that is relevant for parenting a child. Psychological status may be important to examine, but it is irrelevant if it does not actually impair the individual's ability to parent; that is, there has to be a demonstrable nexus between the psychological state and parenting behavior.

Child's Psychological Needs

Second, the APA guidelines recommend that evaluations that inform decisions based on the BIC Standard should assess *the child's psychological needs*. This corresponds to legal decision makers' need for information about children and their development. In describing this construct, the 2009 custody guidelines urge the forensic practitioner to include the child's educational and physical needs (APA, 2009). The 1994 guidelines additionally recommended that an evaluation should include "an assessment of the psychological functioning and developmental needs of each child and of the wishes of each child where appropriate" (APA, 1994, p. 678). An assessment of a child focuses on the current status of her "cognitive, emotional, social, and academic needs and abilities" (Otto & Edens, 2003), but it also includes her physical needs (APA, 2009) or special needs (AACAP, 1997a). Family and developmental history provide a context to help the evaluator better understand a child's needs, and they offer ideas about what the child will require in the future.

Courts also need to know the caretaking history—how each parent understood and addressed each child's needs—so as to have some foundation for decisions that would affect each child's immediate future. In addition, most concepts central to the needs of children are dynamic due to child maturation and changing family circumstances (such as the divorce or separation itself).

For example, the concept of a child's need for security may be defined differently depending on the age and emotional maturity of the child, much like the assessment of a child's wishes. In terms of physical needs, one parent may be better at providing the basic care needs of an infant, but that skill would be less salient in parenting an adolescent. Other special circumstances in a family may arise. For example, if one child has unusual medical needs, the relative abilities of each parent to address those needs may be of primary significance in that assessment.

The Resulting Fit

The resulting fit refers to the congruence between the parents' functional capacities and the children's needs. The *fit* construct corresponds to the court's need for information about the relationship between parents and their children. Central to this concept is the reciprocal relationship or interaction between parent attributes and child psychological and physical needs (Schutz et al., 1989). How do the skills and deficits of each parent respectively complement or conflict with the needs and abilities of each child? The earlier APA (1994) guidelines suggested an "assessment of the functional ability of each parent to meet these needs, including an evaluation of the interaction between each adult and child" (p. 678). The AACAP child custody practice parameters (1997a) urge evaluators to assess "parenting style to see how good a fit there is between each parent and the child" (p. 7), while the AFCC model standards urge direct observations of each parent and each child to gather "data reflecting on parenting skills and on each parent's ability to respond to the children's needs" [§10.2 (b), p. 20].

This concept of "fit" is consistent with Grisso's (2003) explanation that all legal competencies have an "interactive component." Stated another way, "Does this person's level of (parenting) ability meet the demands of the specific situation with which the person will be faced (i.e., the child's needs)?"

BEWARE Do not evaluate a parent's ability to be sufficient or deficient according to an absolute standard; instead focus on the parent's ability to meet the needs of a particular child.

(Grisso, 2003, p. 32). Once one has evaluated a person's capacities (here, the parent's abilities) and has determined the caregiving demands of the situation he faces (here, the child's needs), the forensic evaluator must assess the "match or mismatch" (Grisso, 2003) between the individual's abilities and those demands. A parent's capacities are judged to be sufficient or insufficient not according to some absolute standard, but according to whether they meet the needs of a particular child. A parent who can capably manage healthy elementary school children might be less competent with a chronically ill toddler or a disrespectful adolescent.

Co-Parenting Relationship

The APA (2009) custody guidelines base child custody evaluations on three primary psycho-legal constructs. They do not focus on the nature of the relationship between the parents, an essential aspect of any post-separation/divorce family assessment that has robust findings in postdivorce research (Gould & Stahl, 2000; Johnston & Roseby, 1997; Melton, Petrila, Poythress, & Slobogin, 2007) and consensus among child custody evaluators. This is also an important factor of interest in statute and case law. As is summarized in Chapter 3, the postseparation parenting relationship is strongly related to outcomes for children (Amato & Booth, 2001). The APA custody guidelines allude to this factor when they "encourage" the forensic evaluator to consider "family dynamics and interactions" (APA, 2009, p. 6), while the AFCC model standards merely note that an evaluator should have an understanding of family dynamics as part of her professional toolkit (AFCC, 2007). The AACAP (1997a) practice parameters are silent on this issue.

Having described how factors derived from the BIC Standard and its legal interpretation have been translated into psycho-legal constructs, we now turn to psychological "things to be assessed." These are the factors that form the psycho-legal constructs and provide useful information to the courts in child custody cases.

How Can the Psycho-Legal Constructs Be Translated into "Things To Be Assessed"?

Given the APA's three basic psycho-legal constructs included in a custody evaluation and the fourth, research-based one, the next task is to translate them into "things that can be assessed."

- What parenting attributes are relevant to measure?
- What needs of children should be considered?
- What concepts can help us analyze the "fit" between parent and child?
- How do interparental relationships affect parenting abilities and the needs of children?

Parenting Attributes

In child custody disputes, the focus is on comparing the strengths/weaknesses of two parents who are both presumed to be competent. This is in contrast to child protection cases, in which the focus is on comparing a parent to a minimal standard of parenting (Budd, 2005; Budd, Clark, & Connell, 2011)).

There is no consensus in the mental health field about what skills or attributes constitute "parenting" or what level of ability constitutes "good enough" parenting. This is not unexpected, given the diversity in parental values and the complexity of family dynamics. However, much research has been done to suggest how parenting might affect child outcome, and different writers have suggested essential parenting abilities to assess. The following list, adapted from Gould and Martindale (2007), is representative of the literature on parenting attributes:

- The ability to create a positive relationship with the child:
  - Can a parent provide the level of physical care, the degree of responsiveness and attunement, and the consistency of family environment needed to develop a sense of trust and security in the child (Kraus, 1999)?

- An understanding of the child's needs and characteristics as an individual:
  - Can a parent appreciate the uniqueness of the child and understand her educational, social, physical, and emotional needs? (Gould & Martindale, 2007).
- An understanding of those needs and characteristics in a developmental context:
  - Does that appreciation account for whether expectations for the child are developmentally appropriate (Thomas & Chess, 1977)?
- The ability to place a child's needs ahead of one's own:
  - Can a parent give primacy to a child's needs when appropriate (Ackerman & Schoendorf, 1992; Schutz et al., 1989)?
- Flexibility or adaptability in one's responsiveness to a child:
  - Can a parent modulate his or her responses to the changing needs of a child or to the feelings of a child, when appropriate (Fisher & Fisher, 1986)? Are the boundaries between parent and child or between the child and the world outside of the family fixed and permanent or malleable depending upon age and circumstance?
- Ability to communicate effectively with a child:
  - Can the parent provide a setting in which he can have a dialogue with a child, elicit as well as understand a child's feelings and perspective, and communicate his view (Baumrind, 1967; Fisher & Fisher, 1986)?
- Appropriate parenting style:
  - Can a parent establish appropriate limits, administer discipline when those limits are violated, and communicate moral and family

values in a context of love
and concern (Baumrind,
1967; Schutz et al., 1989;
Stahl, 1994)?

These dimensions of parenting form
a core of general abilities that evaluators
consider when assessing parents.

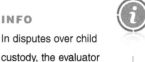

INFO

In disputes over child
custody, the evaluator
compares the strengths and
weaknesses of two parents
who are both presumed to
be competent.

Child's Needs

Gould and Martindale (2007) propose
that positive developmental outcomes for
children in general are associated with
the development of competence, "a pattern of effective adaptation
in the environment, either broadly defined or in terms of the major
developmental tasks expected of a person of a given age and
gender . . ." (Masten & Coatsworth, 1998, p. 205). Such adaptation might depend on cultural or social norms and might have
more specific areas of achievement, such as academic or athletic.
Children bring their own *bio-psycho-social* qualities to the process,
and the nature of their functioning can impact parent behavior in
as significant a manner as the reverse (Lewis, 1981). That is, the
nature of influence on behavior is "bi-directional and interactive"
(Collins, Maccoby, Steinberg, Hetherington, & Bornstein, 2000,
p. 222).

Children have general sets of needs that, when met, would
increase the likelihood of mastering developmental tasks and supporting the growth of competence. These needs (as adapted from
Gould & Martindale, 2007) include the following:

- Secure attachment:
    - Can the child rely on her parent(s) to provide a
      sense of safety, physical comfort, emotional
      nurturance, and consistency of environments
      (Main, 1996; Solomon & George, 1999;
      Whiteside, 1998)?
- Stage-appropriate self-regulation:
    - Can the child learn to modulate his own
      emotions, manage distress, and appropriately

comply with external rules (Masten et al., 1995; Rothbart & Bates, 1998)?

- Special needs met:
  - Does the child have any special physical/medical, emotional, religious, or cultural needs, or any special abilities or talents (Schutz et al., 1989)?
- Peer relationships:
  - Can the child make friends, develop prosocial behavior, and learn to negotiate with peers for mutual benefit (Coolahan, Fantuzzo, Mendez, & McDermott, 2000)?
- Academic achievement:
  - Can the child learn and perform in school commensurate with her abilities and adapt to or cope with any impediments to learning (Kelly & Emery, 2003; Masten & Coatsworth, 1998)?
- Relationship with siblings:
  - Can siblings provide physical and emotional support for one another, particularly in stressful circumstances (such as divorce or separation) (AFCC, 2007; Cicirelli, 1991; Schutz et al., 1989)? In addition, can older siblings be role models for their younger brothers or sisters (Nichols, 1986)?
- Child's preference:
  - Does the child express a desire for any particular outcome, as understood in the context of his age, cognitive ability, and emotional maturity (AFCC, 2007; Larson & McGill, 2010)?
  - If such a desire was expressed, did the child do so freely or did a parent influence or prompt it (AACAP, 1997a)?

INFO

Evaluate the developmental strengths and weaknesses of each child, and the influence those factors might have on parenting

The Resulting Fit

As noted above, the "fit" concept relates to the degree of congruence, or the "match," between a child's needs and a parent's capacity to address those needs. A child's development and maturation spur change her psychological and physical needs, just as adult development and ongoing experience can significantly impact one's parenting abilities. Children "may need different types of care at different stages of their lives" (Gould & Martindale, 2007, p. 27), while, similarly, parents may be more or less able at any particular time to provide that care. Variables that address the "fit" between parents and children include the following:

- The congruence between parent abilities and child needs (Bray, 1991):
  - Can parents understand and provide what their children need emotionally and physically, and, conversely, are the children's needs broadly within the realm of what their parents are able to provide?

- The compatibility between child temperament and parental abilities (Caspi, Henry, McGee, Moffitt, & Silva, 1995; Lee & Bates, 1985):
  - Is there a match between parent and children's temperaments? If one child has a difficult temperament, can parents adapt in order to address those issues?

- Agreement between parents' expectations and demands and children's abilities and other characteristics (Thomas & Chess, 1977):
  - Are parents' expectations reasonable/realistic given the child's various developmental strengths and weaknesses, including gender and personality style? If a child has a special need, does the parent understand it and have realistic expectations for the child? How does a parent

BEWARE
The "fit concept" relates to the "match" between a child's needs and a parent's capacity to address those needs. However, be aware that these needs and capacities change over time.

manage a child with special deficits or special talents?

- Presence/absence of support system/network/family to provide assistance to parents (AACAP, 1997a; APA, 2009; Hetherington & Kelly, 2002):

  - If there is a significant special need, does either parent have any back-up or support to help with the parenting of that child?

The Interparental Relationship

As noted above, the nature of the relationship between the parents postseparation or postdivorce has substantial impact on the other psycho-legal constructs. The robust nature of research findings about this issue, together with its being a major factor of interest in many statutes or case laws, support its inclusion in the list of issues to be addressed. Moreover, because high-conflict families are the ones most likely to undergo child custody evaluations (Maccoby & Mnookin, 1992), the issues of parental conflict/ cooperation are central in most child custody assessments.

Some of the variables to be considered within this concept include the following:

- The type of conflict (Goodman, Bonds, Sandler, & Braver, 2004):

  - Does the substance of disputes involve legal issues, negative attitudes in one or both parents about the other, active verbal or physical aggression, or disagreements on parenting rules and styles?

- The level of conflict and how it is expressed (Depner, Leino, & Chun, 1992; Johnston, 2003):

  - What do the parents do or say with respect to each other?

  - How intense are the disagreements?

- Whether the conflict predated the separation (Cherlin et al., 1991; Melton et al., 2007):
  - Did these disagreements exist before the separation (and how long before) or arise as a result of the separation?
- The degree to which the children are directly or indirectly involved (Johnston & Campbell, 1988; Rohrbaugh, 2008):
  - What is the degree of exposure for the children in the conflicts, and are they directly involved (e.g., are they the message bearers or negotiators)?
  - Does the conflict interfere with the children's ability to have an ongoing relationship with both parents?
- Co-parenting skills:
  - Can each parent cooperate with the other parent or caregiver with respect to significant issues in the child's life (Amato, 2001)?
  - Can each parent manage conflict with the other parent or protect the children from existing conflict (Hetherington & Kelly, 2002)?
  - To what degree does each parent support the child's relationship with the other parent? Sometimes called the "friendly parent" clause, this is often one of the factors that many state statutes (e.g., Alabama, Kansas, Iowa, Wyoming) require courts to consider under the BIC Standard.

2
chapter

A Caution About the Factors to Be Assessed

As one can see from the above nonexhaustive list, there are many possible parent and child factors to be assessed related to the psycho-legal constructs.

INFO

High-conflict families are the families most likely to undergo child custody evaluations.

There is no consensus as to any one set of factors an evaluator should address. In addition, as many commentators have noted (Melton et al., 2007; Tippins & Wittman, 2005), there is no empirically justifiable method to weigh or rank relative parent strengths or contrast them with ordinary weaknesses when comparing parents on these dimensions. Occasionally, there will be clear impairments in personal functioning, such as might occur with mental illness or substance abuse, that demonstrably compromise parenting. If one parent suffers from either condition and the other does not, the comparison becomes easier.

That said, the outcome is still not a foregone conclusion, because the determination hinges not on what the particular condition or diagnosis is but on how that condition affects the daily personal and parental functioning of the one afflicted, and on the effects of that functioning on the child (Benjet, Azar, & Kuersten-Hogan, 2003). In addition, the context in which the particular impairment exists is an important consideration. For example, a mother who has performed nearly all of the hands-on caretaking tasks of parenting while being an at-home parent may have developed a prescription drug addiction or clinical depression that emerges during the divorce, or even some time afterward. The issue of her impairment has to be contextualized in terms of her support system, motivation, efforts toward recovery, level of acknowledgement of the problem, and daily care of the children, as well as the children's developmental status and relative attachment to and comfort level with each parent. With family support and/or medical or judicial oversight, that parent might progress in recovery quite well, with minimal negative impact on the children. In contrast, without support, the parent may be unable to commit to her treatment and take care of the children at the same time. Thus, the weight a forensic evaluator gives to that personal challenge in parenting depends on the context in which the parent must manage it. The comparison of relative parental abilities and deficiencies is not straightforward, because some parents will be able to shore up apparent weaknesses through the existence of compensatory relationships and resources, while others will not. In addition, the interplay with the developmental status of the children is significant, as the level of risk to a young child is obviously much greater than to an adolescent.

A similar caveat applies to assessments of the "goodness of fit" between the range of parental

BEST PRACTICE
If one parent has an impairment (such as clinical depression), evaluate that impairment and its effects on parenting within the overall context.

abilities and that of child needs. It is not always evident whether a relatively poor fit between a parent's ability and a child's need will have a negative outcome for the child, because often that comparison is embedded with other comparisons of good "fit." It can be difficult to determine whether one child's needs should be given priority over a sibling's needs. There is no formula to estimate the relative contributions of a parent–child match and a parent–child incompatibility to predict how they will affect the outcome. Furthermore, if one adds to the analytic equation the circumstances related to parental cooperation or conflict, the complexity of the psychological "calculus" increases dramatically, particularly because these are all qualitative analyses.

What Is the Proper Role of Psychological Information in Assisting the Courts in Child Custody Cases?

The caveat offered above requires us to consider the proper role of this multifaceted psychological data in a child custody evaluation. Is it sufficient merely to describe those conditions and to explain their significance, as Grisso (2005) has suggested? Alternatively, can we make predictions of outcome and offer recommendations, as most judges and attorneys wish (Bow & Quinnell, 2004)? To begin to address this controversial question, we will look briefly at the role of such information in child custody evaluations, a topic that we again consider in Chapter 6.

One way to construe this controversy is as a debate between "description" and "interpretation." Few doubt that descriptions of parents and children, when they focus on the data outlined above, are of value to the courts as long as the data are collected in reliable ways. However, commentators in the field of child custody evaluation disagree on the extent to which child custody examiners should go beyond description and basic clinical inferences to offer judgments about the implications of those data.

Most arguments fall into one of two broad positions. One position argues that psychological information in child custody cases should be confined to descriptions of parents' attributes and children's needs, as well as structuring those descriptions to make the degree of "fit" or the "mismatch" self-evident. In essence, this position would discourage the evaluator from offering an ultimate issue opinion or from making recommendations on the legal questions. The opposing position argues that the information should be used to offer courts interpretations regarding the likely outcomes of various custody arrangements, despite the fact that those interpretations require going into the realm of prediction and beyond that which can be reliably verified.

Depending on the jurisdiction, courts may allow or prefer either approach. Most legal professionals prefer the latter position, and most custody evaluators' practices are consistent with court and attorney preferences (Bow & Quinnell, 2001, 2004). The current professional discussion of the topic does not endorse either of these approaches, but all child custody examiners should understand the two perspectives, so that they can make informed decisions about their own practices. The following discussion, therefore, offers examples from the literature that represent these two points of view regarding the proper use of psychological information in child custody proceedings.

The Descriptive Approach

This approach includes two categories of knowledge. The first, *observational,* involves primary sensory data—that which the evaluator sees or hears himself—without any other higher-order abstraction related to the sensory observations (Tippins &Wittman, 2005). For example, an evaluator might report, "During the home visit, Jimmy stomped his feet on the floor and screamed when his father would not allow him to watch a TV show that Jimmy wanted to see." A related form of this might include behaviors that either parent or a child reports. For example, "Jimmy's father states that his son has problems with self-control, while independently a teacher reports that Jimmy exhibits similar behaviors (e.g., stomping and screaming) in school when frustrated." Tippins and Wittman (2005) would consider sensory description, or "what the clinician observes" (p. 194), to be an example of Level I, or a first-order level, in a hierarchy of inferences.

A second-order level, called *inferential,* occurs when the evaluator combines a set of observed behaviors and makes higher-level inferences or conclusions about some abstract capacity or concept related to what she observed, such as, in the above instance, the category of self-regulation. For example, Jimmy's observable lack of control, confirmed by teacher report, leads to a conclusion about problems he has in self-regulation under frustration—a factor that explains an important aspect of the child's needs as well as the demand it can create on a parent. Tippins and Wittman (2005) would consider this to be an example of Level II in their hierarchy, "what the clinician concludes about the psychology of a parent, a child, or a family" (p. 194). More basically, this entails what the evaluator concludes about what he saw or heard (or what others reported they saw or heard). Neither observational nor inferential statements are about the legal issue before the court, but they are related because they address relevant mental health constructs (such as parent attributes and child needs/capacities). The first-and second-order levels of analysis (Levels I and II) constitute descriptive modes of analysis, as there is no judgment implied as to their relative merit in a child custody context.

INFO

The first-order level of analysis, *observational*, and the second-order level, *inferential*, are *descriptive modes of analysis*: there is no judgment implied as to their relative merit; the evaluator is simply stating what *is*, based on observation by self or others.

The reporter is simply stating what *is*, based on observation by self or others. Most writers in the area of forensic psychology aver that this kind of case-specific, descriptive data is the most reliable sort of information (Gould & Martindale, 2007; Melton et al., 2007; Tippins &Wittman, 2005). Together with the relevant psychological literature (Kelly & Johnston, 2005), these two levels of description permit evaluators to make inferences that are useful to the court and are within the areas of competence of the mental health field.

The Interpretive Approach

The forensic evaluator moves beyond the descriptive approach when she uses Level I observations and Level II inferences to make conclusions about custody-specific, psycho-legal constructs, such as comparing the "fit" between each parent's attributes and child needs (Tippins &Wittman, 2005). This third-order level (Level III) of inference argues for a more expansive use of the psychological information in providing guidance to the court and the parties as to what is best for a particular child in regard to the legal decision. It could include such practices as stating which parent is a better "match" for a child or suggesting what risks or benefits specific parenting plans might pose for a child, "as long as they are grounded in case-specific facts and reliable empirical literature" (Tippins & Wittman, 2005, p. 200). Kelly and Johnston (2005) support the value of this approach and go on to suggest that evaluators might offer general probability statements or qualified predictions (such as "specific, risk-focused conclusions") when the facts of a case and research data converge (Tippins & Wittman, 2005, p. 200). The argument against this practice stems from the fact that there is neither consensus about how to measure degree of "fit" nor empirical data to support predictions of specific risk/benefit analyses; therefore, the forensic evaluator who would make such conclusions would be impelled to reach beyond what the data can support.

The fourth-order level (Level IV) of inference occurs when, combining convergent, multisourced data from observation and higher-level mental health constructs, the evaluator offers an opinion on the legal question ("this should happen") or provides some prediction of outcome ("this is likely to happen"). This is the most controversial use of custody-related psychological information, having fueled a 30-year debate between many forensic academic scholars and forensic clinicians (Grisso, 2005). At this level of interpretation, the evaluator may either recommend a specific parenting plan or opine on a legal question, such as the award of custody to one parent or the other or whether one parent should be permitted to move out of state with a child.

The various standards speak to this debate in different ways. AFCC (2007) and APA (2009) note the controversy but take no position on the issue, while AACAP (1997a) supports offering specific, custody-related recommendations. The vast majority of forensic clinicians and legal actors prefer to provide this level of interpretation (Bow & Quinnell, 2004), and a segment of academic and legal scholars support it (Dessau, 2005; Stahl, 2005). However, "there is no evidence in the empirical literature that current interview protocols, traditional psychological tests, or custody-specific tests are in any way able to reliably predict child adjustment to different access plans" (Tippins & Wittman, 2005, p. 204).

INFO

The third-order level of inference occurs when an evaluator uses both Level I observations and Level II inferences and moves beyond describing to concluding. The fourth-order level of inference takes this even further: combining data from many sources (including observation and mental health constructs), the evaluator offers an opinion on the legal question ("this should happen") or provides some prediction of outcome ("this is likely to happen").

What Are the Differences between Child Custody and Other Types of Evaluations?

It is important to consider the differences between child custody evaluations and other forensic evaluations in which similar capacities are assessed. The assessment of parental capacity is central to most child protection cases, as it is to child custody cases. There are many similarities in issues to be assessed and evaluation methods. The important differences between the evaluations are listed in Table 2.4. The primary difference is that in child custody cases, the parental capacities and parent–child "fit" are considered in comparison to the other parent; in child protection cases, parental capacities are considered against a standard of minimally adequate parenting (Budd et al., 2011).

Because many forensic evaluators are also child clinicians, however, a thorough understanding of the role differences between clinical and forensic evaluators is essential in order to avoid ethical pitfalls (Heilbrun, Grisso, & Goldstein, 2009; Rohrbaugh, 2008). Some of these differences are noted in Table 2.5. In particular, a forensic evaluator must be aware that in most cases, the court, not the family, is the client (Kirkpatrick, 2004); there is no doctor–patient *confidentiality*; payment is by the family or court but not by health insurance; and one's role is noninterventionist and impartial.

In this chapter, we have traced the process by which legal definitions of the BIC Standard combine with directives from professional organizations and from social science research and form the basis of what to evaluate. We then listed components that make up the four broad assessment areas.

Table 2.4 Comparison of Child Custody and Child Protection Evaluations

Child Custody	Child Protection
Presumption of minimally adequate parenting	No presumption of minimally adequate parenting
Stakes involve distribution of parenting time and responsibility	Stakes involve conditions of access (e.g., visitation) and eventual reunification versus termination of rights
Focus on child's best interest	Focus on child's best interest and parent's rights
Animosity between parents likely	Animosity between parents and state likely
Varied socioeconomic status	Typically low socieconomic status
Broad focus of evaluation	Narrow focus of evaluation

Reprinted with permission from Budd et al., (2011).

The resultant assessment model is relevant to the legal matter and consistent with knowledge and ethics in mental health. The chapter also reviewed the controversy regarding opinions and recommendations to the court in child custody. Finally, the differences between child custody and child protection evaluations, as well as the differences between child forensic and child clinical evaluations, were described. In the next chapter we move on to a discussion of the research that can inform the evaluator about separation and divorce, parenting impairments, child outcomes, and the evaluation process itself.

Table 2.5 Differences Between Child Clinical and Child Custody Evaluations

	Clinical	Child Custody	Caveat
Purpose of evaluation	Diagnose, treat, and advocate for client/patient	Inform judicial decision making	
Who is the client?	Child and/or family	Court	
Confidentiality	Yes	No	Essential that custody evaluator give warning of limit of confidentiality and document in report
Sources of information	Primarily patient and parents who are viewed as reliable	Multiple sources; validation of parental views are sought	
Evaluator's demeanor	Helpful, empathic, rarely challenging	Impartial, objective, skeptical, sometimes challenging	A clinical evaluator conveys a sense of interest and desire to help; the forensic evaluator conveys a sense of interest with neutrality; either type of evaluator must be warm, fun, and flexible enough to engage children of all ages in meaningful dialogue

Table 2.5 Differences Between Child Clinical and Child Custody Evaluations (*Continued*)

	Clinical	Child Custody	Caveat
Documentation	Written documentation must support diagnoses and meet institutional and health insurance requirements	Written documentation details data obtained during evaluation and impressions and bases for evaluator's impressions	Because of the possibility of deposition or testimony, and because the evaluation is not likely to be modified or discussed in a collaborative setting as clinical evaluations are, there is a higher standard of documentation than in the clinical role
Access to report	Parents or legal guardian	Report is controlled by court, which determines who may have access	
Responsibility for fees	Health insurance/ self-pay	Determined by court; often retainer is paid by parties or evaluations are provided by funded court clinics	Health insurance does not pay for forensic evaluations (not medically necessary)

Empirical Foundations and Limits | 3

As we note in Chapter 2, the BIC Standard in itself offers little assessment guidance for custody evaluators, although statutes and case law have provided factors to be addressed in such evaluations. We also note the four psycho-legal constructs that will guide the evaluator's assessment methods toward an understanding of the psychological best interests of the child.

Here we examine the literature that describes research relevant to children and parents in divorce and separation. This literature helps to determine what "things to address," and it also informs evaluators' interpretations of the data they collect in their child custody cases. In a best practice forensic model, the mental health evaluator applies that group-data-based knowledge to the dynamics of the individual case, particularly to how the particular case elements might affect child outcomes. In this chapter, we give a brief overview of the demographics of parental separation and then summarize some of the relevant areas of research of which the forensic evaluator should be aware.

Parent Demographics

In 2001, an estimated 20% of all first marriages ended in divorce or separation within 5 years (U.S. National Center for Health Statistics, 2004), while 32% to 47% ended in divorce within 10 years (Bramlett & Mosher, 2002). In general, when heterosexual parents divorce, mothers obtain primary responsibility for children

BEST PRACTICE
In a best practice forensic model, consider how relevant research applies to the dynamics of the individual case. Focus, in particular, on how the case elements might affect child outcomes.

at least 80% of the time (Maccoby & Mnookin, 1992). Postdivorce, only about 25% to 30% of separated parents are able to form cooperative relationships with their ex-partners (Ahrons, 1994), whereas 20% to 25% remain in conflictual relationships (Maccoby & Mnookin, 1992). Notably, the largest group—close to half— develop a detached parenting or *parallel parenting* relationship marked by low levels of conflict, infrequent communication, and overall disengagement from each other (Kelly & Emery, 2003; see Fig. 3.1).

In 2004, 2.4 million married women and slightly over 1 million unmarried women gave birth to a child (U.S. Census Bureau, 2007). In contrast to marriages, 49% of never-married, cohabitating relationships dissolve within 5 years (Bramlett & Mosher, 2002). In the past decade, the incidence of never-married parent cases that appear in family court has approached that of divorces, although there are no data on what segment of the former group litigates custody issues.

Over 90% of divorcing parents settle their dispute without a trial. Of the other 10% who remain on the litigation path, perhaps half of them undergo a child custody evaluation (Maccoby & Mnookin, 1992). Fewer than 2% of divorcing parents proceed to a complete trial (Dessau, 2005; Maccoby & Mnookin, 1992).

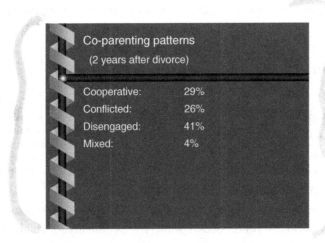

Co-parenting patterns
(2 years after divorce)

Cooperative:	29%
Conflicted:	26%
Disengaged:	41%
Mixed:	4%

Figure 3.1 Post-Separation Parenting Relationships

Parents who undergo court-ordered evaluations are more likely to represent a subset of high-conflict families (Johnston & Roseby, 1997) that, overall, make up about a quarter of divorcing parents (Ahrons, 1981, 1994; Maccoby & Mnookin, 1992; Wallerstein & Kelly, 1980). Domestic violence, while reported in about 75% of families who contest custody (Johnston & Campbell, 1988), is not unique to that particular group, because similar rates of aggressive behaviors generally exist in couples headed for divorce (Lawrence & Bradbury, 2001). Finally, a common experience among many custody-litigating parents is engagement in some form of parent-alienating behavior (Johnston & Kelly, 2004). .

In summary, a small percentage of divorcing or separating parents receive custody evaluations; they are often characterized by high conflict, continuing anger and mistrust, periodic verbal or physical aggression toward each other, and significant difficulty with communication and cooperation. Many of these parents cannot separate their personal issues from their children's needs or protect the children from direct knowledge of their conflicts (Johnston & Roseby, 1997). Their decision to engage in the legal adversarial process itself may intensify the kinds of behavior noted in such families (Wolman & Taylor, 1991).

3
chapter

Influence of Culture and Ethnicity

Child custody evaluators assess families from many different ethnic, religious, and cultural backgrounds that reflect the diversity in their locales. The American Psychological Association's (APA) child custody guidelines (APA, 2009) and the model standards of the Association of Family and Conciliation Courts (AFCC) (2007) both advise the development of cultural competence and sensitivity, while the practice parameters of the American Academy of Child and Adolescent

INFO

Only a small percentage of divorcing or separating parents undergo custody evaluations; these couples are often characterized by high conflict, continuing anger and mistrust, periodic verbal or physical aggression toward each other, and significant difficulty with communication and cooperation.

Psychiatry (AACAP) (1997a) focus on developing an understanding of how religion might affect family life.

Culture is a synthesis of a social and moral code of conduct together with activities that symbolize those codes (Stuart, 2004). It may also be defined as "shared experiences or commonalities" of groups or of individuals within groups "in relation to changing political and social contexts" (Warrier, 2008, p. 540). In socializing their children, parents impart these shared experiences or behavioral norms, although children are not passive recipients of their parents' values (Stuart, 2004). Custody evaluations typically compare the practices of two competent parents and how those parents respond to the temperaments and behaviors of their children. They usually do not involve child protective issues, which themselves might involve value-laden interpretations of what constitutes maltreatment (Budd et al., 2011). There is no consensus for what constitutes good-enough parenting. Moreover, there may be nonabusive parenting practices normative to one region, culture, or religion, such as the use of corporal punishment or enforcement of social restrictions (e.g., whom one can have as friends), to which most middle-class, modern-day Americans would not subscribe or for which research on child development has not accounted. When dealing, then, with an immigrant family or with a family that does not practice a mainstream religion, it behooves the evaluator to be aware of typical practices or beliefs, but at the same time to understand that each participant in the family will have his own unique interpretation of those things.

BEST PRACTICE
The APA's (2009) child custody guidelines and AFCC's (2007) model standards advise you, as a forensic evaluator in child custody cases, to develop cultural competence and sensitivity, while the AACAP's (1997a) practice parameters recommend that you develop an understanding of how religion might affect family life.

Thus, the evaluator cannot rely on cultural stereotypes (Hughes, 2006) and instead needs to view these practices—where relevant to court concerns—through the perspective of each family member. As Stuart (2004) has noted, where cultural differences exist, what is known about the culture in question "is a useful guide for developing a set of hypotheses, each of which should take the form of a question, rather than a set of assumptions that are routinely accepted" (p. 8).

Impact of Divorce on Children

Since the landmark study by Wallerstein and Kelly (1980), there has been a dramatic increase in the empirical knowledge base regarding families and divorce, as well as an emerging literature on never-married parents and their children (Amato, 2001; Amato & Keith, 1991). Below, we provide brief summaries of some of the empirical findings about basic issues that a forensic evaluator is likely to confront in performing child custody evaluations, especially the effects of various conditions on children. It is essential that an evaluator have reasonable and current familiarity with these major bodies of knowledge in order to be minimally competent to assess the issues that each family member presents and to consider the relative risks and benefits.

Despite significant research on factors associated with divorce and its effects on children, currently there is no empirically based way to add up or assign weights to the various relevant factors when applied to a specific family. Also, because these disputes are so fact-specific, it is hard to extrapolate from research findings to the individual case. Amato (2001) cautions, "Knowledge of group averages, therefore, cannot predict how a particular child will adjust to family disruption" (p. 366).

In addition, research in this field rarely attempts to answer a specific legal question regarding divorce or child custody (O'Donahue & Bradley, 1999). Because judicial decisions are based on unique facts about each family that change over time, the relevant research-based factors provide context and might provide information about the risks or benefits of different outcomes, but they are not decisive. This, of course, makes child custody evaluations similar to most other areas of

BEST PRACTICE

An evaluator must have reasonable and current familiarity with major bodies of knowledge regarding the impact of parental separation on children in order to be minimally competent to assess families involved in custody disputes.

BEWARE
There is no empirically based way to assign weights to the various relevant factors when applied to a specific family.

forensic assessment. No forensic evaluation ever warrants a definitive prediction that anything will happen in a specific case. Forensic mental health evaluations describe general levels of the risk that some particular outcome might occur.

Effects of Separation and Divorce on Children

The current state of knowledge regarding the effects of divorce on children stems from several types of studies, including long-term longitudinal studies (Ahrons, 1981; Hetherington & Kelly, 2002; Wallerstein & Kelly, 1980), large-sample repeated surveys (Furstenburg, Peterson, Nord, & Zill 1983; Zill, Morrison, & Coiro, 1993), small-sample cross-sectional studies, and meta-analyses of a variety of different studies (Amato, 2001; Amato & Keith, 1991; Bauserman, 2002). Some studies have prospectively explored children's behavior before separation and followed them through divorce (Block, Block, & Gjerde, 1988; Cherlin et al., 1991), while a few have looked at older children's (or young adults') retrospective views of their parents' separation or divorce (Braver, Ellman, & Fabricius, 2003; Marquardt, 2006). Often these studies compare the developmental course of children of divorce with children from nondivorced families (Amato & Gilbreth, 1999; Simons, 1996). With the dramatic increase in never-married parent cases appearing before family court judges (Carlson & McLanahan, 2006), the children of those parents have more recently been included as an important group of study (Insabella, Williams, & Pruett, 2003).

DISTRESS AND DISORDER

In the first year or two postseparation, children often exhibit temporary behavioral changes (Hetherington, Cox, & Cox, 1982; Wallerstein & Blakeslee, 2003). Younger children may have problems in emotional regulation or disturbed sleep patterns, while older children can show short-term behavioral or academic problems, grief reactions, and loyalty conflicts (Wallerstein, Corbin, & Lewis, 1988). This is a period when the loss is most acute and the stress of divorce and single parenthood may compromise parents' caretaking abilities (Hetherington & Kelly, 2002; Wallerstein & Kelly, 1980). The well-being of the primary parent and the level of parental conflict are two major influences affecting outcome (Hetherington & Kelly, 2002). However, the majority of parents and children return to predivorce baseline functioning. There are small differences in results by gender, with boys having more problems in behavior and social relationships than girls. Age differences in adjustment, particularly after the initial separation period, have been difficult to establish, as many studies do not distinguish between age at separation and age at the time of the research or age since separation (Amato, 2001; Amato & Keith, 1991).

Results of meta-analyses indicate that children of divorce experience small but significant decrements in behavioral adjustment and achievement compared to those of nondivorced families (Amato, 2001). While most children do not experience *enduring* behavioral or emotional disorders, many will be distressed about the divorce process (Laumann-Billings & Emery, 2000; Marquardt, 2006). In other words, they recall painful feelings about the process, sometimes for years afterward, usually as a result of some of the social and familial dilemmas associated with divorce (Emery, 2004; Marquardt, 2006). Interestingly, after parental divorce, the children of high-conflict marriages do better than children of low-conflict marriages (Amato, 2001; Amato, Loomis, & Booth, 1995). The children of high-conflict parents gain some relief from parental fighting, whereas children with low-conflict parents cannot understand why their parents are no longer together and feel a great sense of loss.

Children of divorce are twice as likely as children of married parents to manifest behavioral difficulties (and to seek therapy more often) and to have lower levels of academic achievement (Amato, 2001; Zill et al., 1993). They are also more likely to drop out of school and to engage in sexual activity at a younger age, and they are twice as likely to bear children in adolescence (McLanahan & Sandefur, 1994). For example, whereas approximately 11% of children from nondivorced families manifest behavioral, academic, or family problems, about 21% of children of divorce will exhibit such difficulties (Zill et al., 1993). In a more optimistic vein, it is important to note that 75% to 80% of children of divorce will not have such developmental challenges or be negatively affected in the long-term by their parents' divorce (Kelly & Emery, 2003).

FACTORS INFLUENCING RISK

Studies that have examined *risk* (of negative effects) and *resilience* (ability to resist negative effects) in children of divorce find several factors that encourage resilience. Among them are the following:

- the parent with primary responsibility is competent and psychologically well-adjusted (Hetherington & Kelly, 2002; Wallerstein & Kelly, 1980);

- the nonresidential parent has regular and consistent contact and takes an active interest in the activities and school performance of the child (Amato & Gilbreth, 1999; Nord, Brimhall, & West, 1997);

- the parents are cooperative or, failing that, protect the child from direct exposure to interparental conflicts (Hetherington & Kelly, 2002); and

- the parent with primary responsibility has extended family support (Hetherington & Kelly, 2002).

Many factors that increase the risk of negative effects obviously are the reverse of these protective factors. Experiences that make it more difficult for children to cope with divorce include the following:

- stress of the initial separation (Kelly & Emery, 2003);

- diminished parenting (Hetherington et al., 1982);

- loss of significant relationships (including extended family, e.g., grandparents) and friends (Amato & Booth, 2001);

- parental conflict (Depner et al., 1992)

- multiple moves (including change of schools and loss of friends) (Braver et al., 2003; Hetherington & Kelly, 2002);

- economic disadvantages (the stress of which can affect parenting style or quality) (Duncan & Hoffman, 1985);

- the repartnering of either parent (Hetherington & Kelly, 2002; Kelly & Emery, 2003);

- loss of post-separation parenting time (Maccoby & Mnookin, 1992); and

- having parents who had a low-conflict marriage (Amato et al., 1995).

Two of the above factors deserve special attention regarding their negative impact on children. The first is *parental conflict.* One of the most robust factors that relates to outcome for children is the nature and level of postseparation and/or postdivorce parental conflict (Depner et al., 1992; Johnston & Campbell, 1988; Kelly & Emery, 2003). Intense expressed anger and conflict between parents can alter the developmental trajectory of children (Johnston, 2003); interfere with the security of their attachment to either parent, in particular to the father (Cummings, Schermerhorn, Davies, Goeke-Morey, & Cummings, 2006); create severe loyalty conflicts (Marquardt, 2006; Wallerstein & Kelly, 1980); affect children's health (Fabricius & Leucken, 2007) and their ability to learn to self-regulate (Schermerhorn, Cummings, DeCarlo, & Davies, 2007); and contribute to possible resistance or refusal to see one parent or the other (Kelly & Johnston, 2001; Warshak, 2003).

The second is *parenting time.* Studies have examined the manner in which children spend time with each parent postseparation. Parenting schedules are remarkably similar across Western-oriented cultures and have not changed much over time

(Maccoby & Mnookin, 1992; Resetar & Emery, 2008). While data from the 1980s suggested that fathers' contact with their children diminished over time (Amato & Gilbreth, 1999; Furstenburg, 1990; Zill et al., 1993), later studies showed more lasting paternal commitment and contact (Amato, 2001), with children who had regular contact with their fathers demonstrating better adjustment than those who did not (Hetherington & Kelly, 2002). Shared decision making, structured parenting plans, and overnight contact were contributing factors to that change (Amato, 2001; Isaacs, 1988) and are predictors of enduring paternal involvement. While parents often argue over the parenting plan, the data demonstrate that it is the quality of the parent–child relationship rather than the quantity of time spent together that is critical to child outcomes (Baumrind, 1967; Insabella et al., 2003).

In summary, divorce or parental separation has a significant but small impact on child adjustment, with the largest effect experienced just prior to or soon after the separation. While most children of divorce show resilience over time, many experience painful struggles unfamiliar to their peers in nondivorced families. Regular contact and positive relationships with two parents who engage in minimal or contained conflict, have sufficient financial resources, attend to the child's academic and extracurricular interests, and have extended family support predict better outcomes for children (Hetherington & Stanley-Hagan, 1999).

Domestic Abuse and Marital Conflict

One of the most damaging forms of interparental conflict is intimate partner aggression, often called domestic abuse or domestic violence. Allegations of this sort are frequently reported in custody evaluations (Johnston, Walters, & Oleson, 2005). A voluminous clinical and scientific literature on this issue with respect to custody disputes has led to changes in statutes and in case law across the country. As of 2008, 20 states and the District of Columbia had a legal presumption against either sole custody or joint legal or physical custody to a parent who is found to have perpetrated an act of domestic violence (as defined by statute). Another 29 states explicitly consider the existence of domestic violence to be one of the best interest factors of which the court must take notice. One state, Washington, implicitly addresses domestic violence by considering the need to protect the child from physical, mental, or emotional harm (National Center for State Courts, 2008).

Effects of Domestic Violence

Reports of domestic violence and abuse are substantial in contested custody cases. Horvath, Logan, and Walker (2002), in their review study of 102 custody evaluation reports and corresponding court records, found that roughly 72% of the cases filed involved confirmed domestic violence (type unspecified). After reviewing 105 custody evaluation reports, Ayoub, Deutsch, and Maranganore (1999) reported that almost two-thirds of the reports they reviewed had noted domestic violence (also type unspecified) in the family, and in over half of the cases children had witnessed the reported violence. These reports of domestic abuse are similar to rates reported by Johnston and Campbell (1988) in their high-conflict sample and to the rates reported by divorcing couples in general (Lawrence & Bradbury, 2001).

The direct and indirect effects on children of witnessing interparental physical aggression or significant fear-generating intimidation are multiple, affecting their mood, behavior, health, and cognitive/academic status (Kelly & Johnson, 2008). Many studies of children who have witnessed violence in their close family relationships report symptoms consistent with posttraumatic stress disorder (Chemtob & Carlson, 2004; Lehmann & Ellison, 2001). Younger children who witness violence may suffer from developmental delays (Lieberman & Van Horn, 1998). In their custody evaluation report review study, Ayoub et al. (1999) found that the effects on a child of witnessing domestic violence

INFO

There are many direct and indirect effects on children who witness domestic violence. The child's mood, behavior, health, and cognitive/academic status can all be impacted.

were as harmful as those of being the victim of child maltreatment.

A child's witnessing of *psychological abuse* between parents has both a direct effect on her adjustment (Teicher, Samson, Polcari, & McGreenery, 2006) and an indirect effect as a result of compromised abilities in the victimized parent (Cummings et al., 2006). Thus, children who are exposed only to this form of partner abuse (i.e., where there has been no physical abuse between parents) are more likely to exhibit increased anxiety, distractibility, and acting-out behaviors (Cummings, Davies, & Campbell, 2002; Cummings et al., 2006).

Types of Abuse

The matter of classification of domestic abuse into subtypes has been the focus of much professional and political debate. Here we offer one useful typology, as well as information about the effects of each type.

Coercive control refers to physical abuse intended to intimidate and to exert power and control in an intimate relationship (Jaffe, Baker, & Cunningham, 2004). This type of domestic abuse has been termed "intimate terrorism" (Johnson, 1995) or, more recently, "coercive, controlling violence" (Kelly & Johnson, 2008). There is some controversy in the field about whether this form of domestic violence is gendered. Those who study severely abused or battered women, particularly those women in protective shelters, find that the vast majority of perpetrators are men who typically (but not exclusively) use physical means to intimidate and exert power and control over the women with whom they share an intimate relationship (Jaffe et al., 2004). Conversely, others who study large, representative, and national (e.g., United States, Canada) samples find that coercive violence is reported by comparable numbers of men and women (Dutton, Hamel, & Aronson, 2010;

Grandin & Lupri, 1997; Whittaker, Haileyesus, Swahn, & Saltzman, 2007). In this type of severe abuse, the perpetrator uses various forms of aggression—including physical, sexual, and psychological *aggression*—to maintain control over the partner. However, the size and strength differences between genders result in more injuries to women, except when a woman is the sole aggressor (Dutton et al., 2010).

Conflict-oriented abuse involves less severe forms of aggression (physical: slap, kick, push; verbal: insult/put-down, curse) and is very common (Straus & Gelles, 1988). This type of aggression is reactive and related to conflict between the partners, but it is not motivated by the need to have power and control over the other partner (Johnson & Leone, 2005; Kelly & Johnson, 2008). Such intimate partner abuse also has been called "common couple violence" (Johnson, 1995), "common couple aggression" (Zibbell, 2005), or, more recently, "situational couple violence" (Kelly & Johnson, 2008). In these community or national samples, females report being as aggressive as males across a variety of relationships (such as dating couples, same-gender couples, and cohabiting or married couples) (Smith-Slep & O'Leary, 2005). In addition, unmarried couples who date or who live together have higher rates of these forms of aggression than do married couples (Capaldi & Crosby, 1997).

Other forms of domestic violence include "violent resistance"; aggressive acts often committed in self-defense (Johnson, 1995; Miller, 2005); and "separation-instigated violence," wherein violence was not characteristic of the relationship but occurred suddenly in reaction to the pain or trauma of dissolution (Johnston & Campbell, 1988; Kelly & Johnson, 2008).

Domestic violence can co-occur with child abuse and neglect, depending upon the definition of domestic violence and the population surveyed (Dutton et al., 2010).

3 chapter

INFO

Types of domestic violence include the following:

- Coercive control
- Conflict oriented
- Violent resistance
- Separation instigated

The broader the definition (and the greater the severity of the aggression—such as that reported by women in shelters), the more prevalent is the co-occurrence of child maltreatment (Appell & Holden, 1998; Ayoub et al., 1999; Fantuzzo & Mohr, 1999). There is also a co-occurrence of domestic abuse and substance use/abuse (Hesselbrock & Hesselbrock, 2006; Moore & Stuart, 2004; Stuart et al., 2006).

Psychological aggression refers to partner conflict without physical violence (O'Leary & Mauiro, 2001). Also called emotional or mental abuse, it can be a precursor to physical violence (O'Leary & Slep, 2006), although many partners who engage in different forms of psychological aggression never progress to any physical abuse (Frye & Karney, 2006). Nonetheless, it is likely that certain forms of psychological abuse/aggression (e.g., stalking, intimidation, severe ridicule, and social isolation) have effects on the victim's state of mind and emotions that may be as traumatic as those of physical violence (Murphy & Cascardi, 1999). Psychological aggression is very common in severe marital conflict (Smith-Slep & O'Leary, 2005) and in divorcing families (Lawrence & Bradbury, 2001).

In summary, allegations of domestic abuse are the most frequent type of negative behavior reported in custody disputes (Dutton, 2005). These rates of reporting are consistent with reports of various forms of interpartner aggression in divorcing couples in general. Differentiating types of abuse helps to inform the forensic evaluator about the dynamics of the family, the potential risks for a victimized partner, and the nature of the risk for children who are exposed to those behaviors.

Child Maltreatment

Allegations of child maltreatment in custody disputes are amongst the most difficult to assess. Here we describe the research on child maltreatment, but less will be said in the remainder of this volume about the assessment of child abuse. Child custody examiners frequently must deal with such issues; readers can consult other texts (e.g., Kuehnle & Connell, 2009; Faller, 2007) for information on assessing child sexual abuse.

Frequency of Child Maltreatment

In 2007, there were 3.2 million referrals to child protective agencies for alleged maltreatment. After screening and investigations, about 500,000

BEWARE Allegations of child maltreatment in custody disputes are among the most difficult issues you will be called upon to assess as a forensic evaluator. It is critical for the forensic evaluator to have specialized training and knowledge regarding the evaluation of these claims.

children were found to have been the victim of some form of maltreatment. The majority of allegations involved neglect (60%) or physical abuse (10%), while about 7.6% involved sexual abuse (U.S. Department of Health & Human Services, Administration on Children, Youth, and Families, 2009).

In the context of custody disputes, the incidence of reported allegations has been estimated to be between 1% and 2% (Bala & Schuman, 1999; Brown, 2003; Thoennes & Tjaden, 1990). In their review of documents from completed custody evaluations, however, Horvath et al. (2002) found allegations of child abuse (undifferentiated) in court case records about 56% of the time, although the custody reports noted them only 37% of the time. Mothers made allegations about three times as often than fathers did. Allegations that arose after the divorce was finalized were more likely to be supported as compared to allegations that emerged while the divorce was pending.

Regarding substantiated reports, Ayoub et al.'s (1999) review of child custody reports found that allegations of various forms of child maltreatment were supported between 25% and 33% of the time, consistent with the findings of Johnston, Lee, Oleson, and Walters (2005) in their sample of 120 custody-disputing couples. Allegations of abuse against fathers in custody evaluations are substantiated about 60% more often than allegations against mothers (Johnston, Lee, et al., 2005), mirroring the rate for other forms of child protection cases that do not involve custody conflicts (McGleughlin, Meyer, & Baker, 1999). Where child sexual abuse

3
chapter

INFO

As in noncustody cases, allegations of abuse against fathers in custody evaluations are substantiated about 60% more often than are allegations against mothers.

is confirmed, other forms of maltreatment are likely, including domestic violence (Erickson & Egeland, 1987). There is also twice the risk of child physical and sexual abuse when a parent is a substance abuser (Walsh, MacMillan, & Jamieson, 2003).

One might expect that there is a greater likelihood of false allegation of child maltreatment in the context of parental separation, but there are no solid research findings supporting this claim (Kuehnle & Kirkpatrick, 2005). The incidence of child sexual abuse claims in the general population tends to vary with societal trends, but it may be underreported (Kuenhle & Kirkpatrick, 2005). The Canadian Incidence Study noted that about 6% of separated parents had made allegations of sexual abuse (Bala, Mitnick, Trocmé, & Houston, 2007). In that study, a total of 45% of those sexual abuse reports were either substantiated (11%) or suspected (34%), whereas 54% were either unsubstantiated (36%) or intentionally false (18%).

Impact of Child Maltreatment on Children

Post-traumatic stress disorder and acute stress disorder are common reactions to child maltreatment, affecting between 25% and 50% of child victims of physical abuse (Famularo, Fenton, Kinscherff & Ayoub, 1994) and up to 70% of child victims of sexual abuse (Kendall-Tackett, Williams, & Finkelhor, 1993). Of course, this also means that 30% or more of children who have experienced sexual abuse and up to 75% of children who have experienced physical abuse do not manifest post-traumatic stress disorder. Some research has shown that child *neglect* can have more negative developmental effects than child physical *abuse* (Erickson & Egeland, 1996). Children who have been victims of multiple forms of abuse have a higher risk of perpetrating some maltreatment when they become parents themselves

(Widom, 1989). Adolescents who have been victims of parental verbal and physical aggression and have witnessed such aggressive acts between their parents are more likely to be aggressive toward their significant others or spouses in adulthood (Cui, Durtschi, Donnellan, Lorenz, & Conger (2011). However, early traumatic experience is not determinative, given that less than one-third of such children progress to become abusive as adults in their own families (Kaufman & Zigler, 1987). Nevertheless, "victims of all forms of family violence are at an increased risk for a variety of psychological problems," including conditions ranging from "aggression to anxiety to depression" (Emery & Laumann-Billings, 1998, p. 128).

Some childhood sexual behavior is normative (Friedrich, 2005; Friedrich, Fisher, Broughton, Houston, & Shafran, 1998), so it is often difficult to differentiate sexualized symptoms in those children who have been sexually maltreated from normative sexual behavior or symptoms in those who are emotionally disturbed but have not been abused. While inappropriate sexual behavior is more common among sexually abused children (Friedrich et al., 2001; McLellan et al., 1996), the presence of such sexual behaviors is not necessarily indicative of sexual abuse (Drach, Wientzen, & Ricci, 2001; Friedrich, 2002). It may be related to other forms of trauma, such as physical abuse, witnessing domestic violence (Silovsky & Nice, 2002), or other factors that increase behavioral dysregulation (Friedrich, 2005). The stress of divorce, particularly high-conflict divorce (Johnston & Campbell, 1988; Johnston, Kline, & Tschann, 1991), can result in children's reporting clinically significant behavioral or psychological problems that are similar to the reports of sexually abused or maltreated children, depending upon which measures of child adjustment one uses (Hetherington, 1999; Kendall-Tackett et al., 1993).

Other emotional difficulties or nonabusive forms of boundary violations (such as co-sleeping, co-bathing, or inadvertently witnessing sexual relations) can also

INFO

While inappropriate sexual behavior is more common among sexually abused children, the presence of such sexual behaviors alone is not necessarily indicative of sexual abuse.

produce symptoms in children (Johnson, 2005). Allegations of sexual abuse in a high-conflict divorce significantly complicate the assessment of the abuse claims. Moreover, children's inappropriate sexualized behaviors warrant consideration of possible abuse, but in themselves are not conclusive of it. At the same time, because there is no specific profile of child abuse symptomatology, the absence of symptoms does not per se eliminate the possibility of abuse where it has been alleged.

One critical area of investigation with respect to child maltreatment, and to sexual abuse in particular, has been the process of eliciting information from alleged child victims and assessing the validity of such data (Kuehnle, 1996). The literatures related to children's language (Saywitz, 1995), memory (Goodman, Hirschman, Hepps, & Rudy, 1991), age (Lamb et al., 2003), and suggestibility (Bruck & Ceci, 2009; Ceci & Bruck, 1993; Ceci, Kulkofsky, Klemfuss, Sweeney, & Bruck, 2007; Kulkofsky & London, 2010) and the context of investigative interviews (Davis & Bottoms, 2002) have led to guidelines about the structure and process of such interviews (AACAP, 1997b; American Professional Society on the Abuse of Children, 1997; Lamb, Sternberg, & Esplin, 1998; Lamb, Sternberg, Esplin, Herskowitz, & Orbach, 1999; Poole & Lamb, 1998). In addition, methods have evolved to elicit the most accurate information possible (Reed, 1996), particularly with respect to open-ended questions and nonsuggestive interview techniques (Bruck & Ceci, 2009).

The empirical findings about child interviewing and accurate reporting (Lamb, Orbach, Sternberg, Herskowitz, & Horowitz, 2000) indicate the need for a heightened level of skill and caution, the addition of recording technologies, and the use of a structured protocol (Hewitt, 1999). Due to the severity of the possible consequences to the child, to the accused, and to the accused parent's access to the child, there are serious implications of committing a type I (false positive, where abuse is substantiated but did not occur) or type II

BEST PRACTICE

The empirical findings about child interviewing and accurate reporting in child maltreatment cases indicate that you need (1) a high level of skill and caution, (2) the addition of recording technologies, and (3) the use of a structured protocol.

(false negative, where abuse is not substantiated but did occur) error. For a review of these issues, see Carnes (2000) or Kuehnle & Drozd (2005).

Parental Psychiatric Disorder

One frequent reason for the court to appoint a mental health forensic evaluator stems from questions about the impact of adult psychiatric disorder on parenting and on children. In fact, many statutes require consideration of the mental or psychological health of the parents as one of the best interest factors (see Appendix A). A substantial body of literature exists on psychiatric disorders and parenting, including information about risk and protective factors.

Frequency of Parental Psychiatric Disorder in Custody Cases

There are no national data on the number of adults with mental illnesses who have custody of children. However, mothers have been the primary focus of research on the effects of mental illness on parenting (Jenuwine & Cohler, 1999), probably because women are far more likely to be the primary caretakers of children than men are (Nicholson, Biebel, Hinden, Henry, & Steir, 2001; Styron, Pruitt, McMahon, & Davidson, 2002). While having a severe psychiatric disorder increases the risk of losing custody, that risk decreases with familial and social support (Benjet, Azar, & Kuersten-Hogan, 2003). Fear of losing custody can deter a parent from seeking appropriate mental health services and community support (Hearle, Plant, Jenner, Barkla, & McGrath, 1999).

In studies that reviewed custody evaluation reports, Horvath et al. (2002) found that those reports addressed issues of psychiatric illness about 26% of the time (undifferentiated by gender or type of psychiatric illness). In contrast, Ayoub et al. (1999) stated that their sample of reports addressed psychiatric disorders in 59% of the mothers and 61% of the fathers, an equivalence that does not reflect national morbidity data and whose proportions are more than twice those of the Horvath et al. research. One possible explanation is that their report sample came from a forensic service in a major urban hospital, which arguably could draw more cases with parental mental disorder as a presenting problem.

Impact of Parental Psychiatric Disorder on Parenting

It is essential to consider how any psychiatric disorder may affect parenting (Otto et al., 2003), as the current obligation for experts is to examine the "documented functional significance of the disorder for the child" (Benjet et al., 2003, p. 241.) or, as suggested in Chapter 2, the nexus between the disorder and parenting ability. For the most part, mothers with severe mental illness are as concerned about their children and give the same priority to their children's needs as mothers in general (Benjet et al., 2003). However, the more severe the mental disorder, the more likely it is that mothers will lose custody of their children (Joseph, Joshi, Lewin, & Abrams, 1999). Parenting in the context of the multiple demands of maintaining a household is stressful and can exacerbate preexisting mental illness (Zemenchuk, Rogosh, & Mowbray, 1995). For example, when their symptoms become severe, some parents with mood disorders have been noted to be less nurturing and available to a child (Kahng, Oyserman, Bybee, & Mowbray, 2008; Weinberg & Tronick, 1998). Mothers with mood disorders are more likely to be primary caretakers than are mothers who are psychotic (White, Nicholson, Fisher, & Geller, 1995). Such mothers may interpret their children's misbehavior as indications of nascent emotional disturbance and worry about the effect of their illness on the children (Nicholson, Sweeney, & Geller, 1998). On the positive side, parenting can promote recovery and serve as a motivator for a mentally ill adult, especially when there is sufficient family and community support (Oyserman, Mowbray, & Zemenchuk, 1994).

Impact of Parental Psychiatric Disorder on Children

Children who have a mentally ill parent are at greater risk for a number of psycho-social problems (Nicholson et al., 2001) in addition to having a greater genetic vulnerability for psychiatric illness. They have elevated risks of exhibiting learning problems, developmental delays, attention issues, social skills deficits, substance abuse, anxiety disorders, and somatic complaints (Beardslee, Versage, & Gladstone, 1998). This reflects both genetic risks and the direct effects of parenting by parents who are less resilient in the face of daily stressors. Indeed, the two may interact. For example, a child with intense emotional/social needs or externalizing behaviors places greater stress on an already compromised parent and thereby affects parenting practices (Dishion & Patterson, 2006; Goodman & Gotlib, 1999). There

INFO

Children who have a mentally ill parent are at greater risk for exhibiting learning problems, developmental delays, attention issues, social skills deficits, substance abuse, anxiety disorders, and somatic complaints.

is evidence, though, that the quality of the family or spousal support can mitigate those stressors and enhance parenting (Nicholson et al., 2001).

3
chapter

The literature in the area of mild-to-moderate parental mental illness suggests multiple, interacting variables that mediate child outcomes. This research, in contrast to that regarding severe mental illness in parents, has primarily used middle-class samples of mothers with mood disorders (Nicholson et al., 2001). Children who perceive parents as being unavailable or inattentive—as is more likely to be the case with parental postpartum depression or mood disorder (Jenuwine & Cohler, 1999)—may develop problems in attachment relationships and in the ability to control one's emotions or to self-regulate (Radke-Yarrow, 1991). While almost nine of ten children of psychiatrically disordered parents remain resilient, the remaining group suffers from the effects of living with a mentally ill parent, especially if there are repeated hospitalizations or if the illness is untreated. Repeated hospitalizations are indicative of the severity of the disorder. The separations associated with those admissions are likely to be more stressful for the children than are the psychiatric symptoms themselves (Jenuwine & Cohler, 1999). In addition, frequent parental hospitalizations are correlated with more negative child outcomes (Benjet et al., 2003).

In summary, parental psychiatric illness is one of the more common yet complex issues raised in a custody dispute. As such, it is a natural referral for a forensic mental health evaluator. The literature on parenting and psychiatric disorders underscores the importance of assessing the social and family context in addition to the nature and severity of the psychiatric disorder itself. The forensic evaluator should evaluate at a minimum the link between the demonstrable effects of the disorder on parenting in that particular family and "the impact of that illness on the child" (Jenuwine and Cohler, 1999, p. 303.). Of paramount importance are the nature of the illness, the parent's understanding of the disorder and compliance with treatment, the availability and efficacy of treatment, and the presence of supportive adults who are able to step in and protect the child should the patient/parent deteriorate and to support the parent in obtaining the appropriate care.

Parental Substance Abuse

Parental alcohol/substance use or abuse is an issue often raised in child custody evaluations. Along with parental psychiatric disorder, it is a major reason for parents, primarily mothers, to lose custody of their children, although it also influences courts to circumscribe fathers' contact with their children. Because substance use or abuse is such a frequent complaint in custody evaluations, screening for it and assessment of its effects on parental and family functioning is an affirmative responsibility of the forensic evaluator.

The National Institute on Alcohol Abuse and Alcoholism (NIAAA; 2009) defines a light drinker as one who has had three or fewer drinks per week in the past year and a moderate drinker as one, who, on average, has had more than three drinks but no more than seven drinks per week for women, and no more than fourteen drinks per week for men, in the past year. Between 60% and 65% of adults are light to moderate drinkers, although men are three times more likely than women to drink moderately (Hesselbrock &

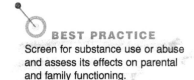

BEST PRACTICE
Screen for substance use or abuse and assess its effects on parental and family functioning.

Hesselbrock, 2006; NIAAA, 2009). Men are slightly more likely to be heavy drinkers than women are (6.1% vs. 4.2%), a pattern defined as, on average, more than one drink per day for women and more than two drinks per day for men in the past year (NIAAA, 2009). Men are also more likely to experience problematic use during early to middle adulthood (Warner, Kessler, Hughes, Anthony, & Nelson, 1994), which coincides with the age range of parenting. If the female partner/spouse in a relationship abuses alcohol, there is a greater chance that the male partner will, too (McCrady, 2008; Vaillant, 1995). Historically, women are more likely to abuse prescription drugs than are men (Courtwright, 1982). As is true with psychiatric disorders, research and treatment studies on substance abuse in general have typically looked at men, while studies on substance abuse and parenting have typically used samples of mothers (Mayes & Truman, 2002).

Substance Use in Child Custody Cases

If alcohol is a mother's substance of choice, she is more likely to have abused it at home, thus avoiding some negative consequences, such as arrest or driving citations. In addition, treatment or recovery can be more complicated in women than it is in men, due to the greater social stigma and disapproval associated with female substance abusers (DiClemente, 2006). On the other hand, the parenting role often has the highest value for mothers and frequently motivates treatment compliance (Benjet, Azar, & Kuersten-Hogan, 2003). Regardless of gender, even substance use or abuse that does not reach a diagnostic threshold of dependency can be problematic, particularly when the result of that use compromises intimate relations and parenting (Douglas and Skeem, 2005).

Two studies have reported on substance abuse allegations in child custody evaluation reports. Ayoub et al. (1999) stated that evaluation reports in 105 acrimonious divorces addressed issues of substance abuse in fathers in 52.3% of the cases and in mothers in 29.1% of the cases. Reviewing 102 child custody cases, Horvath et al. (2002) noted that 42% of the custody evaluation reports addressed that issue, although they did not differentiate by gender.

Substance use or abuse often co-occurs with other forms of psychopathology, such as mental illness or domestic violence (Kessler, Chiu, Demler, & Walters, 2005; Regier et al., 1993). Over 5.5 million adults ages 18 and older suffer from co-occurring disorders, but only about half of those receive treatment (Substance Abuse and Mental Health Services Administration [SAMHSA], 2006). Substance abuse can lower the threshold for committing acts of domestic violence. For example, approximately two-thirds of those who abuse an intimate partner drink alcohol prior to the aggression, as compared to a frequency of about half that for those who are violent toward a nonintimate acquaintance or stranger (Hesselbrock & Hesselbrock, 2006) or abuse a child (Wasserman & Leventhal, 1998). Parental substance abuse is one of the more common reasons for state intrusion in the form of child protection services into family life (Benjet et al., 2003). That noted, many adults are substance-dependent without negative psychological effects (Donovan, 1999; Schuckit et al., 2001).

Impact of Parental Substance Use on Children

About 12% of children live with at least one substance-abusing parent (SAMHSA, 2009). The consequences for children of having a parent who is a substance abuser are varied. Many studies find associations with externalizing (behavioral/acting out/conduct problems) (McMahon & Giannini, 2003) and internalizing (emotional/anxiety/depression) problems in children (Giglio & Kaufman, 1990; Harter, 2000), school difficulties (Harden & Pihl, 1995), and increased likelihood of adolescent-onset substance use or abuse (Chassin, Curran, Hussong, & Colder, 1996; Clark et al., 1997). As they grow into adulthood, children of substance-abusing fathers are more likely to use alcohol and drugs, use them earlier (Hill, Shen, Lowers, & Locke, 2000), and use them more often than are adults whose parents did not abuse substances (Reich, Earls, Frankel, & Shayka, 1993). However, the literature suggests there are few or no *direct* effects of a parent's substance abuse on child outcomes (Mayes & Truman, 2002), as the contexts of abuse often contain multiple and related stressors, such as co-occurring psychological problems (e.g., personality or psychiatric disorders) and environmental problems (e.g., divorce, unemployment, or low socioeconomic status) (Suchman & Luthar, 2000, 2001).

INFO

Children who have a substance-abusing parent are at greater risk for behavioral or emotional problems, school difficulties, and increased likelihood of adolescent-onset substance use or abuse.

Despite a parent's substance abuse, family cohesiveness, adaptability, and parental monitoring of children (Goldstein, 2003) can ameliorate the effect of a parent's substance dependency (El-Sheikh & Buckhalt, 2003). Thus, family contextual factors (e.g., marital cohesiveness), external stressors (e.g., unemployment or economic stress), or co-occurring conditions (e.g., depression, anxiety) all influence the substance-abusing parent and, in the aggregate, have an effect on parenting.

3
chapter

Treatment Issues

The level of support for treatment for substance abuse is critical and predictive of recovery (as it is with psychiatric disorders). Therefore, programs that provide help for family and loved ones are often preferable to those that help only the substance abuser, although these family-support programs appear to be more available for substance-abusing mothers (Luthar & Suchman, 2000). Programs that include children and provide some focus on parenting skills have a greater chance of enhancing motivation to abstain and of promoting improvement in overall parenting. For those addicted to opiates, methadone has been an effective means of maintenance that allows the individual to function normally. In recent years, buprenorphine, an opiate agonist, has been used to block the effects of an opiate, reduce craving for the drug, and allow phased withdrawal from it. It has been a useful pharmacological tool in outpatient treatment/recovery programs. However, effective treatment should include attention to the reasons the person became addicted, as well as to those who can support recovery. Such treatment might include halfway houses, psychotherapy, self-help groups, and family support programs (Stimmel, 2009).

Parental Alienation and Estrangement

One of the more controversial yet common areas of interest in custodial disputes is the issue of alienation of a child from one parent. In its more severe form, typically a child either resists or refuses contact with one parent and complains about that parent in terms disproportionate to the reality. Alternatively, in a moderate form of alienation, a child may complain to one parent about the time spent with the other parent but continue to go along with the parenting plan. If there is litigation, often the disfavored or rejected parent will allege that the preferred or favored parent has initiated a campaign of sabotage of the former's relationship with the child. This problem can be difficult to both evaluate and remedy and has been the source of much debate in the field (Walker, Brantley, & Rigsbee, 2004).

Definition of Parental Alienation and Estrangement

Wallerstein and Kelly (1980) first wrote about this phenomenon, calling it an "unholy alliance." However, Gardner (1992) is generally credited with describing a complex set of behaviors and attitudes within a divorced family that, in its most intense form, he labeled Parental Alienation Syndrome, or PAS. Based on his clinical experience with divorcing families, he posited that PAS consisted of the following three factors:

1. the persistent rejection of the disfavored parent by the child *in the absence* (emphasis added) of prior abuse, neglect, or domestic violence;

2. the child's denigration of the parent in a rigid, black-and-white manner with no guilt or remorse for that attitude; and

3.   the favored parent's instigation of, support for, or
     lack of discouragement of this behavior.

Warshak (**2003, 2011**) labeled this *irrational* or *pathological*
alienation, in the sense that it was not a reasonable reaction to the
rejected parent's actual behavior. He further noted that it needed
to "reach the level of a campaign" (2003, p. 280). Irrespective of
whether the "syndrome" label applied, subsequent clinicians have
offered symptom lists of varying lengths (Darnall, 1998; Ellis,
2007), but there has been a dearth of research to support those
claims.

Others have challenged Gardner's concept of a "syndrome"
(Walker et al., 2004; Warshak, 2001). Kelly and Johnston (2001)
conceptualize alienation as a spectrum of the child's relationships
with each parent and the multiple factors affecting those relationships. This ranges from "affinity," or a naturally greater affection
for one parent with continued attachment and love for the other,
to "alignment," or a strong preference for one parent with ambivalence about the other parent without rejection, to "alienation," or
a near total alliance with one parent with varying levels of rejection
of the other parent. Their multifactorial systems model suggested
that any level of disaffection is multidetermined and results from
qualities in each of the family members (i.e., the favored parent,
the rejecting child, and the disfavored parent). The interaction of
these factors influences the child to reject one parent or align with
the other. Initial research indicates that variables such as the degree
of parental warmth or prior involvement with the child are important predictors of alienation (Johnston, Walters, et al., 2005).

Kelly and Johnston (2001) differentiates alienation from
"estrangement," in that the latter reflected a child's *reasonable*
(emphasis added) aversion to or fear of contact with the disfavored
parent because of painful experiences with that parent during the
marriage (or cohabitation) or the separation period. Such experiences might include child maltreatment, domestic violence, and
inappropriate or ineffective parenting. Given the possibility that
the child's estrangement is secondary to child maltreatment,
any remedies should consider the safety of the child and/or
victim-parent as a primary guiding principle, particularly if the

3
chapter

INFO

PAS assigns responsibility for the breach in a parent–child relationship to the powerful influence of the favored parent. The multifactorial systems model, on the other hand, views the parent–child alienation as a spectrum of the child's relationships with each parent and the factors affecting those relationships.

estrangement occurrs in the context of domestic violence (Drozd, Kuehnle, & Walker, 2004; Drozd & Oleson, 2004). In summary, the multifactorial systems model differs from that of PAS, as the latter gives primacy and assigns blame for the breach in the parent–child relationship singularly to the powerful influence of the favored parent.

Attachment and Parental Alienation and Estrangement

Other writers have placed alienation in the context of developmental and attachment theory. Garber (2004) cited research that suggests marital conflict has a negative effect on a child's attachment. This impact on the child derives from the direct effects of exposure to parental conflict and the indirect effects of changes in parenting itself due to the stress of the conflict. Both of those effects can compromise a child's emotional security (Davies & Cummings, 1994). However, Walker et al. (2004) disagreed, asserting that there were no data yet to link attachment and alienation in children of high-conflict divorces, particularly given that the so-called *alienated child* "frequently does not have attachment problems with other peers, adults, or the non-alienated parent, although other problems may be present in that relationship" (p. 57).

Frequency of Parental Alienation and Estrangement

The reported prevalence of this phenomenon reflects the nature of the samples (Johnston, 2003; Maccoby & Mnookin, 1992; Wallerstein & Kelly, 1980). It seems reasonable to conclude that between 10% and 20% of divorcing or separating families will experience a child's resistance to or ambivalence about seeing one of the parents (Johnston, 2003). In high-conflict families

(Clawar & Rivlin, 1991; Johnston, Walters, et al., 2005), alienating behaviors exhibited by at least one parent (or child alignment) will occur on a regular basis, such that it might be considered normative (Johnston & Kelly, 2004) in the divorcing population. For example, depending on the sample, the frequency of visitation refusal and resistance increases in high-conflict divorces, ranging from 19% to 50% of families in which one child resists visits (but does not categorically refuse) to 6% to 20% of families in which a child completely refuses to see one

INFO
Research suggests that children in separating or divorcing families will at times resist or be ambivalent about seeing one parent, but a child's outright refusal is more likely in a high-conflict divorce.

parent for some period of time (Johnston, 2003; Johnston & Campbell, 1988; Johnston, Walters, et al., 2005; Kopetski, 1998; Lampel, 1996). Canadian courts' data from between 1989 and 2008 show an increase in the number of decisions involving allegations of parental alienation in the second decade of the study, although the rate at which the courts substantiated the claims of alienation (about 60% of claims made) remained about the same in each decade (Bala, Hunt, & McCarney, 2010).

Remedial Dilemmas for Parental Alienation and Estrangement

Another area of controversy involves how to reconcile children who have become alienated from a parent when there appears to have been no significant basis for that behavior, that is, no child abuse, neglect, or domestic violence. Most commentators recommend some plan of family therapy in which all the players are involved, either individually or jointly (Lee & Oleson, 2001), although some have cautioned about what kind of therapy is preferred or whether it should be mandated by the court. In instances of what Gardner would call severe alienation, he recommended that the courts switch custody from the favored parent to the alienated one, citing his own study of 99 cases (Gardner, 2001). It should be noted, however, that Gardner's ideas remain controversial and neither peer-reviewed support nor consensus in the field exists on this issue. Studies that have used multimodal approaches to reconciliation (e.g., individual, joint, or family therapies) (Friedlander & Walters, 2010; Johnston, Walters, & Friedlander, 2001) have shown modest gains over time in the relationship between the alienated child and the non-abusive, rejected parent (Johnston & Goldman, 2010). Johnston and Goldman (2010) report that nearly all the children who refused or resisted contact with a parent reconnected with the rejected parent after the age of majority. Other studies have used small samples of alienated children, limiting the significance of their findings (Dunne & Hedrick, 1994; Lampel, 1986). Reports of more time- and professionally intensive intervention models have been promising (Sullivan, Ward, & Deutsch, 2010; Warshak, 2010), although the challenge is to modify the methods of those intensive approaches to suit an affordable, community-based model.

Much more research is necessary in order to develop reliable measures of alienation, so that researchers may better understand and distinguish what factors in parents and children increase the risk of alienation from those that protect against its development, and what kinds of treatments are effective for such families (Warshak, 2001). In the meantime, current best practice suggests that the forensic evaluator should consider the contributions of the favored parent, the rejected parent, and the aligned child to the rift when assessing families in which alienation is alleged (Friedlander & Walters, 2010).

Parenting Plans and Outcomes for Children

BEST PRACTICE
Current best practice suggests that you should consider the roles of the favored parent, the rejected parent, and the aligned child when assessing families in which alienation is alleged.

Courts frequently ask evaluators to recommend a parenting plan, often in conjunction with a request for an opinion on the "type of custody." The database for this question derives from the same kinds of study designs noted earlier in this area of research. Despite a significant amount of divorce research, there is no empirical basis for recommending specific time arrangements or schedules. In a large meta-analysis, Bauserman (2002) reviewed and analyzed studies related to types of custody. He found that

BEWARE
Despite much divorce research, there is no empirical basis for recommending specific time arrangements or schedules.

joint physical or legal custody had a low to moderate positive effect on child outcome when the level of conflict between parents was low. One limitation of his study is that he included only a small number of studies that measured interparental conflict. However, in those studies with conflict measures, parents with joint custody had lower levels of acrimony. Bauserman (2002) and other writers (Maccoby & Mnookin, 1992) have suggested that such parents were more likely to self-select joint/shared custody than were parents with high conflict. When parents engage in high conflict, the data suggest that court-ordered shared physical custody (where the parent with the lesser share of time has at least 35% to 40% of the overnights) may be the worst of all possible psychological worlds for the child (Johnston, Kline, & Tschann, 1991).

Given the variety of data and the natural limitations of research, the results can provide only broad indicators for families in which determinations are fact specific. Evaluators who recommend parenting plans do so primarily based on the history of the family, child development considerations, and knowledge of practices in their local jurisdictions, with limited guidance from research. Some states (e.g., Arizona, Massachusetts, and Oregon) have promoted model parenting plans to inform parents considering postseparation parenting arrangements. These guides to parenting plans outline factors to consider in devising schedules and recommend various parenting arrangements for children of different ages. The Web addresses for these model plans are available in Chapter 1.

BEST PRACTICE
If you recommend a parenting plan, it is essential to consider the history of the family and to be knowledgeable about practices in your local jurisdictions. Be mindful also of the literature on parenting plans and child development.

3
chapter

Children's developmental needs are paramount in the development of parenting plans. Of particular relevance for infants and toddlers, developments in the field of attachment research have influenced custody determinations and parenting schedules (Sparta & Stahl, 2006). Infants and toddlers in separated and divorced families spend the majority of their time, especially overnights, with mothers (Hodges, 1991), consistent with attachment theory promoting the importance of a primary caretaker (Goldstein, Freud, & Solnit, 1973). However, more recent research suggests that young children are capable of multiple, secure attachments and that it is developmentally important to have regular access to both parents (Lamb & Kelly, 2001), as long as schedules are not erratic (Pruett, Ebling, & Insabella, 2004) and both parents are attentive and loving (Ludolph, 2009). Current thinking suggests that children's temperament and developmental status and each parent's caretaking skills are important contributors to children's secure attachment in separated families (Ludolph, 2009).

The controversial aspect of this change in thinking relates to overnights for very young children with the nonresidential parent (Bruch, 2006; Solomon & Biringen, 2001; Warshak, 2000). Preliminary studies have not demonstrated adverse effects of overnights with nonresidential parents for very young children (Pruett et al., 2004), except when there is conflict between the parents over custody and parenting time (McIntosh, Smyth, Kelaher, Wells, & Long, 2010; Solomon & George, 1999). Currently, attachment theory and research do not provide a consensus on the questions of at what age and with what frequency children can spend overnights with the nonresidential parent, or of what specific parenting plans are age- or stage-appropriate. The role of child attachment in child custody issues, however, continues to be the focus of considerable discussion (Byrne, O'Connor, Marvin, & Whelan, 2005; Calloway & Erard, 2009).

Beyond the question of attachment, in general there is a dearth of research bearing directly on the development of parenting plans. However, an evaluator can extrapolate important guidance from the existing research on parental conflict and child outcome. That literature advises caution with respect to shared physical custody in the presence of interparental conflict. Parenting plans that minimize transitions between households and limit children's exposure to interparental conflict are supported (Baris & Garrity, 1994; Johnston & Roseby, 1997).

Parents frequently alter their postdivorce caretaking arrangements without judicial involvement (Maccoby & Mnookin, 1992), often in response to developmental changes in their children, but also as a practical matter secondary to changes in their own lives. Divorced parents and their children move more often than do married parents (Austin, 2008b), but frequently these moves occur within defined geographic areas (e.g., within the same town or to nearby towns). When these moves require a change of school or change of friends for children, it can increase their stress as they try to cope with the changes in their family structure and the "back and forth" of many parenting plans. As noted earlier, geographic stability is a protective factor with respect to child outcomes. When either parent moves about 75 miles or about an hour's car ride away, contact with the nonresidential parent diminishes, weakening that parent's subsequent relationship with the children (Ahrons, 1981, 1994; Braver et al., 2003; Maccoby & Mnookin, 1992).

In summary, the above synopses of empirical findings reflect the behavioral and relationship concerns that litigants most often raise in family disputes.

Other issues arise in such disputes that have limited empirical data to inform a forensic evaluator. Research is needed in such areas as the relocation of one parent with the children (Austin, 2008a), same-gender-parent disputes (Patterson, 2006; Richman, 2009), supervised visitation (Pearson & Thoennes, 2000), *de facto parenting* (American Law Institute [ALI], 2000), and grandparent access to children (Roberts, 2003; Thompson, Scalora, Limber, & Castrianno, 1991).

Assessment Practices

Research has examined the assessment practices of child custody examiners. In discussions in Chapters 4–7, we frequently refer to practices that are required or recommended by the practice guidelines described in Chapter 2. The present studies help to determine how close child custody examiners come to fulfilling those guidelines. The present section focuses on (a) the nature of the studies, (b) their findings about sources of data obtained by child custody examiners, and (c) their use of psychological testing.

Types of Research on Current Assessment Practice

There have been two kinds of studies examining child custody evaluation practices: self-report surveys and reviews of examiners' reports.

SELF-REPORT SURVEYS

Keilin and Bloom (1986) conducted one of the earliest surveys of child custody examiners, involving 82 mental health professionals, primarily psychologists. Virtually all of them stated they interviewed the mother, the father, and the children in an evaluation, but the frequency of use of other sources of data declined. About half of the sample reported contact with third parties and/or made observations of family interaction. The average amount of time spent on an evaluation, including report writing, was 18.8 hours.

Ackerman and Ackerman (1997) essentially replicated the Keilin and Bloom study, but with a sample of 201 psychologists. The sample reported spending an average of about 21.1 hours in a custody evaluation. The additional time relative to the 1986 survey was spent reviewing pertinent documents and writing reports. LaFortune and Carpenter (1998) also followed up the Keilin and Bloom study; their sample of mental health professionals, 89% of whom were psychologists, also averaged 21.1 hours for an evaluation.

Bow and Quinnell (2001) repeated earlier self-report surveys with a sample of 198 custody-experienced psychologists, 96% of them doctoral-level professionals. They found that after the APA guidelines were published in 1994, the average number of hours to complete an evaluation increased to between 24.5 and 28.5. Ninety-two percent of the respondents said they held office observations of parent and child; 78% of them reported making at least one collateral contact (e.g., pediatrician, teachers, friends, or neighbors), and 91% used psychological testing in the assessment of adults. Bow and Quinnell concluded that their findings "suggest that respondents support the use of multiple methods of data collection" (p. 264), as emphasized in the APA guidelines.

EXAMINERS' REPORTS

Horvath et al. (2002) reviewed the custody evaluation reports (collected from the local courts) of a variety of types of mental health professionals. Although cited often, the study is limited by its small sample of psychologists (N = 24) in one midwestern city. They found that only 76% of psychologists documented an observation of parent and child together, a majority reported administering psychological testing to both parents, and none listed a home visit. Few psychologists indicated that they had interviewed teachers, although about a quarter of them noted that they had interviewed relatives.

In a similar study of the child custody reports of 52 experienced doctoral-level psychologists from 23 states (collected via voluntary submission of reports through mail solicitation), Bow and Quinnell (2002) found that 82.7% of the respondents documented parent–child office observations, 34.6% noted home visits, and about 88% listed the use of "objective" psychological testing on adults.

More recently, Zelechoski (2009) reviewed 142 custody evaluation reports (solicited from family law attorneys) of 72 mental health professionals from three urban areas, three-quarters of whom were doctoral-level psychologists. She found that 91% of psychologists used psychological testing (to "assess response style, history, symptoms, and experiences of the individual[s] being evaluated," p. 30), and 94% of them included collateral contacts as part of the assessment. Zelechoski's study is noteworthy in that it has the largest sample of reports not submitted by their authors, so they are arguably more representative of work in the field. The results indicate that the majority adhere to Heilbrun's (2001) principles of forensic mental health assessment. The practice of the majority of psychologists in Zelechoski's sample is consistent with existing principles for all types of forensic assessments.

These three studies suggest a discrepancy between what psychologists say they do in evaluations and what they actually document, although some of that difference may be explained by when the study was done, the particular custody evaluation method used, and the manner in which the data were collected (voluntary versus involuntary). The reliability of the findings may also be affected by sample size, as Bow and Quinnell and Zelechoski had over twice the number of reports that Horvath et al. had. Thus, while there have been differences between self-report and actual practice in terms of the use of different assessment methods, the clear trend over time suggests increasing adherence to the principles of forensic mental health assessments in general and to the APA guidelines and the AFCC model standards.

Sources of Data

The above-mentioned studies provide some information regarding the degree to which child custody examiners seek information from sources other than interviews of parents and children. Obtaining information from a variety of sources is highly recommended by existing child custody guidelines (AACAP, 1997a; AFCC, 2007; APA, 2009). This is partly because of the shortcomings of relying on examinees' self-reported information in child custody cases. Clients who present for child custody evaluations often do so under court order in an adversarial process. The demand characteristics of the situation itself (Nichols & Maner, 2008) can motivate a parent to present a favorable persona, that is, to "fake-good" (Medoff, 2003), and, conversely, to emphasize negative characteristics of the other parent, given that there is an

ongoing contest in which the stakes
are high (i.e., custody of the children). In addition, children's natural and understandable desire to
be protective of and loyal to both
parents can limit the value of their
reports. Because of those distorting

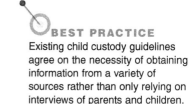

BEST PRACTICE
Existing child custody guidelines
agree on the necessity of obtaining
information from a variety of
sources rather than only relying on
interviews of parents and children.

dynamics, there is consensus that evaluators should use multiple
methods to collect data. Below are some of those methods and
some data relevant to the frequency of their use.

PARENT–CHILD OBSERVATIONS

Besides interviewing parents and children, a recommended data-
collection method involves home or office observations of direct
interaction between parents and children (Hynan, 2003), including the possible use of structured tasks (Rohrbaugh, 2008; Schutz
et al., 1989). There has been an evolution in this particular assessment method. Before the publication of the initial APA guidelines
(APA, 1994), 68% of sampled psychologists self-reported doing
parent–child observations (Keilin & Bloom, 1986); this number
increased to 91% in a postguidelines study (Bow & Quinnell,
2001). By comparison, Horvath et al. (2002) found that just 60%
to 62% of the reports they reviewed documented parent–child
observations, and in the same year of publication, Bow and
Quinnell (2002) found that 84.6% of psychologists listed parent–
child observations in their reports.

HOME VISITS

This method, when performed in each parent's residence, has the
advantage of offering a more naturalistic setting that can also provide, among other things, a glimpse into how organized a child's
home life might be. The data from different time periods and
sources are fairly consistent, as about 30% of psychologists pre–
1994 APA guidelines reported that they did home visits (Keilin &
Bloom, 1986) and 33% of psychologists post–1994 APA guidelines reported using that method (Bow & Quinnell, 2001). By
comparison, Horvath et al. (2002) found that between 32% and

39% of social workers/court investigators did home visits, and none of the psychologists in the sample noted a home visit in his report, although Bow and Quinnell (2002) found that 34.6% of the psychologists in their sample documented that they had made a home visit.

COLLATERAL SOURCES

As noted above, there is consensus that an essential component of a child custody evaluation consists of gathering collateral information from more independent, external sources to confirm or disconfirm data offered by parents or children. The weight one might give to this information will depend on, among other factors, the degree of perceived neutrality of the informant (Austin, 2002). While most evaluators interview collateral contacts by telephone or in person, some send out questions to which sources respond in writing, as in interrogatories (Kirkland, McMillan, & Kirkland, 2005). Keilin and Bloom (1986) found that only about 49% of psychologists reported interviewing collateral contacts, while 16 years later Bow and Quinnell (2002) noted that 86% of psychologists surveyed had reported contacts with professionals (e.g., therapists or teachers). More recently, Kirkland et al. (2005) found that 100% of the respondents in an AFCC sample, most of whom were psychologists, reported that they interviewed collateral contacts. When reports were reviewed to determine what evaluators actually did, more than 94% of such documents reported *collateral sources* of information (Zelechoski, 2009), although earlier report reviews (Bow & Quinnell, 2002; Horvath et al., 2002) showed less adherence to this practice.

DOCUMENT REVIEW

A review of relevant documents provides another source of information. The between-study data sets on this issue are difficult to compare. However, 98% of the psychologists in the Bow and Quinnell (2002) study self-reported some document review, while other studies showed some variation depending upon what documents were at issue (e.g., medical, school). Bow and Quinnell's (2001) study of psychologists' written reports noted that 78.8% listed document reviews, about 20% less than was claimed.

Thus, the data from 1988 through 2009 suggest the evolution of a multimodal, multisourced model of forensic mental health assessment (Gould & Martindale, 2007; Heilbrun et al., 2009). While the review of actual reports shows that there may be variation between self-report and documented methods, the two studies with larger sample sizes and broader geographic representations of professionals indicate a closer match and better adherence to the goals of forensic mental health assessment.

INFO

Another trend over time suggests the growth of a multimodal, multisourced model of forensic mental health assessment, including the use of psychological testing for adults.

PSYCHOLOGICAL TESTING

The use of psychological testing as an additional data source for adults in child custody evaluations has increased over the past 20 years, according to multiple surveys. The reported use of the Minnesota Multiphasic Personality Inventory (MMPI and MMPI-2) in evaluations among psychologists grew from about 61% of the time in the Keilin and Bloom (1986) study to about 84% of the time in the Ackerman and Ackerman (1997) replication (Hagan & Castagna, 2001). Quinnell and Bow (2001) noted that psychologists reported some testing of adults in these evaluations about 91% of the time, while Ackerman and Ackerman (1997) stated that only 2% of the psychologists in their sample reported that they did not use psychological tests.

The reported use by psychologists of personality instruments for adults has varied over time, as is shown in Table 3.1. The data reflect (a) the percentage of participants who reported using the particular test multiplied by (b) the average percentage of time they used the test in their evaluations (Hagan & Castagna, 2001). For example, in the Quinnell and Bow (2001) study, 44% of the respondents said they used the Rorschach, and they reported using it in an average of 64% of their cases.

The reported use of the Rorschach had decreased since the 1986 survey but then appeared to increase again in 2001, to about

Table 3.1 | Reported Use of Personality Tests in Three Surveys

	Keilin & Bloom (1986)	Ackerman & Ackerman (1997)	Quinnell & Bow (2001)
MMPI-2	61%	84%	91%
Rorschach	31%	16%	28%
TAT	15%	25%	13%
MCMI II/III		25%	39%

28% of all reported evaluations. The reported usage of the Thematic Apperception Test (TAT) had a different pattern, as can be seen in Table 3.1, but has decreased to about one in eight assessments. Conversely, the reports of the Millon Clinical Multiaxial Inventory (MCMI–II/III) use (Millon, 1987, 1997) have increased over time to make it the second most frequently administered test in custody assessments.

Psychologists have also employed psychological tests with children in custody disputes, and that usage has changed over time, as is illustrated in Table 3.2.

The data in the latest survey (Quinnell & Bow, 2001) revealed that no one instrument was used in more than one-third of all evaluations. However, certain tests have become more common, such as various "projective" drawing tasks [e.g., the House-Tree-Person/Kinetic Family Drawing (KFD)] that have no standardization, a high degree of subjectivity in scoring and interpretation, a lack of scientific foundation, and a likely inability to survive a *Daubert* challenge (Medoff, 2003). The surveys do not describe the specific ways in which those tests were used, so one cannot determine whether psychologists who administered them scored them according to some formal system, used them in to formulate hypotheses, or employed them as adjuncts to clinical interview

Table 3.2 | Test Usage as a Proportion of All Evaluations of Children

Test	% use Keilin & Bloom (1986)	% use Ackerman & Ackerman (1997)	% use Quinnell & Bow (2001)
Family drawing/KFD	8.5%	15.6%	34.2%
House-Tree-Person	8.3%	14.4%	20.3%
Draw-A-Person	15.8%	n/a	24.7%
Rorschach	22.6%	12.9%	14.7%
TAT/Children's Apperception Test	29.2%	19.6%	16.8%
MMPI-A	n/a	9.8%	18.1%
Millon Adolescent Clinical Inventory (MACI)	n/a	4.5%	7.6%
Sentence completion	21.9%	22.0%	8.5%
Roberts Apperception Test	10.7%	6.9%	4.8%

data. From 1986 to 2001, there was an increase in self-report, "objective" tests, such as the Minnesota Multiphasic Personality Inventory for Adolescents (MMPI-A) and the Millon Adolescent Clinical Inventory (Millon, Millon, Davis, & Grossman 2007), whereas the Rorschach had a curvilinear path, decreasing between the first and second surveys and then slightly increasing in the last survey. There were no references to the Personality Assessment Inventory (Morey, 1991a) in the Quinnell and Bow (2001) survey.

Yet, as an "objective," multiscale measure of personality and psychopathology, its use appears to be increasing in child custody evaluations (Medoff, 2003; Mullen & Edens, 2008) and, after the MMPI-2, it is the most frequently used test in the assessment of adults in other forensic settings (Archer, Buffington-Vollum, Stredny, & Handel, 2006). In the earlier surveys, intelligence testing of children and adolescents was done in about one-third to one-quarter of cases, but that had decreased to about 15% in the last survey (Quinnell & Bow, 2001). Lastly, child/adolescent behavior rating scales completed by parents or other caretakers (e.g., teachers) have become more common in these evaluations, and in the final survey, about 21% of the cases used the Achenbach Child Behavior Checklist (Achenbach, 2001) and about 11% used the Conners Rating Scales (Conners, 1997).

A few studies have examined evaluation reports to determine what psychologists do in these assessments with respect to psychological assessment. Horvath et al. (2002) found that the small number of psychologists in their custody report sample administered psychological testing 71.4% of the time to adults and 47.6% of the time to children. Bow and Quinnell (2002) reported that psychologists documented the use of psychological tests on parents about 84.6% of the time and on children less than 22% of the time, while Zelechoski (2009) reported that about 91% of psychologists documented the use of objective personality tests on adults. The latter two studies, with larger samples, show a closer match in test usage between psychologists who were asked to report what they did and those whose completed evaluations were reviewed.

There is continuing controversy over the value of formal psychological assessment in child custody evaluations, particularly in the area of personality testing. Some commentators note that personality tests, for example, have little research to suggest their reliability or validity with respect to predicting parenting capacity or child custody outcomes (Emery, Otto, & O'Donahue, 2005; Erickson, Lilienfield, & Vitacco, 2007; Melton et al., 2007; O'Donahue & Bradley, 1999; Others (e.g. Caldwell, 2005; Erard, 2005) assert the value of using tests that possess adequate psychometric properties (e.g., MMPI-2, Rorschach), measure response styles, have significant peer-reviewed research history, offer valid information to describe the functional abilities of parents and children, or explain psychopatholgy (Caldwell, 2005; Erard, 2005; Medoff, 2003). The Rorschach, for instance, can provide information about personality constructs such as interpersonal sensitivity, impulse or

BEWARE There is continuing controversy over the value of psychological testing in child custody evaluations, particularly in the area of personality testing. However, surveys of judges and attorneys indicate a high level of expectation that, if a psychologist is performing the forensic evaluations, he will employ psychological tests.

affect regulation, coping strategies, or balance of self or other focus, among others that are related to parenting abilities (Medoff, 2003; Otto & Collins, 1995; Otto & Edens, 2003).

Such instruments may also be the source of hypotheses about the examinees, for which a forensic evaluator can find support in the other components of the assessment. Moreover, certain psychological tests (e.g., MMPI-2, Rorschach) can be as valid and reliable as many common medical diagnostic tests (Medoff, 2003; Meyer & Archer, 2001), with the Rorschach having the additional virtue of being able to circumvent the self-reporting bias of many of the other tests (Erard, 2005). Additionally, the MMPI-2 has context-specific normative data on custody litigants against which parent responses can be compared (Bathurst, Gottfried, & Gottfried, 1997; Greene, unpublished data as reported in Caldwell, 2005), as does the MCMI-III (McCann et al., 2001). While new, nongendered norms for the MCMI-III have made the McCann et al. (2001) data outdated, those norms have not yet been validated (Ackerman, 2010). As noted above, the Personality Assessment Inventory (Morey, 1991b) is useful in assessing parents and has the advantages of fewer questions (i.e., 344), a solid research base, and nonoverlapping scales (Cox, Thorpe, & Dawson, 2007). In addition, a recent revision of the MMPI-2, the Minnesota Multiphasic Personality Inventory-2-Restructured Form (MMPI-2-RF), uses a 338-item subset of the larger, original MMPI-2 item pool (Tellegen et al., 2003). The goal of this revision was to respond to criticism about the overlap among MMPI-2

3 chapter

items; that is, the same items are included in more than one scale (Ackerman, 2010). The instrument needs more empirical support before one can have confidence in its validity for child custody evaluations (Ackerman, 2010; Ben Porath & Flens, 2010). In summary, surveys of judges and attorneys indicate a high level of expectation that, if a psychologist is performing the forensic evaluations, she will employ psychological tests (Ackerman, Ackerman, Steffen, & Kelley-Poulos, 2004; Ackerman & Steffen, 2001). When not administering psychological tests, the psychologist-evaluator may have to explain his rationale for that decision.

CHILD CUSTODY ASSESSMENT INSTRUMENTS

Almost every area of forensic assessment has seen the development of specialized measures intended to obtain information specific to forensic questions. The area of child custody evaluations is no exception, although, as with personality assessment in this forensic area, some controversy has surrounded their use. Otto and Edens (2003) have provided the most recent reviews of research on these instruments. Below, we summarize their review regarding some of these instruments: the Ackerman–Schoendorf Scales for Parent Evaluation of Custody (ASPECT), several scales by Bricklin, the Parenting Stress Index, and the Parent–Child Relationship Inventory.

The ASPECT "is a composite measure that aggregates data from several sources" (Otto & Edens, 2003) in an evaluation, including interviews, testing (of children and adults), and observations. Additionally, parents answer 57 open-ended questions about parenting and custody. The scoring of multiple sources of information, including structured interviews, unstructured observations, answers to parenting questions, and structured (e.g., Wechsler Adult Intelligence Scale-IV) and unstructured tests (e.g., family drawings), is handled through 56 yes/no items whose totals can be disaggregated into three dimensions of parenting and one overall index, the Parental Custody Index or "PCI." Otto and Edens (2003) and, later, Connell (2005) questioned such basic issues as the combining of structured and unstructured methods in the scoring, the reliability of the data collection itself, the lack of test–retest statistics, and problems in the normative standardization group. They noted that this was an important effort in integrating diverse sources of data, but more research was necessary before forensic use of the ASPECT was warranted. They also questioned whether an evaluator can base complex custody decisions on a single PCI index (although for the developer's view, see Ackerman, 2005).

The Bricklin Perceptual Scales (BPS) (Bricklin, 1990a) purports to be a projective measure of a child's perceptions of parenting behavior, including parents' competence, supportiveness, follow-up consistency, and possession of admirable traits (Otto & Edens, 2003). Using a stylus to poke a hole through a black line on a paper, a child answers 32 questions about specific behaviors of each parent (64 items in all). One endpoint of the line represents "very well," while the other endpoint represents "not so well" in terms of how the parent performs the behavior in question. Bricklin posits that the child's choices reflect "unconscious preferences," which, he claims, is a superior criterion to any self-report measure, such as what the child has reported about the parent. That is, the selection theoretically represents what the behavior means to the child. The test is scored by summing the difference scores of each paired item (i.e., mother versus father) in each of the four domains of parenting. Reviews of this instrument emphasize the untested and unverified assumptions about the psychological processes that stimulate a child's choices, small sample sizes, lack of a normative sample, inadequate reliability/validity data, and absence of publication in peer-reviewed journals. The data noted in the manual appear to represent reports by various psychologists to Bricklin about how the test compared to their clinical impressions of the families in their evaluations (Otto & Edens, 2003). Melton et al. (2007) suggest that the instrument "may facilitate gathering useful responses regarding parents' attitudes, knowledge, or values" with respect to child rearing, but they warn against using the formal scoring procedures in the assessment process.

The Parent Awareness Skills Survey (PASS; Bricklin, 1990b) is "designed to illuminate the strengths and weaknesses in the awarenesses a parent accesses in reaction to typical child-care situations" (Bricklin, 1995, p. 88). It asks parents to report verbally what they would say or do in response to 18 different child-care problems. The scoring assesses first the initial parent response, then an answer to a "gentle and non-directive" probe, and finally a reply to a more "direct" probing question. Otto and Edens (2003) note that the test evaluates common parenting issues but has no standardization. While there are general scoring guidelines, the examiner retains the ability to make a "final judgment of the adequacy of the parental response" (Bricklin, 1995, p. 90), thus injecting a subjective element into the scoring. Bricklin does not report any reliability data, nor has he established any norms; therefore, there is no way to compare a parent's scores with any reference group. Therefore, Otto and Edens (2003) cautioned that its use be restricted to being part of a semistructured interview where it "might be able to identify potential strengths and weaknesses at a more global level." That data could then be integrated with other information from the evaluation.

The Perception of Relationships Test (PORT) is intended to evaluate children age 4 or older (Bricklin, 1989). This test asks children to make multiple drawings of individual or all family members in seven different situations, making sure to include themselves in each picture. He considers this test a "data-based projective test developed specifically to assist informed custody decision-making" (Bricklin, 1995, pp. 80–81). The criteria involve measuring the distance between the child and her parents in each representation, reflecting "the degree to which the child seeks psychological 'closeness' with each parent in varying situations" (Bricklin, 1995, p. 80). The critique of this instrument mirrors that of the BPS in that the theoretical foundation is not well described, the administration and scoring procedures are not standardized, inter-rater reliability data for the scoring are not presented, and normative group data are absent. Additionally, there are no test–retest reliability data, although Bricklin (1989) asserts that this form of reliability is not relevant, as the test is responsive to changing situations and perceptions. Lastly, Otto and Edens (2003) suggest that the problems with the test's validity make it inadequate for use in forensic evaluations. In summary, there is little empirical support for the use of the Bricklin scales as psychological tests in child custody evaluations, although they may have some utility as interview data and as asource of hypotheses about the child or family.

PARENTING STRESS INDEX

There are two other instruments that, while not originally developed specifically for custodial determinations, provide data that could be helpful in assessing parenting. The first one, the Parenting Stress Index (PSI) (Abidin, 1995), was designed to assess the kinds and degree of stress in parents with children under 12 years old. Abidin's idea was that parental stress stemmed from three sources: characteristics of the child (e.g., mood, activity level), characteristics of the parent (e.g., depression, marital issues), and significant stressors in the adults' lives independent of parenting (e.g., death of a loved one, loss of job, moving). The self-report test also has a scale that measures response style. In its development, the vast majority of the test's questions were reported to have been selected based on at least one research study. The PSI used 2600+ mothers for a reasonably diverse standardization sample of convenience, but it had a much smaller sample of fathers (i.e., 200) of preschool children, who were almost exclusively Caucasian. The comparison of parents' responses on this test is likely to be more valid when the test is renormed, as there will be a substantial group of fathers in the standardization sample (Austin, Kirkpatrick, & Flens, 2010). For further information on this test, see Abidin, Flens, and Austin (2006).

Otto and Edens (2003) note that the test-construction process for the PSI was superior to that of many instruments in use. Rohrbaugh (2008) reported that the PSI had been used in over 200 published studies with good test–retest reliability over 3 weeks (i.e., 0.55–0.95). The instrument could be one source of parenting information (and of perceptions of the child) that might be used to suggest hypotheses about the parent–child match and to compare parents on their views of their child and stresses that result from the parent–child relationship.

A related test for parents of children 11 and older is the Stress Index for Parents of Adolescents (Sheras, Abidin, & Konold, 1998), an upward extension of the PSI. Reviewers indicate that the instrument shows promise as a screening tool of parents in need of services, although it should be used with caution pending more empirical support (Jones, 2001; Swearer, 2001).

PARENT-CHILD RELATIONSHIP INVENTORY

The second instrument, the Parent-Child Relationship Inventory (PCRI) (Gerard, 1994) is a self-report survey that measures attitudes toward parenting and children in seven areas: support, satisfaction with parenting, involvement, communication, limit setting, autonomy, and role orientation (Rohrbaugh, 2008). Psychometrically, the internal consistency of the "autonomy" scale was deemed unacceptable (Coffman, Guerin, & Gottfried, 2006). There are two validity scales, one that measures social desirability and another that measures the consistency with which parents respond to questions of similar content. The test–retest reliability of the PCRI was between 0.44 and 0.71 after 5 months (Rohrbaugh, 2008). Otto and Edens (2003) note the absence of studies of the predictive validity of the instrument. Thus, one cannot conclude whether one parent's superior scores over the other will result in better developmental outcomes for the children. In another study, mothers' reports and those of their adolescents were more convergent than those between fathers and adolescents, suggesting a foundation only for the validity of mother's reports on this inventory (Coffman et al., 2006). However, because of the lack of validity for fathers' reports, Coffman et al. (2006) conclude that "the existing empirical findings on the PCRI do not as yet render it suitable for assisting psychologists in formulating recommendations in clinical or legal arenas." (p. 214). Moreover, that differential in validity for mothers' versus fathers' reports makes it inappropriate to compare one parent's scores against the other for the same child, at least with opposite-gender parents.

Surveys also have reported on child custody examiners' use of these custody-specific forensic assessment instruments and the two

Table 3.3 | Use of Custody-Specific (1) or Custody-Related (2)
Instruments by Evaluators in Two Surveys

(1)	Ackerman & Ackerman (1997)	Quinnell & Bow (2001)
ASPECT	10%	12%
BPS	23%	17%
PASS	7.5%	12%
PORT	n/a	n/a
(2) PCRI	8.0%	31.7%
PSI	3.5%	27.5%

Data represent the percentage of respondents using the test times the average
percentage of the time the users estimated they administered it (e.g., for the BPS, 28% of
psychologists said they used it an average of 63% of the time, resulting in its use in 17%
of all of their evaluations [Quinnell, F., & Bow, J. (2001). Psychological tests used in child
custody evaluations. *Behavioral Sciences & the Law, 19*(4), 491–501]).

other tests that custody evaluators have used. As can be seen in
Table 3.3, the most popular of the custody-specific assessment
instruments was the BPS, yet the more recent survey found that it
was used in less than one-sixth of the evaluations, with the other
Bricklin instruments being used less than one-eighth of the time.
The survey data did not report the manner in which the instruments were used, that is, either primarily as clinical tools to collect
information or as formal forensic assessment measures. With
respect to the PSI and the PCRI, however, the Bow and Quinnell
(2001) data as shown in table 3.3 highlight the fourfold increase
in the use of the PCRI and the eightfold increase in the use of the
PSI since the 1986 survey.

In summary, the available custody-specific instruments, such
as those from Bricklin and the ASPECT have psychometric

BEWARE
There is
insufficient validity to warrant the
formal use of the various Bricklin
custody-specific tests, although they
may have clinical use as adjuncts to
interviews. As a custody-related
instrument, the PSI has shown
promise because of improved
methods of test construction.

challenges, and writers agree that they should not be relied upon in evaluations. They may have utility as clinical instruments to elicit information about parents or children, but they should not be formally scored. Parenting inventories, particularly the PCRI and the PSI, have better psychometric properties, and their use in custody evaluations is increasing.

Conclusion

This chapter is a wide-ranging synopsis of the ever-growing bodies of knowledge in those areas of concern and practice most relevant to child custody evaluations. The research on parents and children in divorce cases is important in deciding what type of information to collect and how to interpret it. The research on current practices demonstrates improvement across the years in the degree to which child custody examiners employ multiple sources of information and include standardized methods that can improve the reliability of their evlutions and increase adherence to the principles of forensic mental health assessments. We are now ready to turn to the process of child custody examinations, beginning with the preparation for an evaluation, and then moving to data collection and interpretation of data for the courts.

APPLICATION

Preparation for the Evaluation | 4

An evaluation begins well before the family members arrive at the evaluator's office. To avoid clinical/ethical missteps, it is essential to be thoughtful about the conditions under which one enters a child custody evaluation. This chapter considers two main questions: (1) When is one qualified to perform child custody evaluations? (2) How can one identify likely problems before starting, in order to avert difficulties after the assessment is already underway?

Qualifications for Conducting Child Custody Evaluations

Child custody evaluations require a high degree of specialized knowledge. Neither child clinical expertise nor forensic expertise alone qualifies a mental health professional to perform child custody evaluations; one must have both types of expertise. In addition, one might be qualified to perform child forensic evaluations in juvenile delinquency cases but not in custody cases. In this section, we explain what mental health professionals need to consider when deciding whether they are qualified to accept child custody evaluation referrals. These considerations pertain to specialized clinical, legal, and ethical knowledge and skills.

Specialized Clinical Knowledge and Skills

Any mental health professional who undertakes child custody evaluations must, first of all, have solid *clinical experience and academic training associated*

BEWARE
To avoid clinical or ethical missteps, give thought to the conditions under which you enter a child custody evaluation.

with child and adolescent psychiatry or psychology. Child custody evaluations are essentially driven by concerns about children's development. As such, the clinician's child experience and training must be broad, pertaining to all aspects of child development, personality, and psychopathology. Theory and research on child development and variations of development and assessment methodology, including relevant psychological tests, form the requisite foundation of knowledge for engaging in this work. But in addition to knowledge, specialized skills—such as in interviewing children and adolescents in ways that do not bias one's results, knowing what to observe in parent–child interactions, and knowing how to assess infants and toddlers—must be in the evaluator's repertoire of abilities. Child development and child clinical specialization may seem like simple and noncontroversial requirements. However, this has important implications, because it means that most forensic mental health professionals should not accept referrals for child custody evaluations, inasmuch as very few forensic clinicians are child-trained or child-experienced. More specifically, forensic mental health professionals should accept referrals for child custody evaluations only for the developmental ages for which they have had adequate training. Some "child" forensic evaluators decline cases involving very young children because they are not knowledgeable about infant/toddler development, and some "adult" forensic mental health professionals who are trained in adolescent assessment accept custody evaluations involving older children.

But child custody examiners are not merely specialized child psychologists, psychiatrists, or social workers. All child custody evaluations require the assessment of adults, including a complete *knowledge of theories and assessment methods related to adult personality and psychopathology.* Most parents in

BEST PRACTICE

A mental health professional must have solid clinical experience and academic training associated with child and adolescent psychiatry or psychology in order to undertake a child custody evaluation. This means that most forensic mental health professionals should not accept referrals for child custody evaluations, because very few are child-trained or child-experienced, and those who do have child experience should accept referrals for child custody evaluations only for the developmental ages for which they have had adequate training or experience.

child custody cases do not have mental disorders, but when they do, the clinician must have adequate knowledge of the diagnosis, prognosis, and treatment of adult mental disorders. Because child custody evaluations involve the assessment of adults, knowledge of and experience in adult assessment are essential.

In addition, child custody examiners must have clinical knowledge and experience in several other *special areas of research that play a significant role in formulating custody evaluations.* Among them are knowledge of theory and research regarding family dynamics, including parenting practices, alternative lifestyles, and blended families (e.g., Baumrind, 1967; Condie, 2003; Minuchin, 1974; Nichols, 2010; Patterson, 2006); research on domestic violence (e.g., Ellis & Stuckless,1996; Jaffee, Baker, & Cunningham, 2004; Kelly & Johnson, 2008); research on cultural and ethnic differences among families (e.g., Elwyn, Tseng, & Matthews, 2010; McGoldrick, Giordano, and Garcia-Preto, 2005); and, of course, research on the effects of divorce on children (e.g., Emery, 2004; Hetherington & Kelly, 2002; Kelly, 2000; Wallerstein & Blakeslee, 1989).

Specialized Knowledge of Law, Legal Process, and Practice Standards

4
chapter

When clinicians accept a referral to perform a child custody evaluation, they are acknowledging that they know the laws in their state that control child custody determinations, the legal (court) process by which those determinations are achieved, and the legal regulations and practice standards that control child custody examiners' evaluations. Family law is an ever-changing field of which the forensic mental health professional must keep abreast. The risks of inadequate or wrong legal information are multiple. Courts can disregard the results of financially and emotionally draining, extensive

BEST PRACTICE

Child custody evaluations involve the assessment of adults as well as of children, so mental health professionals also need adult assessment knowledge and experience. In addition, they must have clinical knowledge and experience in several other special areas such as family dynamics, including parenting practices, alternative lifestyles and blended families, domestic violence, cultural and ethnic differences among families, and the effects of divorce on children.

BEWARE
Adequately attend to case-specific or jurisdictional legal standards and rules, or the courts may disregard the results of extensive evaluations. Know the rules and practices for evaluations in the jurisdiction where the evaluation is requested.

evaluations if a child custody evaluator does not adequately attend to the case-specific or jurisdictional legal standards and rules. It is also worth noting that child custody examiners who take cases outside their "home" jurisdiction must research the law in the jurisdiction where the new case will be heard, because laws controlling child custody determinations may vary across states.

First, child custody evaluators must know *the law that controls child custody cases in their jurisdiction*. These laws do more than define what standards the court will use to determine child custody; they describe the process by which custody cases are filed, the steps and procedures that the case must follow as it proceeds through the courts, the parties' rights and obligations, rules of evidence, and the roles of various participants in the process. For example, in some states, court-appointed guardians ad litem, typically attorneys, are responsible for investigating relevant issues. In other instances, children may have legal representation. Sometimes a state's laws will influence how child custody evaluations look, or what examiners report in child custody evaluations. For example, if a state's statutes have adopted a list of factors to weigh, using the language of the Uniform Marriage and Divorce Act (UMDA § 402, 1970), that may create part of the structure for the evaluation in that jurisdiction. Judges in some courts have developed their own lists of factors to be evaluated and have informed their local examiners that they want information on these factors in child custody evaluations. Other counties or states have developed specific practice standards for child custody evaluators wishing court appointments. Evaluators should not take on child custody evaluations unless they know the rules and practices for evaluations in the jurisdiction where the evaluation is requested.

Second, one must know *how one's courts work*. While a jurisdiction's statutes or administrative rules describe what courts must do, they provide only a very general map of the way courts function. In Chapters 5–7, we describe some of these ways in which one must know much more than law in order to find one's way around in the complexity of child custody proceedings. Even so, those descriptions will be only partially

BEST PRACTICE
As a child custody evaluator, be aware of the child custody guidelines or parameters developed by your professional organizations, and know how your courts work.

helpful, because there are variations across counties and states in practical procedures for child custody cases.

Finally, clinicians who take child custody evaluation referrals must know about *practice standards that guide and limit the ways that child custody evaluations are performed* and entered as evidence in the legal process (e.g., California Rules of Court §5.220–5.235; Massachusetts Probate and Family Court Standing Order 1–08). Over the past decade, child custody evaluations have become more uniform, and there is consensus in the field about minimum standards of practice (Kirkpatrick, 2004). It is essential that evaluators be aware of the child custody guidelines or parameters developed by their professional organizations (American Academy of Child and Adolescent Psychiatry [AACAP], 1997a; American Psychological Association [APA], 2009; Association of Family and Conciliation Courts [AFCC], 2007).

Knowledge of Relevant Ethical Issues

One should accept a referral for a child custody evaluation only if one has knowledge regarding the application of professional ethical obligations in child custody cases. Being familiar with the "Ethical Principles of Psychologists and Code of Conduct" (APA, 2002) and the "Specialty Guidelines for Forensic Psychologists" (American Psychology-Law Society [APLS], 1991) is, of course, essential for psychologists. Psychiatrists need to be familiar with the *Principles of Medical Ethics with Annotations Especially Applicable to Psychiatry* (American Psychiatric Association, 2009) and the *Ethics Guidelines for the Practice of Forensic Psychiatry* (American Academy of Psychiatry and the Law [AAPL], 2005). Social workers must, of course, be knowledgeable of and abide by their ethical guidelines (National Association of Social Workers [NASW], 1997).

BEST PRACTICE
One should accept a referral for a child custody evaluation only if one has thorough knowledge about the application of professional ethical principles in child custody cases.

However, knowledge of ethical directives is not sufficient. One must also have a significant grasp on how those principles apply to child custody evaluations. Child custody evaluations raise a host of questions that challenge our interpretation of professional ethics—questions regarding who the client is, what information about themselves or their children parents can release, when one can interview a child's therapist, how to assess and collect fees, when it is required to report suspected child abuse, and how to avoid dual roles, to name only a few. These are complex issues in any forensic evaluation, but they have unique variations in child custody cases.

Specific guidelines or parameters for child custody evaluations have been written and endorsed by professional organizations such as the American Psychological Association (APA, 2009), the American Academy of Child and Adolescent Psychiatry (AACAP, 1997a), and the Association of Family and Conciliation Courts (AFCC, 2007). Clinicians cannot be sanctioned (e.g., with loss of license) if they violate these guidelines—indeed, the guidelines are often called "aspirational," meaning they are an ideal toward which all clinicians should strive, rather than a requirement that all clinicians must meet. Nevertheless, they offer a consensus of one's peers that can have a significant impact on the legal community's perceptions of one's professional competence. We refer to specific ethical guidelines or issues of which child custody evaluators must be aware at relevant points in the following chapters.

Getting Started

Clarification of the Referral Question

Child custody evaluations are typically the result of a court order in a disputed case. One party may initiate an action by filing a motion for an evaluation, or both parties may stipulate that they are requesting an evaluation. Sometimes judges themselves will order evaluations to inform their decision making. As described in Chapter 1, the mechanism for getting to a forensic evaluator differs among jurisdictions.

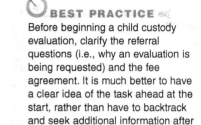

The newly assigned forensic evaluator needs to clarify the referral question and, if relevant, the fee agreement before proceeding. Sometimes, the courts write the referral question(s) in vague terms. Examples include "evaluate issues relevant to custody and visitation" and "do a family functioning assessment." Sometimes they will simply request "a psychological evaluation." The evaluator should translate the referral question(s) into psycho-legal constructs that can be evaluated via psychological means and about which the evaluator is competent to make an assessment, as noted in Chapter 2.

The easiest way to clarify the focus of the assessment is to contact the attorneys, or the parties themselves if they are unrepresented. This can also be done by telephone, either separately or in a conference call. Usually, this conversation clarifies the primary issue(s) and can be paraphrased by the evaluator to ensure all are in agreement. For example, a request to evaluate issues affecting custody and visitation may be clarified to mean an assessment of the effect of the mother's bipolar disorder on her parenting and the children's safety. A request for a "family functioning evaluation" may be rephrased as an assessment of the factors contributing to the 14-year-old son's current refusal to spend time with his father. At times, it may be prudent to write a letter of agreement to each side stating the evaluator's understanding of the reasons for referral, although most often that is not necessary.

If confusion or discrepancies remain, or if either party denies knowledge of why the court ordered a child custody evaluation, then one should ask the court for clarification. Different jurisdictions and even judges within jurisdictions may differ on whether communication should be done through filing a motion; sending a letter; calling the clerk, probation officer, or judicial case manager; or finding another avenue in order to obtain clarity. Direct communications with the judge without the parties or their attorneys present are *ex parte* communications and are ethically inadvisable. Often, when there is confusion regarding the referral question, the evaluator or one of the attorneys will file a motion to ask for clarification of the order. It is preferable to have a clear idea of the task ahead at the outset as opposed to having to backtrack and seek additional information, possibly with more expense and difficulty, after the evaluation is underway.

With the referral question(s) clarified, the potential evaluator can decide whether it is appropriate for psychological assessment and whether it is within his area of competence.

For example, imagine that a court order vaguely requested "an evaluation of issues affecting custody and visitation." When the intended evaluator sought clarification of the specific concerns, it became evident that the parents were disputing the residence of their 5-year-old child with pervasive developmental disorder (PDD). The parental dispute was driven by their disagreement about which school system had better resources for this child. The evaluator advised the court and the attorneys that an evaluator with special expertise in PDD would better serve the family. Alternatively, the evaluator could have asked the court whether a colleague with the necessary expertise could work jointly with her.

If relevant, the evaluator should clarify responsibility for fees at the outset, often with a fee agreement and receipt of a *retainer*. Most evaluators now use written *informed consent* agreements that delineate the reason for referral, fees, procedures, and limits of confidentiality. An inexperienced evaluator can ask a more seasoned colleague for copies of informed consent and fee agreements that conform to local practice, as advised by model standards (AFCC, 2007), or he can obtain samples of such agreements from publications (e.g., Gould & Martindale, 2007; Rohrbaugh, 2008). Model agreements are also available in Appendices B and C.

BEST PRACTICE
Inexperienced evaluators can ask a more seasoned colleague for copies of informed consent and fee agreements that conform to their local practice.

Refusing an Appointment

On occasion, an evaluator should reject an appointment to conduct a child custody evaluation. This is typically uncomfortable for the mental health professional, especially after the court order arrives. Unfortunately, sometimes courts appoint evaluators without confirming that the mental health professional has the time, expertise (APA, 2002, §2.01), and/or desire to take on the case and complete it in the specified timeframe. Occasionally, the court might order an avenue of payment that is not realistic—for example, that the evaluator is to bill one party's health insurance. Occasionally the parties do not send the requested retainer to the evaluator in a timely fashion. Other conflicts, such as personal or professional relationships with a family member, would be valid reasons to decline the appointment (APA, 2002, §3.05).

In these circumstances, the evaluator must send back the court order, decline the appointment, and notify the parties and their attorneys, with reasons stated. This may not be either a popular or a comfortable action to take, but it is, on occasion, ethically and clinically necessary. While it might delay resolution of the custody dispute or divorce, it is better to let the court know as soon as possible if a referral is not appropriate.

When deciding whether to accept or refuse a referral for a child custody evaluation, evaluators must also consider the issue of "dual roles" (AACAP, 1997a, § A.2; AAPL, 2005, §II, commentary; AFCC, 2007, § 8.3; APA, 2002, § 3.05; APLS, 1991, § 6.02). Mental health professionals take care to avoid situations in which they must act as forensic evaluators for former clients—for example, when one has been in a therapeutic relationship with families, adults, or children involved in the child custody case (SGFP, 1991, § 6.02.01–03). The risks of serving as a custody evaluator for a client for whom one has provided psychotherapy are many, not the least of which is the likely violation of confidentiality owed to the therapy client and not to the forensic one.

In addition, examiners sometimes encounter conflicts of interest

BEST PRACTICE
To decline a court-ordered appointment, send back the court order, decline the appointment, and notify the parties and their attorneys, stating your reasons for declining.

in relation to attorneys and family law judges, especially if one is active in professional organizations. While this is often unavoidable, one should try to avoid the possibility or appearance of bias and should make efforts to avoid simultaneous multiple relationships. For example, when actively preparing to co-present with a judge or an attorney at a conference, it is best not to accept cases involving those legal representatives until the conference is over. If that is unavoidable, than any discussion of the case between the judge and the evaluator is strictly prohibited. Any possible conflict of interest should be disclosed at the outset. This serves the goal of transparency and allows parties to object to one's involvement at the start rather than discover the potential problem midway through the assessment.

Defining the Scope of the Evaluation

Forensic evaluations in child custody matters are not "one size fits all." They run the gamut from brief to lengthy evaluations, depending on the nature of the request. Some child custody evaluations can be brief, focused assessments based on one clinical interview of each party and of the children, a few collateral contacts, and minimal record review. Others require comprehensive evaluations that may include psychological testing, multiple clinical interviews, home visits, collateral contacts, and copious review of records. The length and depth of the evaluation is determined by one or more of the following factors.

REFERRAL QUESTION(S)

The number and complexity of the referral questions will obviously influence the length or complexity of the evaluation. Each referral question may require an assessment of several issues. For example, often the court is interested in the impact of an alleged impairment, such as psychiatric illness or substance abuse, on parenting. This requires an assessment of the adult psychiatric illness, an assessment of the impact on the adult's parenting, and an assessment of the children before one can offer an opinion. Similarly, an evaluation of alleged maltreatment or other safety concerns requires multiple steps and "mini-evaluations" in order to address the question comprehensively. The more referral questions asked, the more complicated the evaluation is likely to become.

COMPLEXITY OF THE CASE

Families with multiagency involvement and multiple difficulties— including psychiatric, medical, legal, etc.—will take more time to evaluate simply because there are more data to collect and synthesize. Parents who have had a longer marriage or several children may require more time to assess. Evaluations will take more time and reports will tend to be longer when there are more records to review, more collateral contacts with whom to speak, or more materials to integrate.

TIME DEMANDS

The child custody evaluator should consider the referral questions and the complexity of the case when responding to the court's time demands. When a court requests that the evaluation be completed in a month, yet there are five children with child protective service involvement and an allegation of child sexual abuse, it is either a brave or a naïve evaluator who agrees to take the case without asking for a time extension. A best practices model requires that the forensic evaluator perform a thorough and fair assessment, giving due diligence to the allegations and concerns of each party and to the referral questions of the court. The balance between meeting the time demands and doing a competent, thorough assessment that meets practice guidelines can be difficult to achieve. It would behoove the evaluator to inform the court and the involved parties of the need for more time than was granted if he believes that the time that the court has specified will not allow him to do an adequate job.

4
chapter

FINANCIAL RESOURCES

In most jurisdictions, the nature of the evaluation that a family receives depends on their financial means. If the parties are able to pay privately, they may obtain thorough, lengthy child custody evaluations from court-appointed private practice evaluators. Otherwise, the choices are more limited and depend

BEST PRACTICE

A best practices model requires a thorough and fair child custody evaluation. The balance between meeting the time demands of the court and doing a competent, thorough assessment that meets practice guidelines can be difficult to achieve. At the outset, inform the court and the involved parties if there is a need for more time than was granted.

on the availability of state or grant funding or the existence of court clinics. In some jurisdictions, brief, focused assessments (BFAs) are available without charge to clients. Too frequently, however, the lack of well-trained mental health professionals and/or financial resources results in disputing families' waiting many months in stressful situations for evaluations.

EVALUATOR'S CAPABILITIES

The scope of the evaluation is also limited by the available evaluator's particular capabilities. If it is known at the outset that the referral questions include a topic about which the evaluator does not have expertise, she can either decline the appointment or accept only the evaluation questions that she can competently answer (APA, 2002, § 2.01). For example, the court might order an evaluation of parenting capabilities and of an allegation of sexual abuse in a family. The appointed evaluator might accept the task of addressing the former question but not the latter if he has insufficient training or experience in sexual abuse evaluations. On the other hand, the sexual abuse allegation might not emerge until the evaluation has already begun, in which case the evaluator might ask the court for permission to have that issue independently assessed if he lacks that expertise.

EXPECTATIONS OF COURT, ATTORNEYS, AND PARTIES

The expectations of the court, attorneys, and parties are extremely important to ascertain at the beginning of the evaluation in order to determine the evaluation's scope. While the court is the final authority, the attorneys and their clients often define and give nuance to the referral question in ways that influences the examiner's decisions about the methods and procedures of the ensuing evaluation. The concerns, issues, and preferred outcome of the parties often provide the initial hypotheses and define factors that must be assessed.

LOCAL PRACTICE

The length and depth of a forensic evaluation are partially defined by local practice and availability. In jurisdictions in which BFAs are available, there may be more acceptance of that model than in areas where comprehensive evaluation is the only practice model. Brief, focused assessments can inform the development of temporary orders (Cavallero, 2010). Models of brief evaluations of clearly defined and focused questions have gained increased recognition and are touted as helping families over the acute impasse toward greater stability (AFCC, 2009). Proponents note the low cost, short turnaround time, and adequacy of the brief model for many cases, but caution that it is likely to be insufficient for allegations of

INFO

Forensic evaluations in child custody matters are not "one size fits all." The length and depth of the evaluation are determined by one or more of the following factors:

- referral question(s);
- complexity of the case;
- time demands;
- financial resources;
- evaluator's capabilities;
- expectations of the court, attorneys, and parties; and local practice.

sexual abuse, serious domestic violence, custody determination, *relocation cases*, and cases requiring the assessment of multiple issues. Although there is growing enthusiasm and promising initial reports for BFAs, research does not yet inform the profession about which cases would be appropriate for this model. In the meantime, comprehensive child custody evaluation remains the majority type of assessment in child custody cases.

Unlike some types of forensic evaluations, such as competence to stand trial and criminal responsibility, child custody is not itself a legal construct and does not by itself determine the scope of the evaluation. The referral questions arise not from a client's brush with the law but from parents' disagreements about who should provide care for the children. While the focus in child custody is on a comparison of each party's parenting of the children, the specific concerns in a case, in addition to the four psycho-legal constructs, define the scope and procedures of the assessment.

Contacting Attorneys

If appointed by court order for a child custody evaluation, the evaluator should call each attorney (or party if pro se). Some attorneys prefer to do this as a conference call involving both sides simultaneously, whereas others are comfortable with a brief, individual initial conversation. The purpose of the initial contact with the attorneys is straightforward: to introduce oneself; to clarify the referral question(s); to discuss fees; to request copies of pertinent pleadings, *depositions*, orders, or other legal documents; and to request other relevant records (e.g., medical, educational, police, psychiatric) if counsel has them. Because the responsibility for payment is typically specified in the court order or understood, discussion about fees usually entails informing the attorneys of the likely cost of the assessment (including the evaluator's hourly rate) and requesting a retainer if private pay has been ordered. It is also helpful to clarify whether there are any current safety concerns, for example, the existence of restraining orders when domestic violence is present or alleged.

During the initial call, the evaluator also has an opportunity to briefly inform the respective attorneys about planned procedures, to discuss the assessment timeline, and to ask for the clients' contact information if it was omitted in the referral or court order. The attorneys often ask questions, which typically relate to the evaluator's particular practice, or they may ask for a curriculum vitae or resume if one had not already been provided. Notably, this is likely the

INFO

What are the purposes of an initial contact with the attorney?

● To introduce yourself

● To clarify the referral question(s)

● To discuss fees

● To request copies of pertinent legal documents

● To request other relevant records (e.g., medical, educational, police, psychiatric)

● To clarify whether there are any current safety concerns.

only time the evaluator communicates with the attorneys during the course of the assessment. Should it be necessary to have further substantive communication with the attorneys, the proper protocol is to conduct this through a conference call or written communication to all attorneys of record (AFCC, 2007, § 4.4).

Because a large number of child custody litigants are pro se (that is, not represented by counsel), evaluators may be calling the parties directly rather than communicating through attorneys. In that instance, evaluators may limit the telephone contact to making an initial appointment and requesting advance payment, if specified by the court order, and may wait until the first appointment to discuss the other issues mentioned above.

Current best practice is for child custody evaluators to have a written letter of agreement or contract for services (AFCC, 2007, § 4.1). This may also be considered a memo of understanding or an informed consent document. The document typically includes informed consent statements in addition to information regarding fees, lack of confidentiality, mandatory reporting of suspected child abuse, and other aspects pertinent to one's practice. The evaluator either sends this to attorneys and parties before starting the assessment or presents it at the beginning of the initial client appointment. Sample letters of agreement can be found in Appendices B and C and are further discussed in Chapter 5.

4
chapter

Schedule Initial Appointments

Evaluators should not start a case until they have the legal document ordering or stipulating to the assessment. If the evaluation is private-pay, it is advisable to delay the start of an evaluation until there is an agreement regarding costs and retainer fees. It is critical to receive the retainer before beginning

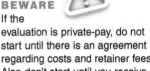

BEWARE
If the evaluation is private-pay, do not start until there is an agreement regarding costs and retainer fees. Also don't start until you receive the retainer; this avoids possible problems with getting paid after the assessment has begun.

the assessment or, at the latest, at the first meeting with a parent. This avoids possible problems with getting paid after the assessment has begun. It is generally impractical and unnecessary to wait for records to begin, as one might do in other types of forensic evaluations. There may not be many records, and commonly the attorneys do not have the records that the evaluator wants (e.g., school reports), so one waits to get signed releases until the first interview.

Typically, the first appointments will be individual ones with each parent. Some evaluators like to start with the custodial parent, others with the parent who is the plaintiff; many yield to the practical solution of interviewing each parent whenever schedules allow. Depending on practical circumstances (e.g., the distance the client has to travel), the first appointment may last from 1.5 to 3 hours to allow adequate time for the initial paperwork and interview, although this practice can vary. It is useful to schedule appointments with each parent in a parallel fashion in order to create the impression of fairness and balance, and to enhance the evaluator's understanding of discrepancies in the parents' views.

The interviews should be individual in a setting that provides privacy and safety, typically the evaluator's office. It is important to know at the outset whether an active restraining order exists and, if so, to take measures to ensure client protection. This can include scheduling each parent on a different day to decrease the possibility of their accidentally meeting each other and taking precautions to keep the time of each parent's appointment confidential. Administrative assistants should be trained to provide protection by keeping parents' appointment information confidential and to be vigilant during appointments with either party. Safety for the evaluator is also of paramount importance; if possible, first appointments should be scheduled at a time when colleagues or office staff will be present. Evaluators should take care as they enter and leave their office if there are safety concerns. The custody evaluator must

be aware of the inherent risks in participating in child custody cases and should
take reasonable steps to increase the
safety of all involved.

BEWARE There are
inherent risks in participating
in child custody cases, so take
reasonable steps to increase
the safety of everyone involved,
including yourself.

In a contested custody case, each
parent likely wonders whether the forensic evaluator is inclined to favor the
other and is sensitive to any inkling of
preference. It behooves the evaluator to treat parents equally
from the beginning so as not to give credence to these concerns.
When possible, it is helpful to make the first call to both parents
on the same day and to offer first appointments in the same
week.

Child-related Logistics

When preparing to interview children, the evaluator first must
decide on the location. The mental health professional's office is
the most common place for the interview. Occasionally a neutral
setting away from parents and conflict is necessary, and the evaluator can make arrangements to interview a child at her school or
in the courthouse. Interviews in the courthouse must be done with
caution, however, due to the anxiety they might provoke in a child,
whereas a school is a familiar and more comfortable setting for
most children. Generally, one avoids lawyers' offices, as they are
often associated with the mother or father; thus they are not, by
definition, neutral. Not only that, but they are not usually a child-
friendly environment, such as might be, for example, a school
guidance counselor's office. Sometimes an evaluator may interview
a child during a home visit; however, one needs to weigh that
choice against the pull the setting might have for the child to
provide information consistent with the parent whose home it is.
That said, it might be preferable to interview children under the
age of 5 or those with special needs in their home environments.
In addition, using the home for the parent–child observation part
of data collection might provide the most useful data about that
relationship, because the observation occurs in a setting more
comfortable and natural for a young child.

4
chapter

BEWARE There is little to be gained from an individual interview of a child younger than 2.5 years of age.

Whether or not a very young child is interviewed is determined on a case-by-case basis. It depends in part on the skill and training of the interviewer, in addition to the child's language, development, and psychological readiness for separation from the parent. A child's inability to separate from a parent and meet with the evaluator alone may make an interview impossible. There is no particular chronological age below which evaluators do not interview children, although below the age of 2.5 years, little is to be gained from an individual interview. Parent–child observation (Chapter 5) remains an important part of child custody evaluations, however, regardless of the age of the child.

With verbal, developmentally on-target children of school age, one can expect that child-trained evaluators can successfully interview them individually. In that case, evaluators generally schedule at least two interviews. As noted earlier, each parent brings the child or children to the evaluator's office once to decrease the chance of influence by the parent who is present in the waiting room. Interviews then occur in a child-friendly space.

Conclusion

At last, having set the stage for the child custody evaluation, the prepared evaluator has clarified the referral questions, fees, expectations, and roles. The evaluator has contacted the attorneys if parents are represented and has made appointments with the parents. With these steps satisfied, he is ready to begin collecting data.

Data Collection | **5**

Chapter 4 sets the stage for child custody evaluations. The present chapter reviews the essentials of the data collection process itself. Child custody evaluations can spring from a range of legal matters before the court and give rise to any number of referral questions. Therefore, no single approach to data collection adequately captures the necessary data in all situations. However, the forensic mental health assessment (FMHA) model includes core methods of data collection central to almost all child custody evaluations: interviews with parents, interviews with children, parent–child observations, review of records, and collateral information gathering. Home visits and psychological testing are often used when they contribute additional relevant information to the evaluation.

Careful documentation is essential during the data-collection phase of an evaluation. Most evaluators take notes during their interviews, and increasingly they do so on laptop computers (Benjamin & Gollan, 2003). No one has reported on the frequency of electronically-recorded interviews in child custody evaluations (Martindale, 2004; Rohrbaugh, 2008), nor is there any consensus on its usage,

INFO

The FMHA model includes methods of data collection central to almost all child custody evaluations:

- interviews with parents,

- interviews with children,

- parent–child observations,

- review of records, and

- collateral information gathering.

Home visits and psychological testing are often used when they contribute additional information to the evaluation.

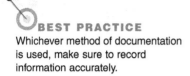

although one must balance the advantage of accuracy of documentation with the extra costs in time and expense. Notably, none of the current guidelines for custody evaluations require electronic recordings. In assessments involving allegations of sexual abuse, however, most authors and guidelines advise audio- or videotaping of interviews to capture an accurate record of children's statements and interviewers' skill, although this practice is not yet universally endorsed (American Professional Society on the Abuse of Children [APSAC], 1997; Kuehnle & Kirkpatrick, 2005).

Whichever method of documentation is chosen, it is essential to record information accurately. When the information is particularly salient, the interviewer should quote the interviewee verbatim, if possible. It is often helpful to note what question the evaluator asked to elicit a particular response, especially during interviews of children, when questions of suggestibility and credibility are most likely to arise. There is a robust literature on young children's vulnerability to leading questions, repetitive interviews, and developmentally inappropriate questioning (e.g., Bruck & Ceci, 2009; Kuehnle, 1996). Extra care in documentation and interviewing must be taken when assessing allegations of child maltreatment in the context of child custody disputes, especially with respect to claims of child sexual abuse (Kuehnle & Drozd, 2005).

Collecting Data on Parents

Child custody evaluators develop an approach and sequence for gathering data that they use routinely, and such matters may vary from one evaluator to another. Some evaluators begin by asking about the current situation that led to the immediate forensic evaluation, while others start with individual history or with the history of the parental relationship. Generally, the data collected from parents must include their individual histories, the history

of the rela⌐   , parenting history
and current co-parenting relationship, information about the children,
and the parents' perceptions of the
current difficulties, including their
preferred outcome. Developing an
approach to interviewing that is relatively consistent across evaluations is
more important than the order of
questioning. However, before initiat-
ing the series of interviews, the forensic evaluator must have a discussion
of informed consent.

BEST PRACTICE
As part of the informed consent
process, the evaluator makes clear
that the assessment is for the
purposes of the court and is not
confidential, unlike, for example, the
reasonable expectations for
confidentiality that people have if
they see a mental health clinician
for psychotherapy. The evaluator
also informs each parent that she
(the evaluator) is a *mandated
reporter*, which means that if she
has reason to believe that a child or
handicapped adult is being abused
or neglected, a report must be filed
with the appropriate state agency.

Informed Consent

Typically, one first introduces oneself and, if asked, offers information about one's background that qualifies the evaluator for the
task ahead. Ideally, the evaluator sends a copy of the fee and
informed consent document to the client and to her attorney
before the first meeting. When reviewing that document during
the first meeting, the evaluator takes care to answer any questions
the client might have about its terms (Association of Family and
Conciliation Courts [AFCC], 2007). Sample documents can be
found in this book (Appendices B and C) and in Gould and
Martindale (2007) and Rohrbaugh (2008). As can be seen in the
two documents provided, they may vary in length and in the scope
of explanation, but they have some common features. In addition
to information about who ordered the evaluation and the purpose
of the assessment, the evaluator gives warnings of the limits of
confidentiality in language understandable to the parent being
interviewed. For example, one makes clear that the evaluation is
for the purposes of the court and is not confidential within the
confines of the legal matter. It can be helpful to contrast that to
the reasonable expectations for confidentiality that people would
have if they were to see mental health clinicians for psychotherapy.
Furthermore, the forensic evaluator advises parents that the

5
chapter

information shared by any participant in the evaluation might be included in the report to the court, and likely will be read by the other parent and participants in the legal process. The evaluator informs the parents that he will tell collateral contacts that their conversations with the evaluator are "on the record," as contemporaneous notes are being taken.

The questions of who is allowed access to the report and who is permitted to have copies of the forensic report are also addressed, and the answers may vary depending on the court order or local practice. In child custody evaluations, the report is sent to the referring court. Whether parties may have copies is determined by local practices. Many jurisdictions allow clients to read the reports in attorneys' offices or courthouses but not to obtain copies, in order to prevent access to sensitive information by children. In addition, the evaluator informs each parent that the evaluator is a mandated reporter, which means that if he has reason to believe that a child or handicapped adult is being abused or neglected, a report must be filed with the appropriate state agency.

Following the discussion about the limits of confidentiality, the evaluator briefly outlines the scope and process of the evaluation, including the likely number of interviews and those who will be included in the interviews. Many parents are anxious to know in what context and for how long their children will be interviewed. They are typically concerned about how to prepare their children for those interviews. It is helpful to offer them simple, but innocuous, suggestions that are appropriate for their children's ages, such as telling the children that the evaluator helps grown-ups (or parents and/or judges) think about the best ways for children to spend time with their parents. Frequently, the evaluator conducts the interviews with children after completing the bulk of the interviews with the parents and will arrange such meetings as conveniently as possible for the children's schedules. The number of interviews with the children depends on the referral questions, the ages of the children, and the evaluator's practices. Often there are two interviews. Each parent takes a turn bringing the children in order to decrease the likelihood of undue influence by the parent sitting in the waiting room. The evaluator also raises the possibility of home visits during this initial meeting with each parent.

In the initial interview, the forensic evaluator informs parents that she will be contacting collaterals, or secondary sources, for information, and she asks for signed releases. The model standards (AFCC, 2007) recommend obtaining signed releases for all collaterals, whether the contact is a professional or a layperson. Evaluators differ in their practice of deciding what type of and how many collateral sources to contact for a child custody evaluation. Some limit these sources primarily to professionals (e.g., pediatricians, school personnel, and psychotherapists), avoiding the likely bias of neighbors, relatives, and friends (Austin, 2002). Others solicit a list of desired contacts from each parent and call some or all of those (or a selected sample of those) requested. On occasion, the court order states a limit on the number of collateral contacts. Nonprofessional contacts may be able to provide observational information about a person or relationship or details of a pivotal event they witnessed relative to the court's concerns.

While there are differences in practice, at a minimum, all evaluations include data from some contacts with direct knowledge of the family or a family member. If the collateral contact is a health-service professional, it is important to have the parties sign a release that is compliant with the Health Insurance Portability and Accountability Act. If the source is a professional for the child (e.g., a pediatrician or teacher), both parents need to sign the release, whereas if it is a parent's personal physician or therapist, then that parent's single signature suffices. If the case involves a modification of a previous custody order and a parent has sole legal custody, then the legal custodian's signature suffices for release forms. If the forensic evaluator is uncertain whether either parent has the authority to sign forms for the children (for example, when a grandparent is guardian or when child protective services is involved), he should seek that information from the parties, their attorneys, or the court.

During this initial explanation of procedures, the evaluator also informs the parent that she will review certain records as part of the evaluation. The evaluator tells the parties whether any records have been provided by the attorneys and which others would be useful. For example, if the attorneys sent court pleadings and *affidavits*, the evaluator may seek permission from the parties to obtain relevant medical and school records.

Other logistics to review at the start of the first meeting with each parent are fees, the general timeline, and issues regarding *testimony* at deposition or trial, should testimony be required. The court order will typically allocate the payment of fees. Those are often divided between the parties, although some courts access state funds to pay for evaluations. For private-pay cases, the evaluator clarifies questions regarding expected fees, including his hourly rate and approximate total cost. At that point, it is helpful for the evaluator to ask the parent whether she has any questions. As described earlier, it is recommended practice for forensic evaluators to provide informed consent statements or memoranda of understanding that review the above-mentioned issues and which parents are asked to sign. Then, having completed the beginning business, the evaluator shifts into the data collection itself.

Topics to Cover in the Interview

Important topics to cover in parent interviews are summarized in Table 5.1.

Table 5.1. Information to Obtain in Parent Interviews

- Background information
  - Name, date of birth, address
  - Family background: where the subject grew up; name, occupation, health, and marital status of parents and siblings; special issues (physical abuse, sexual abuse, alcoholism, substance abuse, mental illness, involvement with social services)
  - Extended family: location, health, involvement with children in evaluation
  - Education/employment: history and current
  - Physical health: major health problems, use of drugs and alcohol
  - Mental health: psychotherapy, medications, psychiatric diagnoses, hospitalizations, current mental status
  - Legal involvement: history and current (other than custody dispute)

Table 5.1. Topics in Parent Interviews (*Continued*)

- Religion: childhood/family background, current practice, area of dispute/agreement with other parent
- Living situation
- Relationship history: history and current significant relationships, other children
  - Spousal/couple relationship in current custody dispute
    - Development of relationship; time line
    - Outside relationships, leisure time
    - Employment and finances
    - Task division: childcare, homework, transportation, housekeeping, finances
    - Conflict management in couple
    - Domestic violence
  - Postseparation relationship
    - How the separation occurred
    - Communication
    - Parenting plan
  - Parenting activities and abilities
    - Activities with children: homework, transportation, medical, recreation, childcare
    - Methods of discipline
    - Understanding and perception of each child
  - Children in evaluation
    - Name, date of birth, age
    - Personality/temperament
    - Health
    - Activities
    - Friends
    - School: school, grade level, teacher, academic performance, abilities/strengths, weaknesses/special needs
    - Favorite thing to do with parent
    - Understanding of parental separation/divorce: what the child was told by parents, child's reaction, how the parents reassure the child
    - Psychotherapy
  - History of current custody dispute
  - Current concerns
  - Desires regarding best outcome
  - Additional issues/concerns

5
chapter

Adapted from Rohrbaugh, J. (2008). *A comprehensive guide to child custody evaluations: Mental health and legal perspectives.* New York: Springer. Reprinted with permission.

BACKGROUND INFORMATION

Information about a parent's family of origin and childhood experiences can provide clues pertaining to current difficulties. For example, knowing that a mother was raised in a home where her father was abusive when intoxicated may provide some understanding of her strong reaction to her husband's having a beer when the children are present. The evaluator inquires about each parent's family of origin including composition, existence of abuse including domestic violence, and parental and sibling functioning. Each parent's legal, psychiatric, medical, educational and occupational history is also obtained. Information regarding past significant relationships or marriages and whether either parent has other children and, if so, relationships with those children and former partners is relevant, as those experiences may color the expectations for the current situation. Often a parent's personal narrative of his life serves as a screening mechanism in that it may inform and help one to understand difficulties and impasses in the present matter. For example, two parents disagreed vehemently about whether their 10-year-old could own a rifle and hunt with his father. In giving his history, the father described his own father as distant and aloof except when they went hunting or fishing together. His narrative helped make sense of the strength of his feeling in the current conflict.

Assessment of a parent's mental status in order to ascertain current psychological functioning is also part of one's evaluation. It is common for people to evidence symptoms of adjustment disorder, including affective distress and/or behavioral disturbance, in the aftermath of family dissolution, so eliciting data that help differentiate current from baseline functioning is an important component of the interview. If the referral question relates to something specific about a parent (e.g., substance use or psychiatric illness), then a more thorough understanding of the development and current status of that difficulty is necessary. The goal of inquiry about

INFO

Often a parent's personal narrative serves as a tool to inform and help one understand difficulties in the present matter.

mental health symptoms is not to
diagnose but to ascertain how they
might functionally impact parenting.

SPOUSAL/COUPLE RELATIONSHIP
When gathering the history of the
parents' relationship, the evaluator
asks each parent the same questions.

BEWARE When you
interview a parent about her mental
health symptoms, your goal is not to
diagnose that adult but to ascertain
how the symptoms might impact the
adult's parenting.

In other words, the second parent interviewed is asked for the same
facts as the first parent, without the assumption that the first parent
reliably reported information. In this way, the discrepancies in perceptions, memories, and stories emerge. It is a common experience
for new evaluators to think that the first parent they interview is
credible and then be surprised that the second parent they interview seems to also be telling the truth, even though their versions
of events are contradictory. The contradictions that are relevant to
the referral questions are noted and further explored during the
course of the evaluation. In general, only the highlights of the history of the relationship are necessary, but the evaluation should
include where and how the couple met, what attracted each to the
other, and how the early relationship/courtship proceeded. One
may ask whether there were "red flags" early in the relationship or
difficulties that signaled its failure. The evaluator should inquire
about issues regarding each pregnancy (e.g., whether it was
planned or unplanned) and the impact of the birth (or adoption)
on the relationship. Significant events or stressors that affected the
relationship or the family—including any moves, illnesses, and
changes in employment—are described. Information about how
the couple negotiated past decisions (e.g., the division of childcare
or housework responsibilities) helps the evaluator understand their
likely ability to negotiate in the future. Not surprisingly, parents
who express intense anger toward each other are less likely to successfully co-parent than those who have adopted a more balanced
view of their ex-partner (Maccoby & Mnookin, 1992). This is relevant because judges typically try to craft orders that will increase
the likelihood of more cooperative parenting in the future (if not
contraindicated by other circumstances, such as safety concerns).

5
chapter

BEWARE When you go over the relationship history with the second parent, ask that parent the same questions you asked the first parent. Do not assume that the first parent interviewed reliably reported information.

The nature of the marital conflicts and their resolution during the relationship are critical areas of inquiry. Whether or not it is part of the referral question, the evaluator asks each parent about the existence of domestic violence. In addition to the obvious and well-known physical safety risks, domestic violence can have a significant psychological impact on adults and children (see Chapter 3). Twenty states have a rebuttable legal presumption against custody to batterers, and 29 additional states consider the existence of domestic violence to be an important factor in child custody (National Center for State Courts, 2008). When allegations of domestic violence are present, the court often wants an assessment.

How to evaluate domestic violence in the context of custody disputes has been described in detail elsewhere (Austin, 2000; Rohrbaugh, 2008). In general, the evaluator asks for a description of the conflict in the relationship and asks whether there have been instances of physical violence. One asks about physical aggression, threats of harm, and sexual aggression. If such issues are affirmed, it is common to ask about the first, worst, and most recent instances of violence. One asks about characteristics known to be associated with the most severe types of domestic violence, for example, social isolation and financial control. Both parents are asked about violence they have experienced and violence they have perpetrated. The role and reaction of the children are always queried, including the whereabouts and ages of the children when the acts of violence occurred, whether any child actively intervened, and what each parent thinks about the impact on each child. Inquiring about interventions—including regarding the involvement of police, medical care, neighbors, friends, or family—and about who was told guides the evaluator to resources to help discern the veracity of the reports. If either parent obtained a restraining order, the circumstances and legal documents are reviewed. In general, the evaluator seeks information that can address three key aspects of domestic violence: the type and level of domestic violence, the impact of the violence on the children, and the risk of violence continuing (Rohrbaugh, 2008).

POSTSEPARATION RELATIONSHIP

The nature of the separation can be significant, so exploring with each party how it occurred may unearth fruitful data. For instance, was the separation planned or the sudden result of a crisis, and were the police involved? If the separation was very distressing or traumatic, then one can ask about the events of the days and weeks following the separation, such as whether a parent was arrested or spent a night in jail, whether children witnessed that arrest, or whether children were able to see that parent in the ensuing days. Throughout the parent's narrative, the evaluator asks about the whereabouts of the children during critical events, their ages at the time, and their exposure to parental conflict and/or violence. Traumatic separations, like other traumas, can have psychological sequelae that might interfere with postseparation individual adjustment and which might impact relationships between and among parents and children (Johnston & Campbell, 1988). For example, a marital separation occurred after a father and 16-year-old son encountered the mother in a romantic embrace with a neighbor. The father reacted angrily and physically assaulted the mother and neighbor. The police were called, and the father was arrested and handcuffed and spent the night in jail. The father was served with a temporary restraining order that prevented him from seeing his children for two weeks. The father became markedly depressed. The son was furious at his mother, whom he blamed for his father's depression and the marital separation. In this situation, the nature of the separation is crucial to addressing the court's questions regarding the parental conflict, the boy's refusal to spend time with his mother, and the custody of the adolescent boy.

BEST PRACTICE
The nature of marital conflicts and their resolution during the relationship are critical areas of inquiry. Whether or not it is part of the referral question, ask each parent about the existence of domestic violence. In general, seek information regarding the type and level of domestic violence, the impact of the violence on the children, and the risk of violence continuing.

5
chapter

BEST PRACTICE
Ask about the parenting history following the separation, because the events after separation can have long-term effects on family members.

The postseparation sequence of events represents important data. Children sometimes do not see the departing parent for days or weeks, especially if there is an existing restraining order, and they may not know or understand why. Depending on their ages and circumstances, children may think they are the cause of a parent's absence; they may also feel abandoned, bereft, embarrassed, or fearful that something has happened to their parent. The remaining parent may be overwhelmed, angry, and/or depressed with concomitant impacts on parenting. It is often a confusing and frightening time for children when their home lives are in flux. Because the events after separation can have long-term effects on family members, the evaluator asks about the postseparation parenting history, including how their parenting plans evolved to the one extant at the point of evaluation.

INFORMATION ABOUT THE CHILD(REN) FROM EACH PARENT

The evaluator asks each parent to describe each minor child and provide a developmental, educational, psychosocial, and medical history, including the child's current functioning and any particular concerns. Child custody evaluators have experience in child assessment and so know how to obtain information about children (for review, see Greenspan & Greenspan, 2003; Sattler, 1998). In child custody evaluations, however, one asks each parent the same questions in order to allow differing perceptions or contradictions to emerge. One asks each parent how the circumstances of the current parental separation may be impacting each child. For example, if the assessment pertains to child safety with an alcoholic parent, then each parent would be asked to explain how that parent's drinking affects the safety of the child. Similarly, in relocation cases, when the custodial parent asks to move out of state with the child against the other parent's wishes, the evaluator asks each parent to discuss the potential impact on the child of allowing or disallowing the move. Their answers yield potentially important information about their abilities to understand their children's needs and how that understanding informs their parenting decisions.

PARENTING ACTIVITIES AND ABILITIES

"Parenting" or child rearing refers to the experiences, skills, qualities, and responsibilities involved in teaching and caring for a child (Encarta World English Dictionary, 2009). The history of each parent's involvement in raising the children is an essential part of the data collection process. Parents disputing custody and parenting schedules commonly inflate their own degree of involvement in the child's care and minimize the contribution of the other parent. Therefore, the evaluator asks each parent separately for a description of his or her involvement and of the other parent's involvement with the children. Evaluators can ask parents for a general list of past and present responsibilities for and activities with their children, including feeding, changing diapers, bathing, homework, school involvement, transportation, recreation, extra-curricular activities, and medical care. It is useful to distinguish between those caretaking functions that are "hands-on," in that they reflect direct care activities (e.g., bathing, feeding, dressing, medical care, or homework assistance), and those parenting functions that are indirect or supportive (e.g., shopping, laundry, paying bills, making appointments, or attending parent–teacher conferences). Evaluators also frequently ask each parent to describe his or her strengths and weaknesses as a parent, as well as the strengths and weaknesses of the other. The data gathered are not assumed to be truth. Relevant discrepancies, strengths, and deficits are noted in order to be further explored through the use of other methods of data collection (e.g., collateral sources, interviews with children, and/or psychological testing).

CURRENT CONCERNS AND WISHES

It is important to have a clear understanding of each parent's concerns regarding the other parent and about the parenting plan. Hearing parents articulate their concerns generally gives meaning and context to referral questions in the court order. Moreover, the concerns or "issues to be addressed" provide an orientation

5
chapter

(i.e., an investigative map) to the evaluator who knows very little about the family. Parental concerns often give rise to hypotheses that are explored during the rest of the evaluation. The notion that parents' concerns help to shape the evaluation may surprise forensic professionals unaccustomed to child custody practice. The current litigation ends when the judge either makes a decision or accepts a stipulated agreement based on the best interests of the child. Ongoing interparental conflict, at home and in legal arenas, is antithetical to promoting children's best interests. Parental concerns help clarify the contributors to interparental conflict. Therefore, understanding and assessing parental concerns that are related to the court's referral questions are an essential part of child custody evaluations. When one parent claims that the other is unable to provide certain types of care for a child, that area of concern becomes a focus of assessment. For example, if one parent alleges that the other parent cannot adequately attend to the medical needs of a young child with diabetes and should therefore not have overnight time, the evaluator needs to elicit specifics regarding that concern. The validity of those concerns can then be explored through collateral sources, such as the pediatrician and school nurse, as well as a review of medical records in the example about diabetes.

DESIRES REGARDING BEST OUTCOME

Each parent's desired outcome is elicited. It is helpful to ask questions in a neutral way (e.g., "So, what do you think the best outcome would be?") as opposed to posing a leading question (e.g., "So, what do you think would be in the best interests of Jeffrey?"). The answer yields important data regarding parents' abilities to appreciate what their children may need, particularly with respect to their relationship with the other parent, and whether they can differentiate that from more self-serving desires. For example, one mother responded that the best outcome would be for her husband to fall off a cliff; perhaps that would be good for her, but her response is not empathic to her child's experience.

Psychological Testing with Parents

As noted in Chapter 3, there is some controversy over the use of psychological tests in custody evaluations. However, the data indicate that most evaluators test parents. They primarily administer the Minnesota Multiphasic Personality Inventory-2 (MMPI-2), but they do not use any other instrument consistently (Quinnell & Bow, 2001). That notwithstanding, a reasonable position is that psychological testing can answer "highly relevant intermediate questions along the way to an opinion about a child's best interest" (Erard, 2005, p. 123) or be indirectly related to the forensic mental health constructs at issue in the case (Erard, 2005). They might address, among others, such issues as affect regulation, interpersonal sensitivity, self-appraisal, range of emotions, coping skills, and adaptability to change. Rather than debate whether or not testing is relevant, it is more useful to ask the following questions:

1. What is (are) the issue(s) or hypotheses I need to address?

2. Are there standard time- and cost-efficient methods of data collection from multiple sources other than testing that can reliably assess those issues?

3. If not, or if the specific legal issue calls for specialized assessments (e.g., allegations of mental disorder), are there instruments to elicit that data? Erard (2005) recommends that testing should start with the "most important concerns flowing from the legal issues" (p. 125) that generate hypotheses that testing (and other data) could address.

4. If appropriate instruments exist, do the parties have the financial resources to afford the assessments?

Once an evaluator has decided to use a certain instrument, he should consider other test-related factors, such as whether it

5
chapter

BEST PRACTICE

Once you decide to use a certain test, consider these test-related factors:

- Has the test been peer-reviewed?
- Does it possess adequate reliability and validity?
- Is the test commercially published?
- Does it have a comprehensive manual?
- Are you qualified to administer the test?

has been peer-reviewed, possesses adequate reliability and validity (particularly for its intended purpose in the evaluation), is commercially published, and has a comprehensive manual (Otto et al., 2003). It is also recommended that the evaluator self-assess whether she is qualified to administer the test. A test that satisfies those criteria can yield empirically based, relevant information that may generate, confirm, or rule out hypotheses about the individual being tested (Gould, 2005).

For example, when one parent alleges that symptoms in the other parent reflect a serious mental disorder (and should therefore limit the other parent's access to the children), selected psychological tests can provide relevant data to address that concern. In addition, standardized psychological tests avoid the problems of possible bias or documentation errors that occur in clinical interviews. Moreover, some instruments—such as the MMPI-2, the Millon Clinical Multi-Axial Inventory-III (MCMI-III), and the Personality Assessment Inventory—include measures of response style or test-taking attitude (Heilbrun, 2001) that suggest the degree to which the person being questioned slanted his answers in a socially desirable manner (i.e., "faked good" [Medoff, 2003]; other instruments make it very difficult for a subject to skew her answers in any particular direction (e.g., Rorschach [Erard, 2005]). Furthermore, the existence of normative data provides a standard of comparison often lacking in other assessment methods, particularly when there are norms on custody-disputing parents (Bathurst, Gottfried, and Gottfried, 1997; McCann et al., 2001).

If testing is appropriate, then the evaluator needs to administer those instruments in standardized ways. For example, a party should not be permitted to complete a self-report test such as the MMPI-2 at home, because this violates the standard method of administration and compromises the validity of the results. Even allowing a party to sit alone in another room or waiting area and complete the test unmonitored might compromise the results (Bow, Gould, Flens, & Greenhut, 2006). Moreover, with all of the information available on the Internet, an evaluator should ask the prospective subject whether he has reviewed any websites that offer guidance in taking the tests or has sought any consultation on the process. If the subject has done so, the evaluator might then have to review the relevant site herself in order to compare the subject's responses to the test with what the website recommended, as the prepared responses might also diminish the validity of the results. Once the test is scored, the results, if considered valid, should be interpreted conservatively, and limitations should be noted.

BEST PRACTICE
If testing is appropriate, administer tests in standardized ways, interpret conservatively, and note limitations.

Three of the standardized assessment instruments most commonly used in assessing adults in child custody evaluations deserve brief mention.

The MMPI-2 is used by the vast majority of psychologists (Bow et al., 2006; Quinnell & Bow, 2001). It is a self-report test that can provide data relevant to personality constructs that relate to the quality of parenting, such as, among others, a tendency for prosocial or antisocial behavior, the ability to modulate emotions, the potential for substance abuse, a capacity to be sensitive to or trusting of other people, and an ability to be consistent and reliable (Caldwell, 2005; Medoff, 2003). The clinical scales on the MMPI-2 can also be helpful when concerns have been raised about the alleged mental illness of one parent that might compromise his caretaking abilities. In addition, the MMPI-2 does have some normative data on custody-disputing parents (Bathurst et al., 1997)

The MCMI-III is used with increasing frequency (39% of all reported evaluations [Quinnell & Bow, 2001]). This third revision of the self-report test is intended to measure personality disorders in adults. The normative sample consisted entirely of individuals who presented with problematic emotional and interpersonal

5
chapter

INFO

Three of the most commonly used standardized tests for assessing adults in child custody evaluations are as follows:

● The MMPI-2

● The MCMI-III

● The Rorschach Inkblot Test

symptoms or who were undergoing professional psychotherapy. This test should be used with caution and skepticism partly because several of the personality disorder scales do not adequately differentiate psychopathology in a population of custody litigants (Widiger, 2001). A similar finding occurred with females in a normative study of the test for use in child custody evaluations (McCann et al., 2001). McCann et al. (2001) also suggested "extreme caution" in using MCMI-III interpretive reports in a child custody context. As noted earlier, the new nongendered norms (intended to rectify the gender differences) have not been validated, so the aforementioned caution still applies.

The Rorschach Inkblot Test is used in about 30% of all reported evaluations (Quinnell & Bow, 2001). This perceptual test relies on the direct observation of the subject's performance and can complement results obtained from self-report tests (Erard, 2005), including, among others, such issues as how one manages emotions and copes with stress, whether one has the capacity to appreciate another's needs, and how flexible or rigid one is in dealing with changing circumstances. It can be useful in checking hypotheses developed from other sources (Calloway, 2005). However, like the MCMI-III, there are varied opinions on the utility of the test in custody evaluations (Calloway, 2005; Hunsley, Lee, & Wood, 2003), so its best use may be "in evaluations where questions of mental health have been raised" (Rohrbaugh, 2008, p. 227).

Collecting Data on Children

As noted in Chapter 2, the court generally seeks information regarding parent functioning, child functioning, parent–child interaction, and the parent–parent relationship—mental health constructs tha [nonly] acknowledged to be fa [int] to the BIC standard and which are included in the APA guidelines (APA, 2009) and AFCC model standards (AFCC, 2007). In addition, the court may have delineated a special issue that it wants the evaluator to assess, such as a child's refusal to spend time with a parent. Every interview provides some data for each of the BIC standard categories, but the child interview uniquely provides information about the child's experience. Understanding and elucidating the child's experience of the family, the parental separation, and its

INFO

Because children do not typically have legal representation in custody proceedings, the child interview may be the only time that the child has an opportunity to be heard and to influence the parenting plan and the outcome of the legal case.

associated events is the most important goal of the interview with the child. Because the child does not typically have legal representation in these proceedings, this may be the only time that she has an opportunity to be heard and to influence the parenting plan and the outcome of the legal case. Specialized forensic interviews of children require general child clinical interview skills and knowledge. It is beyond the scope of this volume to describe general clinical interviews with children, but there are many texts devoted to the topic (see, e.g., Cordell, 2005; Greenspan & Greenspan, 2003; Klykylo, 2005: Sattler, 1998). As with parent interviews, the evaluator begins with an explanation of what is about to happen and a warning of the limits of confidentiality, modified to the developmental age of the child.

5
chapter

Informed Consent

It is best if a parent and child are present together in the evaluator's office when the evaluator describes his role and the limits of confidentiality. By being present, the parent is giving implicit permission to the child to speak to the evaluator, and the parent is supporting the child and resolving any confusion for the child. One has to be aware that children may have some fears about seeing the evaluator, whose role and office are likely unfamiliar to them. One has to be sensitive to children's possible misconceptions. For example, if one introduces oneself as "Doctor" to young children, it may be helpful to explain that you are not the kind of doctor that gives shots, but that you are a worry doctor or a "feelings" doctor who talks to kids about worries, troubles, or concerns they have.

The next step is to give a developmentally appropriate informed consent with limits of confidentiality with the parent present. It is helpful to ask the child about her understanding of why she is there. Sometimes the evaluator can elicit the parent's help in explaining, if an answer is not forthcoming. If not, the evaluator should provide a simple explanation tailored to the age and cognitive ability of the child; the discussion would include the notion that when parents do not live together and cannot decide how children should spend time with parents, judges make decisions with parents. The judge has asked the evaluator to be the judge's helper by getting to know the child and his family, so that the judge can make the best decision for them. For preschool and early elementary school children who do not understand the concept of a judge, one can either explain that a judge is a person who makes decisions when grown-ups cannot decide or bypass the idea of a judge altogether. One can say, "Your parents have asked me to help them to figure out how you will share your time with both of them in a way that works best for you."

The evaluator explains that he will be writing a report, and that the parents will likely read the report. Therefore, if the child does not want them or others to know certain information, then she should not share it with the evaluator. Evaluators can elaborate on this in order to help children avoid questions that they do not want to reply to—for example, to say "no comment" or "I don't want to talk about that."

In addition, as part of the introduction to the interview, the evaluator can encourage the child to respond honestly and tell him not to guess if he does not know an answer. The interviewer can ascertain a young child's understanding of that idea with a simple question and paraphrasing before proceeding. For example, one could ask a 4-year-old, "What is your favorite color?" or "What did you have for breakfast today?" followed by "What is my favorite color?" or "What did I have for breakfast today?" to discover a child's willingness to say, "I don't know." In effect, the evaluator is teaching the child about the rules for answering questions with the goal of eliciting more reliable answers.

The evaluator tailors her explanations to the age and verbal ability of the child(ren). When interviewing more than one child in the family, the evaluator gears his language to the youngest child; at the same time he avoids the perception of talking down to the oldest. Some have wondered at what age children understand these warnings of limits of confidentiality (Condie and Koocher, 2008). Even if a child understands the idea intellectually, it is difficult to know what practical meaning it has to preadolescent children who, by and large, do not have the experience of their lives' being private from their parents. The limits of confidentiality may have only heuristic value, but they still must be discussed in words that are comprehensible to the child being interviewed.

Once the limits of confidentiality are explained, the evaluator asks the parent to leave the room in order to begin the individual interview with the child. As an alternative, some evaluators have a parent–child observation before the individual interview in order to allow children to become comfortable with the evaluator and setting while a parent is present and to gather data on the parent–child relationship. Neither order is preferable. Evaluators need to be able to adapt their usual methods to the demands of the individual case. For example, starting with the parent–child observation session with an adolescent who is furious at her parent is obviously a poor choice, as is starting with an individual interview with a clingy 4-year-old.

Topics To Cover in the Interview

Important topics to cover in interviews with children are summarized in Table 5.2.

Table 5.2. Information to Obtain about Children

- Child's self-presentation (alone and with different family members)
- Activity level
- Attention span and distractibility
- Communication facility: speech clarity, organization, and syntax
- Physical coordination; mannerisms and peculiarities of physical motion
- Frustration tolerance and impulsiveness
- Emotional comfort, mood state, signs of distress or anxiety
- Response to limit setting
- Response to praise
- Social skills and interactions: eye contact, facial expressions, voice tone and quality, presence (and meaning) of sexualized or eroticized behavior
- Cognitive development: ability to analyze logically, recall and report details, empathize, take on role of another person
- Physical condition: general appearance of wellness, cleanliness, clothing
- Child's perception of and relationship with family members
- Child's perception of each parent's home, including structure and routine
- Child's perception of each parent's approach to limits and discipline
- Child's understanding of separation/divorce
- What each parent told the child about the separation/divorce
- Perception of the child's own role in the separation/divorce
- View of each parent as they go through the separation/divorce

- Perception of how the separation/divorce has affected the child's relationships with parents, siblings, relatives, and friends
- Perception of the impact of each parent's new social life on the child
- Child's sense of loyalty in the conflict
- Child's support systems
- Who child confides in (family members, teachers, friends, etc.)
- Child's expression of emotions with different people
- Child's wishes and preferences about custody (addressed indirectly)
- Does the child have information that would help the judge decide what is best?
- What does the child expect it would be like to live primarily with each parent?
- How would the child feel if the judge decided the child should live with the mother/father?
- What three wishes does the child have?
- Would the child like any change in the amount of time spent with each parent?
- Child's psychological functioning
- Child's activities and adjustment in school, community, and neighborhood
- Child's adjustment to changes in family and home
- Child's ability to form and maintain emotional attachments
- Child's self-concept, self-esteem, anxieties, fears, and anger
- Child's overall temperament

From Rohrbaugh, J. (2008) *A comprehensive guide to child custody evaluations: Mental health and legal perspectives.* New York: Springer. Reprinted with permission.

Interviews of 4-year-olds and of 14-year-olds require different techniques, props, and approaches, informed by an understanding of developmental differences in language, fantasy, cognition, attention, and emotional maturity. In clinical interviews with a younger child, the evaluator and child might sit on the floor and use toys such as puppets, action figures, or dolls to facilitate expression. With older children, the evaluator and child typically sit in chairs or on couches, but the child may intermittently play with toys or draw during the interview. Initially, the evaluator tries to quickly establish rapport with the child by asking about school, friends, some aspect of the child's clothing, a pet, some pleasurable activity in which the child engages, or whatever topic may put the child at ease. In so doing, the evaluator begins the inquiry in a manner and pace dictated by the child's developmental age and willingness.

While gaining a sense of the child's overall functioning, the evaluator typically asks the child about his life and functioning outside of the family, including his academic, social, and extracurricular arenas. Electronics, Facebook, favorite music, books, sports, and/or family pets are common topics for adolescents. The children being interviewed have a chance to talk about themselves in a nonthreatening context. The evaluator shifts and asks about their home lives, including household composition and likes/dislikes. The evaluator then asks questions that elicit information about the child's understanding and experience of the parental separation and its impact, the type of interparental conflict (past and present), and the child's view of current familial relationships. The child's experience of the current parenting plan, perception of the availability of each parent, and view of the parents' functioning are also relevant interview subjects. The evaluator takes special care to explore additional areas that pertain to the court's specific referral questions. For example, an evaluator may undertake a specialized assessment if there are allegations of sexual abuse, or one may refer that assessment to another child forensic specialist. If concerns have been raised about a party's allegedly inappropriate behavior, then one elicits detailed information regarding time spent with that parent. In a removal case in which the residential parent is requesting to move out of state with the children, one explores how and when the child connects with the nonresidential parent in order to gain insight into how distance might affect the relationship.

As with any child mental health interview, it is important to ask questions regarding the child's mental status, her overall psychosocial functioning, and any experiences with domestic violence or maltreatment. How and whether one assesses a child's custodial preferences varies according to his social, emotional, and intellectual maturity, in addition to the statutory requirements. Some children, finally being given an opportunity to be heard, will express their opinions with little prompting. Others, when asked what they think would help their families, will suggest parenting plans that reflect their choices. Many children do not want to think that they are choosing between their parents. Forensic evaluators have to be careful to protect them from being in that position. Recommendations for different types of interview questions for children are provided in Table 5.3 (see also Gould and Martindale, 2007; Rohrbaugh, 2008).

Psychological Testing with Children

Other than survey data on the frequency of psychological testing with children and adolescents, there is a sparse literature on the rationale for the use of assessment instruments with children in custody disputes. There might be questions that psychological tests can answer, particularly when parents have disparate views about a child. Erard (2005), for example, suggests a number of concerns about children that testing might address, including, among others, their "cognitive, emotional and social resources" (p. 123) for dealing with their parents' divorce or whether any apparent immaturity reflects a developmental lag or is due to a situational stress reaction. Clark (2008) suggests that testing can add information about the child's special needs; individual problems; or perception of each parent, the family, or the divorce. A common dispute arises when one parent expresses a concern about a child's psychological functioning and consequently lobbies for therapy for the child, while the other parent either does not perceive a problem or attributes the first parent's concern to

Table 5.3. Sample Interview Questions for Children

Sample questions to elicit children's experience of the parental separation:

1. So, how come your parents are getting divorced? Were you surprised or did you see it coming? How do they get along now? [to assess interparental conflict]

2. I talk to hundreds of kids whose parents are getting divorced and they tell me what it's like for them. So what's it like for you? [If no answer:] Some say that they are sad or mad or that it's fine; are you like any of those kids?

3. What's the worst thing about your parents' living apart? What's the best thing?

4. Draw a picture of your family. [Provide a few pieces of paper and crayons/colored pencils/markers. Note who is included and ask about each one. If someone is left out, ask, "What about your mom (dad, brother, etc.)?"]

5. Who do you live with? When do you see [other parent]? Do you think you see Mom/Dad too much, too little, or the right amount of time [same question for other parent]? How is this schedule/plan working for you? If there were anything you could change about it, what might that be?

6. How has this [the divorce/separation] affected you? If there were anything you could change about the divorce, what would that be? [If the answer is to get the parents back together, ask about desired changes if they stay apart.]

Sample questions to elicit information about familial relationships:

7. What do you like to do most with your mom/dad?

8. What is the thing you like best about yourself? If you could change anything about yourself, what would that be? What is the thing you like best about your sibling/mom/dad? If you could change anything about your sibling/mom/dad, what would you change? [Same question for the other parent.]

9. When you have a problem or are upset, whom do you usually go to? Why?

10. Everyone gets mad sometimes. What do you do when you get mad? What happens when you do that? What does Mom do when she gets mad? What happens when she does? [And so on for everyone in the family, including siblings. Alternative: "Who gets the maddest in your family? What happens when that person gets mad?"]

11. How is your mom doing? How is your dad doing?

12. Who is the boss at home?

13. Does anyone get hurt at home? What happens?

14. If I could make any three wishes come true, what would you wish for?

15. Do you have a message you would like to give the judge? If you could talk to the judge yourself, is there anything you would like to say?

Table 5.3. Sample Interview Questions for Children *(Continued)*

Sample questions to elicit information regarding the child's mental status:

16. [For an adolescent] So, how has your mood been? Are you usually happy, sad, angry, worried, or something else?
17. What are you most afraid of?
18. If you could be doing anything you wanted, what would it be?
19. Do you have a best friend? Are you the kind of kid with lots of friends, some friends, or not too many friends?
20. What do you do when you're sad? Mad? Worried? Does that happen a lot of the time, a middle amount of time, or not often?

pathology in that parent instead of in the child. In such an instance, psychological testing can add more objective information for the evaluator that will educate both of the parents as to the nature of the condition as well as inform any relevant recommendations offered to the court.

Once an evaluator decides to seek psychological test data to answer questions relevant to the legal issues, she has many choices, depending on the issues to be assessed. The most common assessment techniques consist of various drawing tasks (i.e., person, house, tree, family), although these should be used to develop hypotheses or as adjuncts to interviews or observations of a child, as there is no empirical foundation for drawing conclusions from them in a forensic context (Rohrbaugh, 2008). Other techniques that address interpersonal, family, or self-concerns are sentence completion items and projective stories, such as the Thematic Apperception Test, the Children's Apperception Test, and the Roberts Apperception Test. In either instance—sentences or stories—the evaluator should explore relevant responses during interviews, but he should be very cautious about drawing forensically relevant inferences because of the limitations in the standardization of the scoring (Medoff, 2003). Standardized instruments used with some frequency are the Rorschach and the MMPI-A (ages 14–18), either of which may be useful in assessing a child's or an adolescent's emotional status, especially when psychopathology is suspected.

BEWARE Child custody evaluators do not draw conclusions from instruments with little or no validity.

The Achenbach System of Empirically Based Assessment (Achenbach, 2001) encompasses ages 1.5–18, the Conners Behavior Rating Scales (Conners, 1997) ages 6–18, the second edition of the Behavioral Assessment System for Children (Reynolds & Kamphaus, 2004) ages 2–25, and the second edition of the Personality Inventory for Children (Lachar & Gruber, 2001) ages 5–19. These instruments have the advantage of eliciting data from school personnel in addition to parents, allowing for comparisons among the different data sources. They provide a broad-based picture of a child's functioning and can be particularly helpful when parents have disparate perceptions of a child's mental health needs. As noted in Quinnell and Bow (2001), there has been a sixfold increase in the use of the Achenbach and Conners child behavior inventories in custody evaluations since 1997. In addition to assessment techniques that screen for a broad range of difficulties in children, there are many instruments geared toward the assessment of specific problems, such as the Children's Depression Inventory (Kovacs, 1992), that can be used selectively. However, the item transparency of this and other behavioral inventories limits their utility in a forensic context.

Assessing Parent–Child Interaction

Setting

Child custody evaluations include an observation and/or an interview of parents with the children (AFCC, 2007; APA, 2009). The setting for this observation can be the evaluator's office and/or the family's home. What is important is that evaluators develop consistent practices to allow comparisons within and across families. The advantages of conducting observations in the evaluator's office include convenience, time- and cost-effectiveness, and constancy, thus allowing the evaluator to more reliably compare familial dynamics across families observed. The primary disadvantage, of course, is that an office is an unnatural

BEST PRACTICE
Develop consistent practices when conducting observations so that you can make comparisons within and across families.

setting for an observa   ereas a home is closer to an in vivo observation.

Role of the Evaluator

Some evaluators strictly adhere to the observer role during a family observation session, sitting in a corner of the office, behind a one-way mirror, or unobtrusively in the home watching the interactions among the children and one parent for a prescribed amount of time. Other evaluators continue in a role as interviewer, asking open-ended questions and noting the family interaction during the session, which is a form of participant observation. There are others yet whose style falls between these observation models, based on the ages of the children or specifics of the case. A common approach is to be a quiet observer with young and elementary-school children while doing a family observation/ interview with older children. Older children are more likely to feel uncomfortable with pure observation, as it is unnatural to them. The promulgated guidelines in this field do not dictate which is the superior method for assessing familial interaction. However, they caution evaluators to be thoughtful in choosing an approach and generally to be consistent in their approach within each case.

Office Parent–Child Observations

When observing parent–child interactions in the office, it is common to tell the parent in general terms what will happen ahead of time. If this is the first time the children and the parent are together in an interview, the evaluator introduces herself, gives informed consent, and tells the children and parent what will transpire. Rohrbaugh (2008) reviews different options for parent–child observations that depend on age and suggests both structured and unstructured tasks for the observation time. For example, a family might be asked to draw a picture together, plan a vacation, build something from a construction toy, or pick up together at the end of a less structured observation session. The length of parent–child observations varies, but sessions of 30 to 90 minutes are typical. Older texts (e.g., Schutz et al. 1989) recommend longer, structured, and more parent–child observations, whereas newer texts

5
chapter

(e.g., Rohrbaugh, 2008) recommend two observations, one with each parent, consistent with the APA guidelines (2009) and the AFCC model standards (2007). Similarly, and consistent with those models, most psychologists report that they include parent–child observations in the evaluation process (Bow & Quinnell, 2001).

Home Visits

The use of the home visit as a component in a child custody evaluation has been discretionary. Survey data indicate that approximately one-third of psychologists report doing home visits (Bow & Quinnell, 2001), although, as noted in Chapter 3, fewer may actually do them (Horvath et al 2002). If one is planning to do a home visit, it is advisable to see the homes of both parents. It is preferable to go when the children are there, so that it becomes an interview/observation opportunity. A home observation is particularly informative when the children are infants or toddlers, as an office interview or observation is likely to be less fruitful for the gathering of developmental and relationship data.

If one parent has made allegations about the problematic nature of the other parent's residence, a home visit is essential so that the evaluator can assess the concerns raised. In addition to providing an opportunity to observe the parent and the children, a visit to the residence can lead to the discovery of relevant information, such as the sleeping arrangements, the types of play materials, safety features, and the level of stimulation or organization in the home. It is noteworthy when one parent has excised the other parent's picture from family photographs or has no pictures of the other in his residence, or, conversely, when a picture with children and both parents remains in a child's bedroom. Rarely do parents provide qualitative information of this sort in office interviews. Asking the children to lead a tour of the residence is a good "ice-breaker" for the family, as well as for the evaluator. Some evaluators like to visit the parent and children at a

BEST PRACTICE

If you plan to do a home visit, it is advisable to see the homes of both parents and to go when the children are there so that the home visit becomes a home observation.

mealtime, because children are more likely to behave as they would at any family meal and one can get a view of the family dynamics that is less veiled than might be the case otherwise.

Home visits can be a stressful experience for those being observed. If the evaluator is at ease with the process, it is more comfortable for all involved. A feeling of awkwardness is not unusual during the evaluator's first forays into other people's ordinarily private spaces, but this becomes easier over time. Moreover, the evaluator develops a particular style and format for home visits that lead to greater consistency and comfort. In summary, a home visit can result in a wealth of valuable information, but, in practice, home visits are not a uniform part of child custody evaluations.

Obtaining Data from Collateral Contacts

Examiners typically obtain information from people outside the family (often called "collateral contacts") when they might have information relevant for the core components in child custody evaluations. These collateral sources consist primarily of those who have had professional relationships with the parents or the children, including but not limited to physicians, therapists, or educators. Although these professionals presumably have little or no interest in the outcome of the dispute, so that bias is less likely to compromise their information (Austin, 2002), evaluators are aware that professionals may have incomplete information and may advocate for their patients. A second group of informants consists of friends or neighbors or those who have worked with the children in a nonprofessional way (e.g., coaches). Each parent suggests a list of informants who may have an opinion about the outcome (and sometimes share it without prompting), depending upon what they know of the dispute. However, these contacts can more readily attest to behaviors of the parents and the children that they have personally witnessed. The third general group of informants includes family members, ex-spouses, or significant others, who usually have a bias about the parties. While their opinions are generally least useful, their observations or information about specific incidents might be germane. They might be most helpful

5
chapter

BEST PRACTICE
Obtain information from people outside the family ("collateral contacts") when they might have information relevant to the custody evaluation. These collateral sources might include physicians, therapists, educators, coaches, friends, neighbors, family members, ex-spouses, and significant others. There is consensus in the field that best practice in child custody evaluations includes collateral contacts.

when they have seen or heard pertinent events (reported by either parent) and can attest to what they witnessed.

When interviewing a collateral contact, either by telephone or in person, the evaluator informs her that her communications are not confidential, that the evaluator is taking contemporaneous notes (or recordings), and that the information will be part of a report for the court. If the collateral contact asks about being a witness, the evaluator has to inform the person of the possibility, however remote, of that occurring. There is consensus in the field that best practice in child custody evaluations includes collateral contacts.

Obtaining Data from Document Review

The evaluator reviews the relevant documents that pertain to the parties or the children. Surveys of child custody evaluators have shown they review some documents in every case (Bow & Quinnell, 2001). These documents include, among others, legal documents (e.g., motions, affidavits, court orders, restraining orders, and prior court decisions); educational, mental health, or medical records; child protective reports; prior custody evaluations; and criminal records. It is recommended that such documents be obtained as copies, not originals, as the evaluator does not want to be responsible for misplacing the latter. Sometimes, one or both parties will submit written histories of their marriage, copies of their journals, or collections of e-mails or letters between the parties. E-mail submissions can be substantial at times, sometimes involving one parent providing e-mails written to a third party by the other parent as evidence of the other parent's moral turpitude. Another form of documentation consists of film or electronic imagery, such as photographs (happy family ones are common), videos of family interaction or premises (usually one in significant disarray), and electronic recordings (e.g., voice mail messages), to name a few. Parents are informed that any documents that they provide are listed in the report and may, therefore, be obtained by the other party.

In summary, data collection is the intensive, hands-on part of the child custody evaluation. Interviews of the parents, interviews of children, family observation, collateral contacts, and review of records are the five components in almost all child custody evaluations. Many also include psychological testing and/or home visits.

Having amassed a mountain of information, the forensic evaluator now faces the challenge of organizing and interpreting that data.

INFO

Surveys indicate that, when available, custody evaluators review legal documents (such as motions, affidavits, court orders, restraining orders, and prior court decisions); educational, mental health, and/or medical records; child protective reports; prior custody evaluations; and criminal records.

5
chapter

Interpretation | 6

This chapter provides a framework for interpretation with attention to legal and ethical issues that inform the process. Most new custody evaluators feel daunted by the task of integrating and understanding the copious amounts of data. Experienced custody evaluators have developed ways to think through the gathered information in order to present comprehensive, but not overly inclusive, opinions to the courts.

A Strategy for Organizing Data to Improve Interpretation

There are many ways to approach the interpretation of assessment data. One is to organize the data as pertains to the four factors (parent; child; fit; parent-parent relationship) with attention to the referral questions and statutory requirements. We illustrate with the following case example: The Court orders an evaluation after a father files for custody of his 10-year old son. The mother and collateral sources raise concern regarding the child's safety in light of father's alleged history of violence. Police reports and collateral contacts document episodes of violence; mother presents as fearful of father; mother's therapist reports diagnoses of PTSD and depression; father angrily insists that he has been treated poorly by a judicial system that favors women; and the child says little and asks to leave when questioned about familial relationships. When observed together, the child directs his mother to draw with him and praises her efforts. The evaluation reveals well-documented episodes of violence, including chronic domestic violence. The evaluator interprets the data based on the referral question (issues relevant to custody), the mother's

BEST PRACTICE

Your task is to organize the psychological "facts" of the family's current and past life and analyze them in light of the questions posed by the Court.

concerns (safety with father), and statutory requirements (to screen for parental domestic violence, a significant best interest factor). The evaluator reports the father's parenting weaknesses, in this case, his marked difficulty with anger, as well as his strengths, e.g. his "can-do" attitude and support for his son.

Table 6.1 │ Model for Interpretation

	Interviews/ Psych Testing	Observations	Collaterals	Record Review
Parent A: Strengths +Weaknesses	[+]empathic, cooperative [-]depression, dependent	passive		
Parent B: Strengths +Weaknesses	[+]"can-do" attitude [-]angry outbursts, blames others	Late or no show for appointments	[-]pedi/sch report that fa has been inconsistent and disruptive	
Child(ren) Needs +Abilities	m.h. and school issues, needs parent collaboration	Anxious, leaves room, avoids talking about parents	teacher reports often tardy when with mother	school evals, ch psych evals
Fit Parent-Child "Match"	fa informs ch of adult issues, mo nurturant but does not get him to sch consistently	tense fa-child relationship, warm mo-child relationship		
Parent-Parent Level + type of conflict/ cooperation	fa reports mo refuses to talk to him, mo states not safe for communication	tension when both present in clinic/angry communication.	school reports interparental conflict at school event	history of restraining orders, documented domestic violence

The mother's strengths and weaknesses are similarly reported, including chronic depression that might be secondary to domestic abuse. The child's needs are described particularly as they impact parenting. In this case, the 10-year old boy has a history of school failure, oppositional behavior, and a diagnosis of Bipolar Disorder. He requires parents who can work collaboratively with psychiatric and educational systems, advocate for his needs, and are consistent in follow-through. The parent-parent relationship is marked by conflict and anger, so shared parenting could pose dangers.

Using Table 6.1 as a way to organize the above data, the evaluator considers the areas central to child custody evaluations as well as the statutory requirements and case specific variables. She analyzes the psychological "facts" of the family's current and past life in light of the questions posed by the Court. The data gathered from multiple sources (interviews/tests, observations, collateral contacts, and review of records) provides the material that fill in the boxes on the grid in Table 6.1. Which specific 'parental attributes' and 'child needs' to address are informed by the referral questions, concerns of other parent, statutory requirements and, if relevant, unique issues.

Tips/Guidelines for Interpretation

Generate and Analyze Hypotheses

During the course of the evaluation, the evaluator is guided to appropriate methods of inquiry by hypotheses that emerge as the process unfolds. Hypotheses about the family's functioning are derived from several sources, including the following:

- the court's reason for referral,
- each parent's expressed concerns about the other,
- clinical interviews and observations,
- collateral contacts,
- psychological testing, and
- reviewed records.

For example, in the above case vignette, the mother's expressed concerns and confirmed reports about domestic abuse would suggest hypotheses about the father's ability to manage his anger in parenting their child. The father's expressed concerns about the mother's mental health would lead the evaluator to think about the mother's ability and energy to cope with the demands the boy will place on her parenting, but also to consider the possibility that her depression was secondary to abuse (and that her functioning will improve once she feels safe). In this context, knowledge of research in the area of domestic violence might also direct the evaluator to inquire about the presence of child maltreatment during the time the parents lived together.

The significant mental health and educational needs of the child might lead the evaluator to produce hypotheses about each parent's ability to handle a child with such temperament and behavioral challenges. Given the domestic abuse, one would question the parents' ability to cooperate in ensuring that school and service professionals meet the boy's needs. In such circumstances, if the parents were to work at cross-purposes, it could be detrimental to the child. The hypotheses inform the assessment and highlight which issues are addressed in the report. These hypotheses provide the primary issues about which interpretations or impressions are formed.

Consider Alternative Hypotheses

As in all forensic evaluations, the evaluator looks for disconfirming information that may temper or change his interpretations. During the assessment phase, the forensic evaluator forestalls closure on any potential hypothesis. Amidst an overabundance of collected information, one should focus on the data that are relevant either to the legal questions asked by the court or to the basic forensic mental health constructs, or both. Those data "must relate to the pertinent inquiry" (Gould, 2004). The evaluator follows the relevant "facts" and discovers what patterns or combinations of data make the most sense in order to understand the psycho-legal questions and the existing hypotheses about the nature of the family's functioning.

Corroborating information from independent sources (i.e., convergent validity) increases confidence in conclusions drawn from such data. In order to minimize confirmatory bias, it can be helpful to assume a ledger-type approach (i.e., pro/con) to hypothesis testing, such as enumerating the major hypotheses and listing the supporting and disconfirming data for each one.

BEWARE
Weigh events in light of their probable impact on parenting. Something that may at first sound like a significant individual problem may have little impact on parenting, and something else that does not sound problematic may be harmful for the children involved.

Consider the Impact of Parental Deficits on Parenting

There is a tendency for us to place greater or lesser weight on a family problem or event depending on our own perception of its magnitude or importance. In contrast, custody evaluators need to weigh such events in light of their probable impact on parenting. Something that may at first sound like a significant problem may have little impact on parenting, and something else that does not sound problematic may be harmful for the children involved. A parent's prescription drug abuse may not be so significant if it is limited to times when the children are with the other parent. Alternatively, concern about a parent's dating may seem inconsequential until one learns that the parent is dressing seductively and displaying inappropriate affection for the new partner in front of adolescent children who are embarrassed and distressed by these behaviors.

Consider a Child's Special Needs/ Developmental Stage in Terms of the Demand on Parenting Skills

Children's parenting needs are multidimensional and dynamic. Beyond the universal needs for food, shelter, and protection and the societal expectations of education and socialization, different children may demand different qualities from parents, and a single child may demand different qualities due to diverse developmental stages or changes in life circumstances. An 8-year-old with

6
chapter

INFO

Children's parenting needs are multidimensional and dynamic, and the assessment of an individual child clarifies the parenting skills most relevant *for that child* in order to allow an analysis of the parent–child fit.

Asperger's disorder needs specialized intervention and parents who are able to advocate and be consistent. A 15-year-old with sickle cell anemia needs parents who can monitor the illness, adhere to a medication regimen, and support their child when she is in pain and in the hospital, as well as encourage age-appropriate independence when possible. A child with a special interest or talent, such as exceptional musical or athletic abilities, does best with a parent who recognizes its value to the child and has the time, interest, and energy to support that ability. The assessment of the child clarifies the parenting skills most relevant for that child in order to allow an analysis of the parent–child fit.

Consider the Fit between Parents and Children

The fit between parents and children is a key component of child custody evaluations. The evaluator analyzes the congruence between child needs/skills and each parent's abilities to meet those needs or support those skills, addressing particular concerns raised by the court and parties. The combinations of relative parent abilities and child needs/skills that are congruent can be considered "matches." Clinically, matches are more likely to enhance positive child development and are protective factors in a risk/benefit analysis. In contrast, those relative parent deficiencies vis-à-vis child needs/skills that reflect incongruence can be considered "mismatches" and are risk factors that are more likely to impede healthy child development. This is essentially a nonmathematical, clinical calculus that considers parent–child interactions.

INFO

The fit between parents and children is a key component of child custody evaluations.

In the above example of a special talent, one parent's hectic schedule and difficulty with organization likely will affect his ability to get the child to the particular activity consistently. That might result in the child's falling behind peers in that activity, getting discouraged, and wanting to quit what might otherwise be a significant source of self-esteem and personal skill. In another example, the father of a 6-year-old boy with moderate to severe attention-deficit/hyperactivity disorder gives him medication on schooldays, but his mother fails to follow through on her weekends, likely contributing to the boy's extremely active and impulsive behavior when in her care. If the weekend drug "holiday" is medically prescribed, as is frequently the case, then one might examine whether the mother continued with an unsuccessful approach or sought advice from the physician who made the original order.

A historical perspective on parenting and child development is important in examining parent–child fit, because current functioning is in part predicated on past parenting practices and earlier child development. Moreover, parents may have different skills that fit better with the child's needs at different developmental stages. For example, Ms. Rodriguez, who is organized and detail-oriented, has always successfully coordinated 9-year-old Roberta's complicated special education services. Alternately, Ms. Silver's careful attention to details and her involvement in most aspects of 16-year-old Rachel's life may have been parenting strengths while her daughter was young but are now contributing to parent–child conflict. Rachel's desire for more independence is developmentally appropriate.

One can often compare parents on the same parenting factor. For example, in the area of child management, Mr. Smith's directive style of parenting is effective in helping 6-year-old Dan deal with the typical impulses and frustrations of a boy his age without resorting to harshness or unreasonable consequences. In contrast, Ms. Smith's permissive style of parenting is not effective in helping Dan to learn to self-regulate; in fact, it appears to encourage the very behavior she wishes to eliminate. Mr. Smith's style of discipline and his ability to adapt it to his son's particular needs constitute one of his parental strengths, while Ms. Smith's permissive style is ineffective and possibly deficient for Dan, who requires clear structure and expectations.

Consider the Current Co-parenting Relationship

An important contextual aspect of family functioning that relates to a best interest determination is the ability of each parent to cooperate with the other after the separation or divorce. It involves each parent's willingness and ability to encourage, or at least to not discourage, a relationship between the children and the other parent, as long as it is safe. Sometimes called the "friendly parent" doctrine, this is an important BIC Standard factor, which is explicitly endorsed by the statutes of 26 states (see Appendix A). Some of the variables included in the ability to cooperate are as follows:

- how the parents cooperated during the marriage or during the cohabiting relationship (i.e., the historical perspective),

- what challenges they have experienced postseparation,

- what values in child rearing and what goals for the children they have, and

- whether they exhibit respect for each other's child-rearing practices or whether they can agree to disagree without being disagreeable.

For example, parents' opposing beliefs about appropriate discipline likely exacerbate the already contentious nature of their relationship. They accuse each other of inappropriate parenting with respect to discipline and believe the other's parenting practices are contrary to the child's best interests. In contrast, a parent might think the other is too permissive but decide to maintain a set of reasonable yet flexible standards for behavior without trying to change or criticize the other parent's methods. An evaluator considers the manner in which parents raise their children in synchrony with each other, in conflict with each other, or independent of each other. The evaluator can then generate hypotheses

INFO

An important aspect of family functioning, as it relates to the BIC Standard, is the ability of each parent to cooperate with the other after the separation or divorce.

about how the interparental relationship impacts parenting and the children's adjustment.

Consider Special Issues, Including Cultural and Ethnic Context

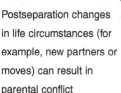

INFO

Postseparation changes in life circumstances (for example, new partners or moves) can result in parental conflict

Special issues include ethnic and cultural aspects, as well as external circumstances or demands that influence the family in ways relevant to the legal matter. For example, Joe is a 13-year-old boy who lives primarily with his mother and shares many interests with his father. He expresses a strong desire to live with his father, prompting the father to file for custody. The mother's initial willingness to consider this request changes dramatically when the maternal grandmother expresses harsh disapproval and tells the mother that children belong with their mothers. Johnston and Campbell (1988) call this "tribal warfare," in which members of the extended family, the community, or legal professionals exert strong pressure for a certain outcome, increasing the level of hostility and possibly precluding a negotiated solution. Evaluators need to be sensitive to factors external to the immediate family that may be salient to the referral questions.

It is not uncommon for a formerly cooperative parent to become hostile when the other parent develops a new romantic relationship. Conversely, the opinions of a new person in a parent's life may affect formerly flexible and cooperative parenting arrangements. Environmental and situational circumstances can also be important in child custody evaluations. For instance, one might raise safety concerns regarding a 6-year-old boy when the parent who is raising him lives on the bank of a river or on a busy street— but such concerns would not be raised if the same parent lived in a home with a fenced-in yard in a cul-de-sac. The risk level for the latter would appear to be less than for the former. Parenting plans and custodial arrangements are also impacted by life circumstances. For example, if one parent's job requires extensive travel, she is less likely to be favored as the residential parent.

6
chapter

Interpret Conservatively

The most frequent criticism of child custody assessments is that evaluators are prone to go beyond the data and state opinions that lack sufficient empirical support (Melton et al., 2007). In Chapter 2, we address the role of psychological information in these evaluations and note that there is greater empirical support for descriptive types of statements than for interpretive opinions. The latter require higher levels of inference with less clear validity and less scientific support (Tippins & Wittman, 2005). Given these limitations, the evaluator needs to be cautious about analyzing data beyond the descriptive levels of inference. Nevertheless, an evaluator can have more confidence in hypotheses that are supported by multiple sources, including research findings, as those data are likely to be more valid (Gould, 2004). A conservative approach to interpretation in keeping with ethical standards warrants an explanation of the limitations of conclusions, as well as the discussion of data that may support alternative explanations or conclusions.

In summary, in this chapter we present a framework for interpreting or explaining data gathered during a custody evaluation. Using a system of data analysis

BEWARE
The most frequent criticism of child custody assessments is that evaluators are prone to state opinions that lack sufficient empirical support. Given these limitations, be cautious when analyzing data beyond the descriptive levels of inference.

BEST PRACTICE
Tips/guidelines for interpretation include the following:

● generate and analyze hypotheses;

● consider alternative hypotheses;

● consider the impact of parental deficits on parenting;

● consider the child's special needs/developmental stage in terms of the demand on parenting skills;

● consider the fit between parents and children;

● consider the current co-parenting relationship;

● consider special issues, including cultural and ethnic contexts; and

● interpret conservatively.

assists the evaluator in understanding which of the multiple hypotheses about the family functioning best fits the available data and in drawing conclusions about the forensic mental health constructs or statutory factors. In the next chapter, we turn to the last two functions of the forensic evaluator: report writing and testimony.

6
chapter

Report Writing and Testimony | 7

The Report to the Court

The psycho-legal report documents the information the forensic evaluator has gathered on psychological and behavioral issues relevant to the legal questions in dispute (Melton et al., 2007; Schutz et al., 1989). The report is a detailed statement of the assessment process (i.e., the method), the content of the evaluation (the data sections), the interpretation or analysis of the data (the discussion/conclusions section), and/or opinion relevant to the psycho-legal question(s) (the recommendations section).

General Considerations

Gould and Martindale (2007) recommend that the report should focus on "historical truth" or "psychological fact finding" that "helps to understand how people behaved in the real world (pp. 14–15)," but it ought not be written in an accusatory manner or in a style that focuses on psychopathology. It is common for a parent to share painful revelations about the marriage. Thus, information in custody reports is often very personal and potentially embarrassing or hurtful to one or both parents at a time when they are likely to be emotionally vulnerable. Notwithstanding that fact, if the expressed parental concerns or allegations are relevant to the legal questions, relevance being a core organizing principle of a forensic evaluation (Heilbrun et al., 2009), an evaluator must attend to them. An unemotional, matter-of-fact approach to those concerns can mitigate the possible sense of personal affront to the one accused, given that the parents in the case will likely continue to have some form of relationship with each other and their children for many years after the evaluation is complete.

BEWARE
Evaluators will often feel caught in the tension between accurate reporting and the ethical principle of nonmaleficence, or "do no (unnecessary) harm".

Thus, the forensic evaluator must struggle with the tension between accurate reporting and the ethical principle of nonmaleficence, or "do no (unnecessary) harm" (American Psychological Association [APA], 2002, Principle A). Concerns that are provocative or emotionally charged but which are not relevant (e.g., a parent's affair that did not alter competent parenting) might simply be noted yet left unexplored. Moreover, the evaluator does not have to describe them in the specific (and sometimes demeaning) language of the parent who made the accusation. Information that is irrelevant to the legal issue should be left out, or, alternatively, the evaluator could offer a simple explanation as to the rationale for setting aside certain issues that do not change the conclusion. To cope with this tension between reporting accuracy and parental sensibilities, Rohrbaugh (2008) suggests that the report present information "in a way that preserves each family member's dignity by describing their particular strengths and weaknesses in a sensitive, impartial manner" (p. 323).

After submitting the report to the court or to the court's designee, such as a guardian ad litem or attorney for the child, the evaluator does not have control over how the report is used. Pursuing their preferred outcome, the parties and their attorneys will decide how to utilize its contents—either as leverage in settlement negotiations or as evidence at trial. A report often contains personal information that could potentially harm the well-being of the parties or the children if it were released. Therefore, to protect the parties, the forensic evaluator has an affirmative responsibility to distribute the report in compliance with the rules or with the practices of the local jurisdiction and the court order. When uncertain, evaluators do not release the report absent instruction from the court. In general, however, the rules are fairly simple. If the court ordered the evaluation, the report goes to the court, or the evaluator sends it to whomever the court designates.

Intended Functions of the Report

A report serves many purposes, all of which influence how one constructs and writes a child custody report. Five main purposes are worth considering:

1. The report has a *documentary* function. The report delineates in a transparent manner the methods employed and the relevant data obtained (Melton et al., 2007). As noted in Chapter 2, the role of the report in performing this function is a focused one, in that the legal questions posed by the court and the relevant constructs direct the evaluation and the subsequent contents, which Heilbrun et al. (2009) consider to be "the heart of the forensic mental health assessment" (p. 109). In other words, a primary purpose of the report is to tell the reader what the evaluator did and learned during the assessment.

2. The report has *an organizing functi*on. It forces the forensic evaluator to impose some order on the information and select data that are relevant to the legal questions posed by the court (Melton et al., 2007).

3. The report has an *interpretive* function, as discussed in Chapter 6. It explains to its several audiences what meaning the reported "facts" have for the psychological and behavioral functions (i.e., "custody-relevant constructs") (Tippins & Wittman, 2005) that underlie the legal questions posed by the court.

4. The report has an *evidentiary* function. In the event of a trial, it will be an exhibit in the proceedings and the primary basis upon which attorneys will examine the forensic evaluator-witness. While the report is the focus of expert testimony, the forensic evaluator should be aware that, in case of a trial, one or both sides are likely to summon the evaluator as a witness and require that he take to court the entire

INFO

A child custody report serves many functions, including the following:

- a *documentary* function,

- an *organizing* function,

- an *interpretive* function,

- an *evidentiary* function, and

- an *advisory* function.

file, including all notes, documents, and psychological testing results. That also requires record-keeping "to be of the highest quality because of the potential for judicial review" (Kirkpatrick, 2004, p. 66).

5. The report may have an *advisory* function. It may provide recommendations, depending on the respective practices of the court and the evaluator, as well as the circumstances of the case.

Unintended Functions and Effects of the Report

There are at least four possible unintended functions or effects of a child custody report.

(1) The report often has a *mediation* function. It can serve as the basis for the parties to settle their child-related disputes (Melton et al., 2007), and might, in fact, serve that function far more often than it is used as evidence in a trial (Association of Family and Conciliation Courts [AFCC], 2007; Bow, Gottlieb, & Gould-Saltman, 2011; Maccoby & Mnookin, 1992). The report provides data for the parties to use in a cost/benefit analysis with respect to either proceeding with litigation or settling their dispute without trial. It may also provide a series of parenting plan solutions from which parents can choose in self-determining the outcome. In one study, 71% of the cases settled after learning the results of their child custody evaluation (Ash & Guyer, 1986). However, forensic evaluators have to

be careful not to view settlement as a goal of their evaluations, even though most agree that settlement is preferable for families as opposed to emotionally and financially draining litigation. The evaluator contributes to unintended, but not unwelcome, settlement discussions by doing a careful evaluation, following sound forensic principles, assuring that parents and children are heard, and documenting thoroughly with the expectation that the case will continue to trial (AFCC, 2007).

(2) The report may have a *third-party information function.* This occurs, for example, when the court permits its distribution to a therapist who is working with a child, a parent, or the family. Additionally, the report can provide important guidance for a parenting coordinator or special master who might have limited decision-making authority over the parties after they are divorced.

(3) The report can have a *healing* or *restorative effect.* One or both parties might come to a different understanding about their failed relationship or the needs of the children, which can facilitate getting beyond the "impasse of divorce" (Johnston & Campbell, 1988). Thus, the report can be emotionally restorative for parents when they read about their parenting strengths and positive influences on the children.

(4) The report can also have a *negative* or *hurtful* effect. Despite a writer's best efforts to limit the inclusion of inflammatory information, one might report revelations previously unknown by a party in the dispute, information that wounds the pride of that person and leaves unintended but lingering pain. This might inadvertently make settlement less likely, fuel conflict over the children, or extend the litigation longer than necessary, because the

emotionally wounded party cannot find a way to salvage some pride in the process.

These unintended functions or effects can be directly related to what the evaluator-writer deems relevant and how she reports that information. Both parents will read the report and will likely continue to have some form of co-parental relationship, with the knowledge of what each has said about the other. It is here that the respectful tone of the reporting and the avoidance of unnecessary, irrelevant, or inflammatory claims can have the most salient effect. Writing the report "in a manner that respects the family system and encourages a parenting plan that accentuates each parent's positive qualities" (Gould & Martindale, 2007, p. 15.) enhances that possibility.

Considering the Audience

There are at least three audiences for a report, and it is the responsibility of the evaluator-writer to make the report understandable to all three.

(1) The court or the court's designee: As the customary source of the referral and the primary client (Kirkpatrick, 2004), it is the agency to which the report belongs and for whom the evaluator is writing. In addition, in the event of a trial, the report will be an important piece of

evidence and the basis of *direct* and *cross-examination* of the evaluator. Despite its preeminent position, the court is the least likely party to read the document (Felner, Rowlison, Farber, Primavera, & Bishop, 1987) because fewer than 2% of divorcing families are likely to proceed to trial (Maccoby & Mnookin, 1992). There are no data regarding what percentage of families who undergo a child custody evaluation actually proceed all the way to a full trial, but clinical experience suggests it may be less than 1 in 10 (Melton et al., 2007). Despite its infrequency, a trial is the logical conclusion of the legal process; therefore, the evaluator "should always anticipate that testimony in a deposition, hearing, or trial will be associated with the evaluation" (Heilbrun, 2001, p. 13).

(2) *The parties to the legal action*, typically the parents, represent the second and most likely audience for the forensic report. They have the most vested interest in knowing how well the forensic evaluator heard them, understood their issues and those of the children, and performed a comprehensive evaluation. Respecting this audience has become more important in recent times, as the number of pro se litigants has been increasing dramatically. Thus, the writer uses language that is "precise, austere, and free from jargon, legal terms, vague abstractions, psychological terms that have been corrupted by popular usage, and any terms that are pejorative in reference to any party" (Schutz et al., 1989, p. 94). The report avoids psychiatric diagnoses (Rohrbaugh, 2008), although if a parent or child has a documented, diagnosed psychiatric illness, that usually is explained in the report. If the forensic evaluator finds that there are undiagnosed, multiple psychological or behavioral problems in a parent or child, the consensus is that the role of the evaluator

7
chapter

is not to provide a diagnosis (Gould & Stahl, 2000), but to describe those symptoms and how they are linked to parent–child relations. In addition, the evaluator may request formal diagnostic procedures (e.g., psychological testing or psychiatric evaluation) as part of the custody evaluation process or in the recommendations section of the report.

(3) *The parties' attorneys* are the final important group of readers, although, as noted above, increasing numbers of parents involved in custody disputes are unrepresented by legal counsel. Attorneys are interested to know whether the evaluation was fair and thorough, whether the information and conclusions support their clients' position, and what aspects of the findings will be advantageous in settlement negotiations. Conversely, an attorney whose client's position is not supported might be interested in whether there are weaknesses in the report in order to attempt to impeach the forensic evaluator's findings in the event of a deposition or trial. If the forensic evaluator offered recommendations, each side will want to know whether she based the opinion on conclusions reasonably supported by the data.

The report needs to be written in language understandable to all three audiences.

Contents of a Report

There are many ways to organize the contents of a child custody report. However, almost all approaches include some basic areas of information. One possible organizational structure follows.

INFO

There are at least three audiences for a child custody report:

1. the court or the court's designee;

2. the parties to the legal action, typically the parents; and

3. the parties' attorneys.

ORIENTATION TO THE EVALUATION

Ideally, in order to provide a snapshot of the assessment, the first page or two of a report will reflect such basic data as the following:

- what court referred the family,
- the legal questions at issue or the reason(s) for referral,
- the basic demographics of the family,
- a summary of activities,
- dates and length of interviews,
- dates and length of contacts with collaterals,
- lists of records reviewed, and
- a summary of the background of the dispute, including
- the parenting plan at the time of the referral.

PARENT DATA

For each parent, the report should include the following:

- major concerns about the other parent,
- responses to expressed concerns of the other parent,
- the individual biopsychosocial history,
- a history of adult relationships,
- areas of partner conflict and issues of domestic abuse,
- the history of parenting and co-parenting during the time the parents lived together as well as during the separation period,
- psychological test data, if tests administered,
- the existence and impact of special circumstances (e.g., cultural/ethnic issues), and
- preferred outcomes for dispute.

This information provides the context within which to report and understand the current concerns either parent has about the other as a parent and provides data about the nature of their strengths and challenges as parents. While that may appear to succumb to a "he said/she said" approach to data collection, it is important to remember that a parent's story provides multiple hypotheses that are subject to verification from alternative sources of data. "Just because a story is compelling does not make it true" (Gould & Stahl, 2000, p. 408). That data section should also include any special issues in their relationship, such as reports of domestic abuse prior to or after separation, psychiatric or substance abuse problems of the parents, or concerns about maltreatment of the children. The report may also contain each party's responses to the relevant concerns that the other parent or other sources expressed.

CHILD DATA

The report summarizes the developmental history and current functional status of the children, as well as any current concerns about the children's adjustment (the second psycho-legal construct). As noted in Chapter 5, the report should include the following information about each child:

- significant developmental history;
- social skills;
- emotional development, including ability to self-regulate;
- intellectual/academic functioning;
- adjustment within the family, including sibling relations;
- any special developmental needs or exceptional abilities;
- the child's understanding and experience of the parental separation;
- psychological test data, if tests administered; and
- the child's current concerns and wishes.
- parental concerns regarding child.

COLLATERAL AND DOCUMENTARY DATA

- Summary of interviews with professional and lay contacts
- Summaries of relevant documents (e.g., medical records, school records, legal records, etc.)

INTERPRETATION OF THE DATA

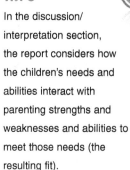

INFO

In the discussion/ interpretation section, the report considers how the children's needs and abilities interact with parenting strengths and weaknesses and abilities to meet those needs (the resulting fit).

In the discussion/interpretation section, the report considers how the children's needs and abilities interact with parenting strengths and weaknesses and abilities to meet those needs. This is consistent with the third psycho-legal concept in the APA (2009) guidelines: the resulting fit. For example, if parental psychopathology or other illness is one of the major concerns, the forensic evaluator explains how the person functioned as a parent while managing the particular condition. The discussion section also includes a focus on the parents' capacity to cooperate and manage conflict—the fourth psycho-legal construct. It is essential to explain how existing parent conflicts affect parenting and child adjustment. This co-parenting variable is an important predictor of the postdivorce adjustment of children and one factor in the determination of the type of legal custody.

In encouraging a conservative approach to interpretation, many writers recommend that parenting or child development issues only be "highlighted in the forensic clinician's conclusions *if* [emphasis added] the clinician can infer, based on confirmed case data and the specialized knowledge base of the profession, that these traits can be reliably associated with custody-specific inferences" (diminished parenting capacity, child behavior problems too challenging for a parent, etc.) (Tippins & Wittman, 2005, p. 197). Many authors (Emery et al., 2005; O'Donahue & Bradley, 1999) have expressed concern about communicating "erroneous inferences" (Tippins & Wittman, 2005, p. 198) to the courts or

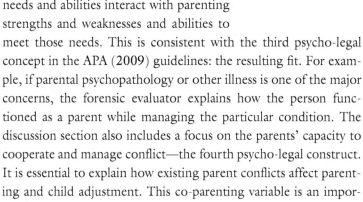

7
chapter

BEST PRACTICE
Parents may raise moral or "character" issues when there has been infidelity in the marriage or when one parent has not been responsible with finances or has not maintained a tidy home. While those issues are important to the parent who raises them, they are not significant for the assessment *unless* there is a demonstrable link to parenting or to some impact on the children.

reporting on parent or child characteristics that are irrelevant to the legal constructs that are the focus of an investigation. As noted earlier, a forensic evaluator obtains a great deal of information about parents and children. The essential question is one of relevance: what behaviors or skills link to factors associated either with the forensic mental health constructs or to the court-ordered questions? For example, parents may raise moral or "character" issues when there has been infidelity in the marriage or when one parent has not been responsible with finances or has not maintained a tidy home. While those issues are important to the parent who raises them, they are not significant for the assessment *unless* there is a demonstrable link to parenting or to some impact on the children.

RECOMMENDATIONS

In the section in Chapter 2 on the role of psychological information in these evaluations, we discuss the question of whether to offer opinions on the legal questions posed by the court, in the report itself and/or during testimony. To recap briefly, most evaluators offer recommendations on legal questions, either in their reports or in testimony, consistent with the expectations of judges and attorneys (Bow, et al., 2011; Bow & Quinnell, 2004; Redding, Floyd, & Hawk, 2001). However, most forensic scholars strongly caution against this practice, noting that it exceeds our expertise. Our professional directives acknowledge the debate. The American Academy of Child and Adolescent Psychiatry (AACAP) (1997a) actively encourages the proffer of recommendations. The AFCC (2007) urges the evaluator, if he is to offer such a opinion, to ensure that it derives from "reliable principles and methods." The APA (2009) simply notes that no consensus has been attained on the issue, but it urges the evaluator to be aware of the debate and to be able to explain her position on the issue. As with the AFCC (2007), the APA (2009) also recommends that such opinions, if offered, derive from "sound psychological data" (p. 18) and focus on the child's best interest.

Advocates for such an advisory role (Fridhandler, 2007; Stahl, 2005) support the idea that the evaluator has the most detailed understanding of family dynamics, can prioritize children's needs, and has the experience of integrating clinical data and current scientific knowledge to make sound clinical decisions. In addition, such a recommendation or opinion testimony is merely one part of a wide range of evidence that a court will consider, and its usefulness "outweighs any dangers implicit in an expert report" and "is probably as good as it gets in the present system" (Dessau, 2005, p. 268).

In contrast, most academic authors posit that there is neither sufficient empirical nor clinical basis to support opinions about what is essentially a value-laden question (Emery et al., 2005; Grisso, 2005; Heilbrun, 2001; Tippins & Wittman, 2005). We may be able to explain legally relevant abilities (i.e., parenting strengths and weaknesses), but we cannot know what levels of those skills are "enough" to meet an often vague legal criterion of "best interest." Melton et al. (2007) note that this level of opinion consists of "judgments based on common sense and personal moral values" (p. 605), while Heilbrun (2001) includes political and community values, all of which are beyond the scope of mental health professionals. Opponents to ultimate issue opinions note that evaluations (most of which include recommendations) often go unchallenged; they can also be instrumental in facilitating out-of-court settlements (Ash & Guyer, 1986). Thus, the findings can be very influential in a legal outcome in the absence of any challenge to the merit or basis for the opinions.

In the context of that debate, if the court asks for recommendations, or if the evaluator's practice is to provide recommendations, his opinion section could include any of the following:

- suggestions as to what is in the "psychological best interest" of the child;

- a possible parenting plan with its attendant risks and benefits;

- an opinion on the legal questions posed by the court (e.g., which parent should have custody or the type of custody, should a parent be allowed to move away with the child); and/or

- other relevant recommendations, such as therapy, additional assessments, etc.

The foundation for recommendations should be clearly explained in the discussion/interpretation section of the report. Heilbrun (2001) suggests that if an opinion on the legal question is offered, then the evaluator should include "cautionary language" that alerts the reader to the idea that it is a clinical opinion about a legal question and is "advisory only" (p. 225). While the extent of this practice is unknown, it underscores the importance of thoughtful consideration regarding proffering ultimate issue opinions.

If the forensic evaluator does not directly address the ultimate legal question, one alternative is to present recommendations as a series of "if-then" possibilities for the court. In this schema, the evaluator suggests a variety of parenting plans, each one contingent on specific legal decisions that the court would make (e.g., sole versus joint legal/physical custody), and would include the probable risks and benefits of each option. By so doing, the forensic evaluator is communicating to the court what the data have revealed about the family and how that might apply to any specific option. It honors the idea that no one outcome is best and provides the various audiences of the report with as much information as possible within the current limitations of knowledge.

BEWARE

No consensus has emerged to resolve the long-standing debate about making recommendations on the legal issues in an evaluation. If you are to provide recommendations to the court, it is preferable to suggest that it is an advisory opinion, to focus on "psychological best interest," to consider offering different options clearly linked to the data along with the risks and benefits of each alternative, and to be conservative in your opinion.

In conclusion, offering a risk/benefit menu of outcome options to the court is consistent with current "best practice." One would still have to be conservative about such a risk/benefit analysis due to the limitations of research in the area of outcome prediction in child custody

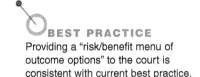

BEST PRACTICE
Providing a "risk/benefit menu of outcome options" to the court is consistent with current best practice.

(Tippins and Wittman, 2005). Moreover, absent a clear distinction between parents (that is, the evaluator finds that both are reasonably capable or both have significant deficiencies), offering opinions on the psycho-legal constructs (e.g., which parent has the *better* "fit" with the child) underlying the ultimate legal issue (i.e., "best interests") or on the ultimate legal question itself (i.e., who should have custody) may be inadvisable, because there is no empirically supportable way to state a preference for one parent over the other. In effect, the issue is "too close to call." If the evaluator offers ultimate issue recommendations in a case in which the best outcome is not clear, then she qualifies the opinions when appropriate, acknowledges inconsistent data, suggests that the opinions are advisory only, eschews the single best outcome by providing alternatives, and states that the opinions are based for the most part on methods that, while reflecting current practice, have not been empirically validated. Most importantly, the "rationale for the opinion should be transparent, so that the Court can understand the bases for the opinion and make its own determination as befits the facts of the case" (Kruh & Grisso, 2009, p. 186).

Tips for Successful Report Writing
READABILITY

A good report is readable. To promote readability, the report is structured and includes headings for major segments of the evaluation (e.g., Parent 1, Parent 2, each child, collaterals, testing, documents, discussion/conclusions, and recommendations) and subheadings for areas of interest within those larger categories (e.g., parents' personal history, relationship history, and parenting history; child developmental history). Such organization facilitates the readers' search for relevant data and provides a cognitive map

7
chapter

for the forensic evaluator who is performing the work. Furthermore, structure aids the creation of clear boundaries between reporting data, offering interpretations, and making recommendations (American Psychology-Law Society, 1991, §13.02; AFCC, 2007, §12.2). To be consistent with that structure, the writer should not include interpretations or conclusions in the data sections or add new data in the conclusions section.

If the report is very lengthy, a table of contents at the front of a report can enhance reader accessibility. One detailed example of report structure is provided by Rohrbaugh (2008). Other writers have proposed more succinct outlines for psycho-legal reports, including Melton et al. (2007), Schutz et al. (1989), and Bricklin (1995). Appendix D includes a format that the authors use.

USER-FRIENDLINESS

A good report is user-friendly. To that end, the length of the report is sufficient to address the legal issues in question, yet not so long as to be daunting to the reader. Most attorneys find that a thorough and detailed report increases chances for case settlement (Bow et al., 2011). Bow and Quinnell's (2004) survey showed that psychologists tended to write longer reports than legal professionals would prefer. The data from each case and the ethical requirement for accurate documentation will largely determine the length of the report. However, it is useful to keep in mind the needs of the respective audiences as one writes. Attorneys can more easily draw attention to a sentence during testimony if evaluators use the line-numbering feature in their word processing program when writing their reports. Another aspect of user-friendliness is whether the forensic evaluator included information in the report that judges and lawyers consider critical. Bow and Quinnell's (2004) survey indicated that these readers believed that the factors of parenting strengths and weaknesses, data about children's history, and information from children's interviews were three of the five most important components of a report. Bow et al.'s (2011) survey of attorneys had similar findings, but included the parent-child observational data as one of the top five components. These factors are consistent with the custody-relevant constructs recommended in the APA (2009) guidelines and the factors to be addressed in the AFCC (2007) model standards and AACAP practice parameters (1997). The other two important components that judges and attorneys valued were recommendations on custody and on a parenting plan.

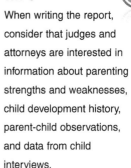

INFO

When writing the report, consider that judges and attorneys are interested in information about parenting strengths and weaknesses, child development history, parent-child observations, and data from child interviews.

Understandability is another aspect of user-friendliness. The level of complexity of sentences and vocabulary, including the amount of jargon or professional terminology, directly affects the degree to which legal professionals or the parties can understand the report. Harvey (1977) found that psychological report writers had great difficulty explaining their findings at levels below the 12th grade in comprehension, even with supervision and review. Word processing programs have readability quotients that can identify for the writer the grade level of text that he has created, as well as the reading ease of the text.

TRANSPARENCY

A good report reflects the transparency of the process (AFCC, 2007; APA, 2009). One form of transparency refers to the clarity and completeness with which the report describes what the evaluator did to collect data. In a recent survey, Bow et al. (2011) found that reporting on the evaluation procedures used was the most important aspect of a custody report for attorneys. To meet this objective, the forensic evaluator makes the evaluation procedures easily accessible to the reader by listing every data source. This begins with every interview in chronological order, including the person interviewed, the dates, and the length of the interviews. This section also includes similar details for secondary or collateral contacts interviewed and a list of the documents the forensic evaluator reviewed. Some evaluators indicate the names of those from whom she obtained the documents and when she reviewed them. This allows the reader or reviewer to understand the chronology of the assessment itself. Home visits or psychological testing should be documented, and it may be necessary in some jurisdictions to explain the rationale if the forensic evaluator omits them.

The reasoning behind the evaluator's opinions should also be transparent to the reader. The reader should be able to follow the sequence of reasoning and understand upon what data and sources opinions are based. The writer should link the observational information and the related psycho-legal concept. It should be apparent to the reader what observations or reports of parent or child functioning support those concepts. For example, if the evaluator writes in his conclusion section that "Mr. Morales is a nurturing parent who is able to appropriately anticipate his child's needs and thus help him through difficult transitions," there should be behavioral descriptions in the data section supporting this impression. For example, "When picking up his son, Mr. Morales had a stuffed animal and a juice box, explaining that Joe was often anxious about leaving his mother and this helped him settle down."

CREDIBILITY

A good report promotes credibility. First, it describes the court order of appointment, including the name of the court, the judge, the dates, and the issues or questions that the court has asked the evaluator to assess and report on. By including a brief synopsis of the background of the dispute, one page can reveal the context of the evaluation, the details of the method, the time spent in interviews and testing, the order of interviews or testing, who was interviewed and how (i.e., in-person or by phone), and a list of documents reviewed. It is easier for the reader to credit the work performed if she can appreciate the thoroughness with which the evaluator performed it.

Second, the report addresses the issue of informed consent. The forensic evaluator documents in the report that he explained to the parties, to the children, and to the collateral contacts the purpose of the evaluation and the absence of confidentiality. If an informed consent agreement was signed, that is also noted in the report. Inclusion of this information in the report is essential in order to avoid the possibility of the report's entry into evidence being denied due to an evaluator's perceived failure to give the warnings of limits of confidentiality.

BEWARE In your report, address the issue of informed consent. Document your explanation about the purpose of the evaluation and the absence of confidentiality to the parties, to the children, and to the collateral contacts. If an informed consent agreement was signed, note that also in the report. Including this information in the report is essential in order to avoid the possibility of the report's entry into evidence being denied due to any perceived failure on your part to warn about the limits of confidentiality.

Third, in the report, the evaluator considers alternative explanations for the hypotheses she has tested or acknowledges those that could not be discounted. This supports the transparency of the thinking process of the evaluator, contributing to the credibility of the evaluator. Continuing with the above example, Ms. Morales, the mother, might have described the father as brusque and unnecessarily harsh with Joe, an observation that a friend of the family confirmed. The evaluator needs to reconcile these seeming contradictions or at least note them in his report. If contradictory data are left out of the report, the risk exists that one side in the dispute will suspect bias, because it will appear that the forensic evaluator highlighted *only* the facts that were consistent with her hypothesis about the case or, worse, the hypothesis suggested by one side in the dispute.

PROFESSIONALISM

A good report presents information in a professional manner. It is an important business document, and its appearance should reflect the pains the writer took to respect the general rules of spelling, grammar, and punctuation. The report represents the evaluator's abilities and, thus, affects the reputation and subsequent livelihood of its author. It is in one's own best interests to ensure that the indirect presentation of self is as positive as possible.

As stated earlier, either side in the dispute may submit the report as an exhibit or evidence in the event of a trial, and it will be the basis of the examination of the forensic evaluator. A neat and organized report with well-documented conclusions based on a thorough evaluation of the issues using reliable methods will make the task of testimony easier for the forensic evaluator in the occasional event of trial. It is to that issue that we now turn.

Testimony

As in other areas of forensic evaluation, the evaluator-witness functions as an impartial evaluator (AFCC, 2007, §P.2; APA, 2009, §5), regardless of whether one side has retained him or whether the court has appointed him as a neutral evaluator (APA, 2009). The function of the evaluator-witness is to provide information "to help the judge make an informed custody decision" (Meyer & Erickson, 1999, p. 20). Thus, the *expert witness* testimony is a means by which the legal actors in the process obtain relevant psychological information. Lubet (1998) asserts, "Teachers no doubt provide the best models for expert witnesses" (p. 9), because the best teachers make the lessons understandable, which enhances credibility. Echoing that, Brodsky (2004) notes that expert witnessing is a form of "performance state," such that the best witness is like a good teacher who has an awareness of how she is coming across and works at improving that kind of communication skill.

The expert witness should stay within the confines of the psychological information that he collected and should refrain from offering conclusions or opinions that go beyond those data. The expert also informs the court of any limitations in the methods or data used (AFCC, 2007, §12.4; APA, 1994, p. 679). Acknowledging the limitations in the data, in the methodology, or in one's ability to know something may actually increase one's credibility as a witness (Brodsky, 2004).

How Is Child Custody Testimony Different from General Expert Witness Testimony?

The role of the expert witness, as just noted, is similar across different forensic domains. Other authors have thoroughly covered much of the area of testimony (Brodsky, 1999, 2004; Gutheil & Dattilio, 2008; Lubet, 1998; Tsushima & Anderson, 1996), explaining how one can perform ethically and competently as an expert witness. There are, however, some unique aspects of testifying when one performs child custody evaluations.

INFREQUENCY OF TESTIMONY

Foremost is the fact that the custody evaluator is likely to be called as a witness in only about 10% of the cases she has evaluated (Melton et al., 2007). Maccoby and Monookin (1992) noted that a very small number of custody litigants in their 3-year study went as far as to have a complete trial. The consensus is that the cases with the highest amount of conflict are most likely to proceed all the way to trial (Maccoby & Mnookin, 1992). While there is no way to predict it in the individual case, one soft measure of the degree of conflict is the size of the court record and the frequency with which the parties have accessed the court.

Because testifying can be the most stressful part of an evaluator's role, its infrequency in child custody litigation can make for a more relaxed professional life. However, cross-examination in court or in a deposition is a way to discover the strengths and weaknesses of one's work product (and one's ability to present and defend it), so its infrequency results in missed opportunities to get feedback on one's work. The other disadvantage of this infrequency is that the evaluator may not go to court often enough to develop confidence in his skills, which can add to the stress of testimony.

BEWARE
Testifying at trial can be the most stressful part of your role as a child custody evaluator; the infrequency of being called as an expert witness results in missed opportunities to get feedback on your work. You may not go to court often enough to develop confidence in your skills.

7
chapter

DEPOSITION—ANOTHER FORM OF TESTIMONY

As noted previously, skill and experience in testifying are challenging to acquire because of the low frequency of trials in custody disputes (Dessau, 2005). However, there exists one other opportunity to hone one's testimonial skills: an oral deposition—"a sworn (transcribed) statement given before trial for the purposes of giving all parties access to the witness's testimony" (Lubet, 1998, p. 138). It is part of the pretrial discovery phase of litigation, in which each side must disclose information and evidence to the other. In a deposition, an attorney for one party— typically the party for whose position the report was adverse— can subpoena the forensic evaluator for testimony in order to assess the strengths and probe the weaknesses of the evaluation report and the forensic evaluator's ability to defend it. The expert witness is entitled to have her own counsel present at the deposition, although that can be costly and is usually unnecessary. There may be occasions, however, when emotions have not been well contained in very high-conflict, litigated cases when the expert witness may wish to have legal assistance present. Because there are fewer rules in a deposition than exist at trial, examiners have broader latitude in the kinds of questions they can ask. The absence of rules for questions can make a deposition more stressful than courtroom testimony, in which attorneys are more constrained in terms of how they can get testimonial information into evidence. The advantage of being deposed is that it gives the witness a preview of the cross-examination style of the attorney and the kinds of questions that attorney might ask. One other feature of a deposition is that in most cases, each side will be represented by an attorney. The lawyer who subpoenas the witness will ask most of the questions, although the

INFO

Depositions can be stressful because they have fewer rules than testimony in court. However, a deposition is a good opportunity to practice testifying about the case, learn about the attorney's style, and obtain a sense of the strengths and weaknesses of one's report.

opposing attorney has a chance to examine the witness briefly when the first attorney finishes.

UNIQUENESS OF THE DATA

What distinguishes child custody assessments from other forensic evaluations is the nature of the data. What is scrutinized is a family system with multiple members interacting over time. In the midst of an often emotional and adversarial process, conflicts between the parents can intensify. Parents' positions can become more polarized, and they may reinterpret history to reflect their current understanding. Parental reports can also be difficult to corroborate.

Another facet of this issue is that the data often reflect complex, overlapping or reciprocal interactions within a family or couple system. Behaviors that may appear negative in themselves can be reactions to provocations or to the acts of a partner, such as sometimes occur when domestic abuse is alleged by one partner against the other. One spouse or partner may behave uncharacteristically inappropriately, for example, by sharing information with the children as a response to discovered infidelity by the other. This challenges the evaluator to understand these interactions, place them in the context of the family's history, and explain them to the court if they are relevant to the legal issues.

TIME FROM REPORT TO TRIAL

Child custody litigation is different from many other forensic areas in that the family system being evaluated is in flux. Many months might pass from the time a forensic evaluator completes an evaluation to the time of trial, and the relevant dynamics/issues might change. When a lengthy period has passed after a custody evaluation, the parties or the court might ask for an update, as the information could be considered "stale" or out of date. Thus, it is possible for a forensic evaluator to be updating an evaluation on a family wherein she has already expressed an opinion that was adverse to one parent. In that case, one or both parents might question the neutrality of the evaluator or be more guarded or even hostile during the update interviews.

TYPICALLY NEUTRAL—THE COURT'S WITNESS

In most cases, the forensic custody evaluator is appointed by the court or is working for the court's designee, such as a guardian *ad litem* or a law guardian (Kirkpatrick, 2004). This is an important and stress-reducing aspect of the process, because performing an evaluation under the umbrella of the court provides quasi-judicial immunity from liability (Kirkland et al., 2006). While such immunity protects one against a lawsuit for money damages by a disgruntled litigant, it does not provide security from a complaint to one's professional board (or to the court, whensuch a complaint process exists). Depending upon the year, these grievances have consistently been the second or third most frequent ethical complaint to the APA, although they have been reported less often since the inception of its guidelines for custody evaluations (APA, 1991–2007).

ABSENCE OF ATTORNEY COLLABORATION ON TESTIMONY

There are few opportunities for a neutral evaluator to consult with the attorney for either side in preparation for testimony. While it is helpful for an evaluator-witness to have some advanced knowledge about what an attorney will ask upon direct examination, that kind of pretrial discussion can be construed as bias toward the litigant with whose attorney the evaluator met, and thus it might be precluded. In addition, the AFCC (2007, §4.4) model standards caution against *ex parte* or one-sided communication while the case is pending.

LACK OF FEEDBACK ON WORK

It is a well-worn adage that without feedback on one's evaluation or testimony, it is hard to know what works and what does not. Testifying is partly an educational task and partly a performance (Brodsky, 2004), but without feedback, it is difficult to understand where one was effective in either domain. It can be helpful to have a colleague attend the trial with the goal of providing a post-testimony critique. However, this area of litigation does not lend itself to that kind of feedback. Most cases do not proceed to trial, as the parties reach a settlement somewhere in the course of the legal process, and attorneys are not wont to give feedback on one's performance if there is a trial. Often the custody evaluator is unaware of a settlement, and unless he has more regular contact with the attorneys through other means (e.g., continuing education, multidisciplinary organizations), it is hard to obtain information about what aspect of the evaluation was useful in settling the case. If one has made recommendations on custody or a parenting plan, one may not learn to what degree the plan upon which the parties agreed reflected what the evaluator had recommended. One often has the impression that the evaluation aided settlement, and there are some data to support that (Ash & Guyer, 1986;

Maccoby & Mnookin, 1992), but typically there is no information as to specifically how it was relevant. A forensic evaluator can be proactive and ask attorneys for copies of divorce agreements or look at the public file in the courthouse. As an additional remedy for this absence of feedback, it is useful for anyone new to this field to ask experienced colleagues to critique one's work.

Types of Witnesses

There are typically two types of witnesses who testify in court proceedings: fact and expert. A fact witness (also called a "lay witness") may "testify only to that which he or she has personally perceived (seen, heard, touched, tasted, or smelled)" (Ewing, 2003, p. 58). Generally, a court prohibits fact witnesses from expressing an opinion or a conclusion, except when they can make "reasonable conclusions that can be drawn on the basis of their sensory perceptions" (Lubet, 1998). Fact witnesses can testify to issues that are in the domain of common knowledge. With respect to expert testimony, prior to 1923, an expert witness could testify if her credentials were considered sufficient by the court and if the proffered testimony itself was thought to be helpful (Flens, 2005). However, *Frye v. United States* (1923) noted that there was a need

7
chapter

for a way to determine whether a witness had "special experience" or "special knowledge . . . when the question involved does not lie within the range of common experience or common knowledge" of the trier-of-fact (at 1014). In addition, the knowledge base on which the expert depended in testimony, particularly with respect to the introduction of novel scientific evidence, had to have achieved "general acceptance in the scientific community" to which the expert belonged. *Frye* held sway for about 50 years and was commonly called the "general acceptance test" (Flens, 2005).

In 1974, the *Federal Rules of Evidence* (FRE) formally defined an expert in federal trials as one who has "knowledge, skill, experience training, or education" that qualifies him as an expert on the subject on which he testifies (FRE 702). The expertise covered not only scientific or technical knowledge but all "specialized" knowledge (Ewing, 2003). The FRE also noted that the other purpose of expert testimony is to "assist the trier-of-fact to understand the evidence or to determine a fact in issue" (FRE 702). Thus, under the FRE there are two primary issues for admissibility: does the witness possess specialized knowledge, and will that knowledge be helpful to the judge or jury? In summary, first *Frye* and later the FRE laid the foundation for the involvement of expert testimony in the legal process, although the U.S. Supreme Court was to refine further the basis for expert involvement in the 1990s. In child custody evaluations, if the forensic examiner has many of the skills recommended in Chapter 4, it is likely that her report and testimony will be admissible in family court.

Issues of Expertise

While *Frye* is still established law in 16 states and the District of Columbia (Bernstein, 2002), it was supplanted in most of the other states by the U.S. Supreme Court case of *Daubert v. Dow Chemical Pharmaceuticals* (1993). *Daubert*, whose ruling was intended to make the test of admissibility of scientific evidence more flexible (*S.M. v. G.M.*, 2005), held that the "Federal Rules of Evidence provide the standard for admitting expert scientific testimony in a federal trial" (at **579**). Further, it directed the trial judge to "decide whether the scientific testimony's underlying reasoning or methodology was scientifically valid (i.e., reliable from a legal perspective) and properly can be applied to the facts at issue (i.e., relevant)" (at **580**).

CASE LAW

Daubert v. Dow Chemical Pharmaceuticals (1993)

- The ruling was intended to make the test of admissibility of scientific evidence more flexible and scientifically valid. The trial judge is the gatekeeper of such evidence, deciding whether it has sufficient validity to be admitted.

One's methodology can be reliable in that it measures accurately what it purports to measure (Flens, 2005), but the information derived from the method may not be relevant—that is, it does not apply to the issue in the case. Both elements are necessary. In a judicial inquiry about the reliability and relevance of such testimony, four judicial considerations bear upon that judgment (Medoff, 2003):

1. Is the theory or technique upon which the testimony hinges testable?

2. Has it been subject to peer review and publication?

3. Is the known or potential error rate acceptable, and are there standards that control the operation of the methodology?

4. Has the technique or methodology gained general acceptance in the scientific community?

Gould (2005) has stated, "Daubert challenges are rarely used in child custody cases" (p. 59). In a personal message (March 8, 2010), he noted that it was unlikely that the comprehensive forensic model of evaluation as a whole would be tested. Instead, a litigant

7
chapter

would more likely seek the test of one of the component parts of an evaluation, such as the interview component (*Matter of W. v. J.*, 2005). A case law search revealed few examples of that sort (e.g., *Robb v. Robb*, 2004; *Smith v. Tierney*, 2005). Were such a legal examination of the forensic model of evaluation to occur, it is likely that it could answer three of *Daubert*'s questions in the affirmative. For question two, for example, it has been subject to peer review and publication in that countless articles have addressed the forensic nature of custody evaluations, including the strengths and limitations of such assessments. Such journals as *Behavioral Science and the Law*, *Family Court Review*, the *Journal of Child Custody*, the *American Journal of Forensic Psychology*, and the *Journal of the American Association of Psychiatry and the Law* have dealt with myriad issues related to such evaluations. For the second part of question three (i.e., standards that control the operation of the methodology), the methodology of the forensic mental health assessment is consistent with established standards in the fields of psychology and psychiatry (*Margo M. v. Martin S.*, 2006). For question four, forensic custody evaluations have gained general acceptance in the fields of forensic mental health, including psychology, psychiatry, and social work, as the professionals in all of those fields work as child custody evaluators and the first two professions have promulgated custody guidelines for its practitioners.

In addition, child custody evaluations continue to be sought by attorneys and courts. It is unlikely, however, to be able to answer the first part of question three—error rate—in the affirmative, as there is no "research with a correct outcome against which the accuracy of the particular measure can be calibrated" (Heilbrun, 2001, p. 108). With no data on outcomes of custody evaluations (and some question as to whether such research could be done, given the unlikelihood of creating control groups), there is nothing to test under *Daubert*. Lastly, it would be difficult to answer the first Daubert challenge: testability of theory or technique. To date, there has been no systematic comparison of the forensic mental health model of evaluation with any other, although there is some consensus that it provides reliable information for the courts.

One subset of custody evaluations that may have more vulnerability to a *Daubert* challenge is that in which there has been some psychological testing (Flens, 2005). In these instances, a significant body of literature exists about the reliability and validity of various instruments (Flens & Drozd, 2005; Medoff, 2003), along with increasing data as to the use of certain tests in custody evaluations, as is noted in Chapter 3. While a

INFO

One subset of custody evaluations that may have more vulnerability to a Daubert challenge is that in which there has been some psychological testing.

review of the literature and case law revealed few, if any, successful appellate challenges (Medoff, 2003; Meloy, 2007; Otto, 2000), anecdotal evidence suggests that the psychological tests with significant research and solid standardization have withstood such challenges, while many of the custody-specific instruments have not (Bow, Gould, Flens, & Greenhut, 2006). Thus, it is reasonable to conclude that a child custody evaluator who adheres to a multi-sourced methodology is unlikely to face a *Daubert* challenge as to the admissibility of his testimony, unless psychological testing was an important part of the evaluation and was solely or excessively relied upon in forming conclusions. However, there is still one other challenge that the evaluator-witness might still face: whether she has the necessary foundation for her claimed expertise.

Qualification of the Expert

Through a process called *voir dire*, a litigant may question the credentials of a witness who purports to have specific expertise by virtue of knowledge, training, education, or experience. Typically, the attorney performing direct examination initiates this process. His goal is to stress the relevance of the expert's training and experience in order to enhance the witness's credibility and to "qualify the witness as an expert, so that he or she may offer opinion testimony" (Ewing, 2003, p. 61). Then the opposing attorney conducts a cross-examination in which she asks questions about the witness's credentials (Tsushima & Anderson, 1996). The goal here is to block qualification of the witness or to limit the weight that the trier-of-fact will attribute to his testimony. The judge has the authority to decide whether the witness has the requisite expertise to offer opinions. However, as a practical matter, if the court has appointed the forensic evaluator, it would be rare for that same court to fail to qualify the evaluator-witness as an expert. It would be even less likely if both of the attorneys or parties had previously agreed to the appointment of the expert. It is possible that the credentials of an expert retained by one side could be more easily challenged than one whom the court selected or who was agreed upon by both sides. It is possible that certain aspects of testimony on the report could be stricken if it were revealed that the evaluator strayed too far from her area of competence (as ascertained in the voir dire) in assessing some aspect of the family.

While much of what we include hereinafter relates mostly to cross-examination, we would like to also stress the value of direct examination in a trial. During direct examination, the expert witness typically has an opportunity to explain the basis for his expertise; to communicate an understanding of the issues in the case; to describe the method he followed; to report the findings he made, including those data that did not fit with the conclusions; and to demonstrate how those findings relate to the psycho-legal constructs in question. Inquiries about any weaknesses in the method may arise on direct testimony, partly as a means to preempt such questions from the other counsel (Kruh & Grisso, 2009). Most importantly, direct examination provides an opportunity to educate the court on the above issues in a way that makes the data meaningful and interesting.

Tips for Competent Testimony

Here are a few suggestions that aid competent testimony and enhance credibility.

BE PREPARED

Probably one of the most important aspects of maintaining credibility is the perception by the court that the expert witness is knowledgeable about the evaluation she has performed. That means being familiar with the basic facts of the parties in the case, the details of the court order and legal questions, the basic methodology used, and the data in the assessment. Nothing diminishes an expert's "credibility" more than appearing unprepared or having to fumble around for basic information requested by an examining attorney. Preparation requires a familiarity with the content of one's evaluation and the supporting documents.

JUST ANSWER THE QUESTION

This is probably the single most important guideline for a witness. One should not try to outsmart the examining attorney, anticipate what the next question will be, or demonstrate how intelligent one is. In some ways, it is a very simple task in a complex legal process.

MAINTAIN CONCENTRATION ON THE STAND

Sustained attention over a day of trial requires more energy than one would suspect, and most evaluators feel drained at the end of a day of testifying. Simply listening to the question and answering it as succinctly as possible requires self-discipline and stamina.

BE CLEAR ABOUT THE ANSWERS ONE IS GIVING

In order to be faithful to one's testimonial oath, clarity is essential. To be clear, the witness needs to understand what the attorney is asking. The meaning of a question is critical in court (as well as in the report), because one word can change its connotation (Loftus & Palmer, 1974). The witness has a responsibility to listen carefully and ask for clarification or repetition of a question or a word within a question, so that the answer can most accurately reflect his experience or opinion. The effects of asking for clarification of a question are several:

- First, it shifts the balance of power from the attorney to the witness, at least temporarily (she is not just a passive respondent).

- Second, it interrupts the pattern or flow of questions of the cross-examination.

- Most important, it forces the examiner to be clear, thus making it easier for the witness to address only the question asked.

BE ALERT TO COMPOUND OR MULTIPLE QUESTIONS

If the expert witness is confused, he should comment respectfully that the examiner asked multiple questions, and then he should ask which one the examiner would like answered first. Sometimes, the attorney will select one and the witness will then have to ask the attorney to restate it. It takes patience and concentration, but the exercise is in the interest of being exact and answering precisely. It also shifts the dynamics; it empowers the witness, at least for the moment; it allows some time to think; and, most important, it results in clearer information for the court.

BE HONEST

The expert witness has sworn to "tell the truth." However, there are times when one comes to realize under examination that one has made a mistake in reporting, overlooked some collateral, failed to corroborate some allegation, or omitted from the report some information that was actually on hand. In the vast majority of circumstances, a conscientious and ethical evaluator's mistakes will not compromise her overall work, although they can prove to be embarrassing. If one comes to realize that a mistake was made and is asked about it, one should not hedge the answer. Brodsky (2004) labeled this as "confabulation," which he called "irresponsible and deficient." (p. 22). If one is faced with data that contradict a conclusion, one should be flexible and admit it. If one has erred or forgotten something, one should simply

BEST PRACTICE

When you give testimony:

- be prepared,

- just answer the question,

- maintain concentration on the stand,

- state your answers clearly,

- be alert to compound or multiple questions, and

- be honest.

acknowledge it, explain it (if asked and if possible), and let the process move on. One must come to accept imperfection in one's self, and in the process, too, because becoming overly defensive on the stand will hurt one's credibility more than admitting some mistake.

Testimony—A Necessary but Stressful Task

Because forensic child custody evaluators receive little constructive criticism of their work (unless they share their reports with peers for review or observe one another in court), being deposed and testifying in court are the important vehicles by which to learn the value of reliable methodology, clear expository writing, and logical thinking. They also encourage the skill of communicating under some stress the methods and findings of one's work, as well as the ability to think on one's feet. Testifying also helps one to gain an understanding of the limitations of any evaluation of the complex issues of a family, especially one undergoing the stress of a custody evaluation. It is hard to imagine a forensic evaluator with any degree of self-awareness who would walk away from a rigorous cross-examination without knowing what he could improve in the next evaluation. It can be enlightening as well as humbling. Knowing at the outset of each evaluation that one might be subject to cross-examination should increase one's motivation to do the following:

- perform that evaluation with due diligence for the important issues and sensitivity to the litigants themselves;

- do the work as if each case were going to end in a trial with cross-examination of the forensic evaluator;

- record the relevant material in a coherent and understandable way in a readable report;

- be aware of what one does know as well as of what one does not know;

- be prepared for that examination, whether or not it ever occurs; and

- if one has to testify, be *very* prepared.

7
chapter

The parents and children who are the subjects of these evaluations—for whom the stakes are very high—deserve no less.

A Final Word

Considering the client–family relationships at stake, an early-career forensic child custody evaluator can feel the weight of an awesome responsibility and the pressure to get it right, as well as the need to perform competently on the stand. With experience, one insight that can result from courtroom testimony is that the forensic custody evaluator is just one component in a complex, occasionally serpentine legal process that can last for months or years. Sometimes the evaluator, especially a court-appointed one, can feel like a pawn in the legal system, and a solitary one at that. At other times, she can feel like a critical part of the solution.

Notwithstanding that, the court and the attorneys will usually treat the forensic child custody evaluator with respect for the role. The court values the information that the evaluator provides, hopes it will be helpful in moving toward the goal of settlement or self-determination, and, in the event of a trial, will use parts of the report or testimony in formulating a decision. It is not always apparent to an evaluator to what extent his work was important in any one case, or even whether any of the principals in the case thought it was good. Sometimes, the only reinforcement one receives from the legal actors in the system is another referral or appointment. As a result, the forensic child custody evaluator needs a kind of code of conduct through which she can aspire to the highest standards. Whether those are professional guidelines, rules of court, or current best practices, they provide the basis for the perception of a piece of professional work well done, despite what happens within the legal process. We hope that this work will be one model that can provide that professional compass and resulting sense of competence.

Appendix A

Custody Factors in 50 States

Key

1. History of relationship of each parent and child = 1. **Pa-ch Hx**
2. Temperament or age or developmental needs of child = 2. **Ch dev**
3. Willingness or ability of each parent to encourage relationship with other parent = 3. **Relat support**
4. Child's Adjustment to home, school, and community = 4. **Adjstmnt**
5. Proportion of pre-separation caretaking of each parent = 5. **% of care**
6. Stability of child's residence and length of time child lived in stable environment = 6. **Envir stabil**
7. Mental and physical health of all individuals involved = 7. **Health**
8. Ability of parents to cooperate with and inform other parent = 8. **Pa coop**
9. Ability of each parent to be involved in child's life (e.g. activities, education) = 9. **Pa involv**
10. Each parent's wishes as to custody = 10. **Pa wishes**
11. Child's informed preference for outcome (and age if stated) = 11. **Ch pref**
12. Relationships with siblings or significant others = 12. **Sib relat**
13. Domestic abuse (1-factor, 2-presumption) = 13. **DV**
14. Evidence of child abuse/neglect = 14. **MalTx**
15. Ability to provide love, affection, guidance = 15. **Nurturance**
16. Criminal history = 16. **Crim Hx**
17. Ability of parents to prioritize child's needs = 17. **Ch. as priority**
18. Geographic viability of parenting plan = 18. **Geog viability**
19. Moral fitness of parents = 19. **Moral fit**
20. Ability to provide for basic needs (e.g. food, shelter, medical care, safety) = 20. **Safety**
21. Any other relevant factor = 21. **Other**
22. Each parent's work schedule = 22. **Pa work**
23. Substance abuse issues in parent = 23. **Pa sub abuse**
24. Gender of child = 24. **Ch gender**

Factors	1. Pa ch Hx	2. Ch dev	3. Relat support	4. Adjstmnt	5. % of care	6. Envir stabil	7. Health	8. Pa coop	9. Pa involv	10. Pa wishes	11. Ch pref	12. Sib relat	13. DV
Alabama		x											2
Alaska	x		x		x	x					x		1
Arizona	x		x	x	x		x			x	x	x	1
Arkansas											x		2
California			x			x					x		2
Colorado	x		x	x	x	x				x	x		1
Connecticut	x	x	x	x	x	x	x	x	x	x	x	x	1
Dist. Of Columbia	x			x		x				x	x		2
Delaware	x			x		x				x	x	x	2
Florida		x	x	x	x	x	x	x	x		x		2
Georgia	x		x	x		x	x		x		x (14)	x	1
Hawaii	x		x			x			x				2
Idaho	x			x	x					x	x	x	2
Illinois	x		x	x		x				x	x	x	1

14. MalTx	15. Nurturance	16. Crim Hx	17. Ch. as priority	18. Geog viability	19. Moral fit	20. Safety	21. Other	22. Pa work	23. Pa sub abuse	24.Ch gender	State	Listing of additional factors unique to each state
					x	x				x	Alabama	
			x				x			x	Alaska	
											Arizona	
				x							Arkansas	
x											California	
			x								Colorado	
x											Connecticut	child cultural background, parent completed education program
											Dist. Of Columbia	
		x									Delaware	
x			x	x	x					x	Florida	anticipated post-divorce division of responsibilities, knowledge of child's friends and care providers, provide consistent routine, protect child from litigation
x	x					x			x	x	Georgia	home environment (safety + nurturance), stability of environment
x			x			x				x	Hawaii	misuse of abuse protection law, protect child from litigation
					x						Idaho	
		x									Illinois	

Factors	1. Pa-ch Hx	2. Ch dev	3. Relat support	4. Adjstmnt	5. % of care	6. Envir stabil	7. Health	8. Pa coop	9. Pa involv	10. Pa wishes	11. Ch pref	12. Sib relat	13. DV*
Indiana	x	x		x		x				x	x	x	1
Iowa	x		x					x			x		2
Kansas	x		x	x						x	x	x	1
Kentucky	x			x		x				x	x		1
Louisiana				x									2
Maine	x	x	x	x		x		x			x		1
Maryland													1
Massachusetts						x							2
Michigan	x		x	x		x					x		1
Minnesota	x		x	x	x	x	x		x	x	x		2
Mississippi											x (12)		2
Missouri	x		x	x		x				x	x	x	2

14. MalTx	15. Nurturance	16. Crim Hx	17. Ch. as priority	18. Geog viability	19. Moral fit	20. Safety	21. Other	22. Pa work	23. Pa sub abuse	24. Ch gender		Listing of additional factors unique to each state
										x	Indiana	
				x		x					Iowa	suitability of parent as custodian, effect on child of lack of contact with a parent, parent agree/oppose joint custody
											Kansas	
											Kentucky	any de-facto custodial care
											Louisiana	
x	x						x				Maine	motivation of each party, methods for and willingness to use dispute resolution, effect of sole legal custody
											Maryland	factors determined by case law
											Massachusetts	welfare of the child
	x				x	x	x				Michigan	
	x										Minnesota	primary caretaker (non-presumptive), permanence of family home or proposed home, child's cultural background
											Mississippi	
											Missouri	child's need for meaningful and continuing contact, each parent's willingness to function as a parent, intent to relocate

Factors	1. Pa-ch Hx	2. Ch dev	3. Relat support	4. Adjstmnt	5. % of care	6. Envir stabil	7. Health	8. Pa coop	9. Pa involv	10. Pa wishes	11. Ch pref	12. Sib relat	13. DV*
Montana	x	x		x		x	x			x	x	x	1
Nebraska	x										x		1
Nevada	x	x	x				x	x		x	x	x	2
New Hampshire	x	x	x	x				x					1
New Jersey	x	x	x		x	x		x			x	x	1
New Mexico	x			x			x			x	x	x	1
New York													1
North Carolina													1
North Dakota	x	x	x	x		x	x				x		2
Ohio	x		x	x	x		x			x	x	x	1
Oklahoma													2
Oregon	x				x								2

14. MalTx	15. Nurturance	16. Crim Hx	17. Ch. as priority	18. Geog viability	19. Moral fit	20. Safety	21. Other	22. Pa work	23. Pa sub abuse	24. Ch gender		Listing of additional factors unique to each state
										x	Montana	whether able parent failed to pay birth-related costs or child support, existence of frequent and continuing contact with each parent
											Nebraska	
											Nevada	level of inter-parental conflict
x	x	x				x	x				New Hampshire	three variations of parent support for child's relationship with other parent, relationship of child with any significant other, parent in prison
				x				x			New Jersey	safety from physical abuse, quality and continuity of child's education, parental fitness, number of children
											New Mexico	
											New York	
											North Carolina	best interest and welfare, safety of child
	x						x	x	x		North Dakota	permanence of family home, child relationship with anyone in home who can affect best interests, extended family, any bad-faith false allegations
											Ohio	history of child support payments, relocation
											Oklahoma	
x											Oregon	primary caretaker preference - if fit, interest in and attitude toward child, desirability of continuing existing relationship

Factors	1. Pa-ch Hx	2. Ch dev	3. Relat support	4. Adjstmnt	5. % of care	6. Envir stabil	7. Health	8. Pa coop	9. Pa involv	10. Pa wishes	11. Ch pref	12. Sib relat	13. DV
Pennsylvania			x								x		1
Rhode Island													1
South Carolina													1
South Dakota													2
Tennessee				x		x	x				x (12)		1
Texas		x	x								x (12)		2
Utah	x		x								x		1
Vermont	x	x	x	x				x					1
Virginia	x	x	x		x		x	x			x	x	1
Washington	x	x			x					x	x	x	1
West Virginia					x			x		x	x (14)		1
Wisconsin	x	x	x	x	x		x	x			x	x	2
Wyoming	x	x	x				x						1

14. MalTx	15. Nurturance	16. Crim Hx	17. Ch. as priority	18. Geog viability	19. Moral fit	20. Safety	21. Other	22. Pa work	23. Pa sub abuse	24. Ch gender		Listing of additional factors unique to each state
							x				Pennsylvania	
											Rhode Island	
											South Carolina	
											South Dakota	
						x					Tennessee	
x											Texas	
					x						Utah	
	x					x					Vermont	quality of relationship with primary care provider, if age/development appropriate, relationship with any other significant person
							x				Virginia	
								x			Washington	the voluntary agreements of the parties
											West Virginia	prior agreements of the parties, approximation formula (ALI), sibling cohesion, if necessary to welfare.
		x					x	x			Wisconsin	regular/meaningful periods of contact, availability of child care, any dating or cohabiting relationship of a party,
				x		x	x				Wyoming	relative competence and fitness of each parent, willingness to accept parental responsibility, parent-child communication

Appendix B

Sample Memorandum of Understanding from the Second Author in Private Practice

Information about Your Child Custody Evaluation

Pursuant to the case of *Parent A v. Parent B*, docket # _____, in its order of *date*, the _____ Court has ordered you and your child(ren) to undergo this evaluation for reasons stated in the court order. What follows is a brief description of important aspects of the evaluation.

What is the general procedure?

- The *first phase* of the evaluation typically starts either with one or two lengthy interviews or with two– to four separate interviews of about 1.5 to- 2 hours each with you alone, followed by observations of you and your child(ren). Then there are interviews with your children alone (depending on their age), with each of you, and, when appropriate to the case, a home -visit to each residence, usually with your children present. One explanation to offer children before an interview is that the evaluator is someone whose job is to help you and their other parent work out how they are going to spend time with each of you after divorce. You may also tell them—as some children are concerned about this—that the evaluator will not ask them with whom they prefer to live. That is not their burden to carry.

  The evaluator will explain to them the limits to confidentiality in language appropriate to their age and level of understanding. The goal is to follow the same interview schedule in parallel with the other parent over a period of about 4 to –6 weeks. The evaluator cannot guarantee that s/he will spend exactly the same amount of time with each of you, because parents vary greatly in how they report background information and the detail with which they answer the questions. There might also be additional interviews with the children, as the need for information dictates.

- The individual interviews commonly cover current issues and concerns;, hoped-for outcomes; and personal (biographical), marital, and parenting history, usually in that order. On occasion, the evaluator might ask you to take psychological tests or complete behavioral checklists on your child(ren). The evaluator might ask you to release criminal, medical, psychiatric, or therapy records. You should have a discussion with your attorney and therapist (if you have one currently) about the pros and cons of agreeing to sign a waiver of privilege, because this information is discoverable, as noted below in the section on confidentiality. The evaluator's interest in such personal information is limited to that which is relevant to the questions asked by the court. If the evaluator uses such otherwise privileged (private) information in his or her report, it is likely that the other parent's attorney will also want to review those data.

- You are welcome to submit any relevant documents, e-mails, letters, reports, etc. to the evaluator. However, you must inform your attorney, if you have one, of these submissions, and you or your attorney must notify the other party in this case or the other party's attorney about such documents.

- In a *second phase* of the assessment, the evaluator will talk to relevant professionals with whom you or your child has been involved, such as teachers or doctors, as well as to a reasonable selection of other people whom you name. All such conversations, as explained in the next section, will be "on the record." This permits the evaluator to collect additional information about you and your family from more independent sources. The evaluator will need written permission in the form of releases of information to talk to the professionals who have worked with you. S/he has the right to select those sources s/he considers most relevant. S/he will send signed permission and information letters to those lay people s/he selects from your list, but you need to first obtain their permission for those conversations. With certain exceptions, generally, family members are the least helpful (likely bias), while professionals are usually the most helpful, with friends, colleagues, or neighbors in between. The evaluator will talk with family members only if you have a compelling reason for why s/he should do so, such as if they witnessed some interaction or incident that you consider significant and important to your case. This is often the hardest part of the process because of the necessary "telephone tag" that occurs.

- After most of this information is collected, the *third phase* of the process involves a final interview 1 to 2 hours in length, the purpose of which is to help clarify the conflicting aspects of the information collected. At this time, you will have a chance to hear and respond to the claims or allegations about you that the other parent has made. The evaluator will then complete his or her report and submit it to the court.

What legal rules apply?

- In the course of the assessment, the evaluator may share any and all information that you offer with the other party, and s/he will use that information in the formation of the report; that is, everything is "on the record," including conversations with your child(ren) and letters, e-mails, or histories that you write, as well as discussions with relevant collateral sources. *Please inform such sources of this* when you ask them to act as references, as some lay people may wish not to be involved. It is also possible that they will be called as witnesses in hearings or trial. Therefore, *confidentiality*, as typically exists with a mental health professional, does not apply in your case or in the case of what your children report, at least within the boundaries of the current litigation. Furthermore, though this issue does not arise often, as a *mandated reporter*, the evaluator is bound by law to inform appropriate authorities [e.g., the office of state child protective services (CPS)] if s/he has a reasonable basis to believe that your children are suffering or in danger of suffering some form of abuse or neglect. If CPS were to call the evaluator about your family pursuant to a child in danger of abuse or neglect complaint filed by someone else, s/he would have to answer questions specific to the allegations CPS was investigating, but s/he would require a court order to release any report to CPS. This evaluation is not a health care service under the Health Insurance Portability and Accountability Act (HIPAA).

- You are encouraged to answer all the questions the evaluator asks, but it is your right not to respond to a particular question if you so choose. If there is some criminal proceeding that is ongoing or foreseeable (such as violation of a restraining order), you have the right not to answer questions about that if doing so would serve to incriminate you with respect to those charges. If you have an attorney, you should consult with him or her first about this kind of concern.

- Except for issues of child maltreatment, as noted above, the evaluator's investigative or evaluative role *does not include intervening* in any way in your legal proceedings. If you have concerns about the other party's behavior, please inform the evaluator either in writing or in interview. If you believe some action is required, you should consult with your attorney, if you have one.

- Consistent with professional responsibilities as needed, the evaluator reserves the right to consult with appropriate colleagues about the issues in your case.

In so doing, s/he will protect your identity, and these colleagues will maintain your privacy.

• Depending on your state's rule, communication by the evaluator with your child's therapist may require a court order. Some states require the appointment of a professional to evaluate and recommend whether that confidentiality should be breached.

• Regardless of who pays the cost, the evaluator is working for the court. Per custom and order of the court, *the evaluator will not give you a copy of his or her report*, though you may be able to read it in the presence of your attorney, if the judge has granted permission to send it to the attorneys. If you represent yourself, you should check with the court clerk regarding where you might read and/or obtain a copy.

What does the evaluation cost and how are you to pay?

• If the evaluation is court-paid, you will not be responsible for the fee, unless the court stipulates otherwise. If you are paying all or part of the fee for the evaluation, in order to start, the evaluator will require a retainer of $_____. If the evaluator exhausts the initial retainer, s/he will request a second retainer, which will be an estimate of the balance required to complete the work. You will receive an itemized statement at the end of the evaluation. The typical evaluation runs between 20 and –30 hours of time at the evaluator's current fee of $_____/hour. Individual circumstances will determine whether the evaluation time will vary, more or less, from that average. From first office contact, the evaluator averages about 90 days per evaluation, though personal (e.g., vacation, illness) or case situations (e.g., legal delays, multiple collaterals, very complex fact patterns) may create some variation from that estimated period. The court has determined the proportion of the fee for which you are responsible.

- If you terminate the evaluation before its completion, you will receive the unused balance of the retainer, after a deduction of expenses and the possible cost of the evaluator's writing a report to the court. The evaluator enters data into his or her report as the investigation proceeds, so the balance returned will reflect that cost to you, depending on when the investigation stops. Because this is a court-ordered investigation, it will require either a court order or a stipulation signed by both parties and attorneys (if you are represented by counsel) to terminate it.

- As part of the cost of the evaluation, the evaluator will bill all telephone calls (in 5-minute intervals), document reading, in-person interviews, correspondence time, test material or scoring costs, travel time (and any significant travel expense), conferences with attorneys, and report writing at his or her current rate. After interview time, report writing is often the largest expense.

- If you miss an appointment without 24-hour notice, the evaluator has the right to bill you for it at the above rate for the time that s/he set aside for the meeting.

What if you wish to depose or have the evaluator testify?

- In the event of a deposition, the court's payment formula does not apply after the report is completed. If you (or your attorney) call the evaluator for a deposition or a hearing on issues other than those the court requested, his or her retainer (payable either a week in advance or before the start of the deposition or hearing) shall include the cost of the time for preparation, travel expenses, and an estimate (at $_____/hour) for the time of the proceeding. If the proceeding for which you call the evaluator runs longer than the estimate covered by the retainer, s/he will bill you for that additional time. If you call the evaluator for testimony at trial on the issues under review by the court, the evaluator will expect a retainer paid at least a week in advance at the rate of

$_____/hour (including preparation and travel time), to be paid by the formula established by the court for the evaluation itself, unless the court changes the formula for payment of witness fees at the time of trial. The evaluator is considered to be the court's witness, regardless of which attorney wants him or her to appear. If the assessment should take less time than anticipated by the retainer, the evaluator will hold the balance in escrow, until such time as s/he receives documentation that the case has settled or is proceeding to trial,at which time the balance is refunded. At the end, the evaluator will provide you and the court with an itemized statement of all of the time and services s/he has provided.

My signature below attests to the fact that I have read the above document and that the evaluator has explained to me the nature of the evaluation, its procedures, the time and costs involved, and the lack of confidentiality. I have had an opportunity to ask any questions about the evaluation, and I understand that I can ask additional questions at any time during the process. I give the evaluator permission to briefly inform collateral sources of the reason that s/he is calling them. I am aware that the court has required me to pay _____% of the estimated cost of the evaluation, or $_____, and that the evaluator will provide me with an itemized statement at the conclusion of the work, a copy of which, by regulation, s/he will submit to the court. The evaluator has also explained to me the process by which I am to pay for this evaluation. I also authorize the evaluator to release the report to the court, as is required, and also to send a copy to anyone whom the court allows by its order.

_____   _____

Litigant   Date

_____   _____

Forensic Evaluator   Date

Appendix C

Memorandum of Understanding from the First Author in a Hospital-Based Clinic

CHILD AND FAMILY FORENSIC CENTER MEMORANDUM OF UNDERSTANDING

1. In the order of the Honorable _____ of the _____ Court held in _____ County on _____, _____, was appointed to serve as *evaluator* for the children of _____ and _____. The order appointing the evaluator specified that the issues to be investigated and/or evaluated are _____.

2. In its order of <u>date</u>, the court specified that the fees for the services of the evaluator are to be paid as follows: _____.

3. It is the policy and practice of the evaluator that unless paid by the [state/district], a retainer is required prior to the start of services. The required retainer amount is $_____ (each party). Payment is by check, made payable to _____ and provided to the evaluator no later than the initial appointment with either party.

4. The hourly rate for the services of the evaluator is $_____. Charges for services include, but are not limited to, time spent performing the following activities: interviews of all parties, and children, document review, travel time, interview of collateral contacts, telephone contact with parties and collateral contacts, other meetings, and report preparation. If the required retainer is expended prior to the completion of the evaluation/investigation, then an additional retainer will be required to cover the additional time as estimated by the evaluator.

5. If either or both parties choose to depose the evalutor or subpoena the him or her to testify in court, then that party shall provide payment for the preparation time, travel time door to door, and time at deposition or court at the rate of $_____ per hour. Payment for the estimated costs incurred for the deposition shall be made to the evaluator 72 hours prior to the scheduled deposition or court hearing.

6. At the completion of all services rendered in this appointment, the evaluator shall provide to the parties a detailed statement of all activities performed in conducting the evaluation and their associated costs.

7. If the retainer amount exceeds the costs of the evaluation, then the parties shall be reimbursed in proportion to payments made.

8. The evaluator conducts the evaluation through a series of appointments with the parents, children, and other involved parties. While every effort will be made to schedule these appointments at mutually agreeable times, please be advised that the flexibility of the evaluator's schedule is limited, and the timelines of the court must be respected.

9. The parties are advised that the evaluator is a mental health clinician performing an evaluation for the purposes of the court, and therefore there is no confidentiality within the legal matter. They are advised that information they share with the evaluator may be shared with the other party and may be included, in whole or part, in the report to the court. Information provided by the children and collateral contacts will be similarly included in the report. The court is the final determiner of what information, if any, from the report is provided to the parties. If you are represented by counsel, your attorney will be allowed to review the report. If you are pro se, that is, not represented by an attorney, you must request the permission of the judge to review the report. Unless otherwise ordered by the court, the evaluator is not permitted to provide copies of the report to anyone other than the court.

10. As a mental health provider, the evalutor is a mandated reporter, meaning that if the evaluator has reason to believe that a

child or handicapped adult is being abused or neglected, a report must be made to the proper authorities in order to promote safety.

11. I, _____, and I, _____, have read, understand, and consent to the conditions of this document. My signature below indicates that I have had an opportunity to ask questions concerning this document.

_____ Date _____
_____ Date _____
_____ Date _____
Evaluator

Appendix D

Sample Outline for a Child Custody Report (adapted from the Child and Family Forensic Center, University of Massachusetts Medical School)

FAMILY

DOCKET NUMBER

THIS REPORT IS CONFIDENTIAL
WITHIN THE CONFINES OF THE PRESENT
LEGAL MATTER. IT CANNOT BE RELEASED
WITHOUT THE PERMISSION OF THE COURT.

DATE OF REPORT:

EVALUATOR:

FAMILY MEMBERS INTERVIEWED:

_____, father,_____mother

DOB:_____   DOB:_____

Age:_____   Age:_____

Child's name:_____

DOB:_____

Age: _____   Years:_____   Months:_____

REASON FOR REFERRAL:

The _____ family was referred for psychological evaluation in an order dated _____ signed by the Honorable, _____ Justice of the Probate and Family Court, _____ Division. The court ordered the evaluator to investigate and report back to the court in writing regarding issues of, (add _____.) briefly, [give brief background e.g., date of marriage, date of separation, current conflict].

DATES OF CONTACT:

Date	Activity	Time

ATTORNEYS INVOLVED:
[Name], who represents _____.

COLLATERAL CONTACTS:
- Name, agency, relationship to case

RECORDS REVIEWED:
- Legal records
- Medical records
- Educational records
- Other

STATEMENT OF THE LIMITS OF CONFIDENTIALITY:
At the beginning of the initial interview with each parent, the nature and purpose of the evaluation was discussed. The parents were told that the evaluator is a [psychologist/psychiatrist/social worker] working at the order of the court to assist the court in decision-making on behalf of [children's names]. Both parents appeared to understand the circumstances of the evaluation and the limits of confidentiality, agreed to participate, and signed an informed consent statement. [Names of children] were informed

of the limits of confidentiality in language appropriate to their age and developmental status. Collateral contacts were similarly informed of the limits of confidentiality by the evaluator.

HISTORY OF THE RELATIONSHIP ACCORDING TO [A] AND [B]:

1. How/when/where the parents met; what attracted them to each other.
2. Early relationship.
3. Impact of having children.
4. Decline of relationship and separation.
5. Domestic violence.

POST SEPARATION HISTORY:

1. Logistics, parenting plans.
2. Significant events.
3. Legal process, including how the evaluation appointment came about.

PARENT A
BEHAVIORAL OBSERVATIONS:

INDIVIDUAL HISTORY:

1. Family of origin:

    Composition, psych/health issues in family, domestic violence/abuse, legal issues, other stressors, current relationship with parents/siblings

2. School history (including discipline problems, special education, etc.)
3. Psych/med/substance use/legal history
4. Work history
5. Relationship history
6. Current living arrangement
7. Parenting history (involvement in caretaking of involved children)

PSYCHOLOGICAL TESTING (if applicable):

PARENT'S CONCERNS AND WISHES:

PARENT B

[Same as for Parent A above]

CHILD #1

DEVELOPMENTAL HISTORY:

PSYCHOLOGICAL TESTING (if applicable):

BEHAVIORAL OBSERVATIONS:

INTERVIEW WITH CHILD:

CHILD #2

[Same as for Child #1 above]

HOME VISIT AND/OR OBSERVATION OF CHILD(REN) AND EACH PARENT:

SUMMARY OF COLLATERAL CONTACTS:

SUMMARY OF (SELECTED) RECORDS REVIEWED:

CONCLUSIONS:
1. Restate reason for referral and brief background
2. Parent A: strengths, weaknesses, address concerns raised by court and other parent
3. Parent B: strengths, weaknesses, address concerns raised by court and other parent
4. Child: developmental status, strengths, needs, attachments, concerns raised by court and/or parents
5. Fit between parental abilities and child(ren)'s needs

6. Relationship between the parents (co-parenting abilities)

7. Specific concerns raised by the court: address if not covered in previous paragraphs

8. Formulation, address concerns raised by the court

RECOMMENDATIONS (if included):

_____

Name

Title

_____

References

Abidin, R. (1995). *Parenting stress index* (3rd ed.) Odessa, FL: Psychological Assessment Resources.

Abidin, R., Flens, J., & Austin, W. (2006). The Parenting Stress Index. In R. Archer (Ed.), *Forensic uses of clinical assessment instruments* (pp. 297–328). Mahwah, NJ: Lawrence Erlbaum Associates.

Achenbach, T. M. (2001). *Child behavior checklist.* Burlington: University of Vermont.

Achenbach, T. (2010) *Achenbach system of empirically-based assessments.* Research Center for Children, Youth, & Families, Burlington, VT.

Ackerman, M. (2005). Transfusion maybe, laid to rest, no: A response to the Mary Connell review of the Ackerman-Schoendorf Scales for Parent Evaluation of Custody (ASPECT). *Journal of Child Custody, 2*(1/2), 211–214.

Ackerman, M. (2010). *Essentials of forensic psychological assessment* (2nd ed). Hoboken, NJ: Wiley.

Ackerman, M., & Ackerman, M. (1997). Custody evaluation practices: A survey of experienced professionals (revisited). *Professional Psychology: Research and Practice, 28,* 137–145.

Ackerman, M., Ackerman, M., Steffen, L., & Kelley-Poulos, S. (2004). Psychologists' practices compared to the expectations of family law judges and attorneys in child custody cases. *Journal of Child Custody, 1*(1), 41–60.

Ackerman, M., & Schoendorf, K. (1992). *ASPECT: Ackerman-Schoendorf Scales for Parent Evaluation of Custody–Manual.* Los Angeles: Western Psychological Services.

Ackerman, M., & Steffen, L. (2001). Custody evaluations practices: A survey of family law judges. *American Journal of Forensic Law, 15,* 12–23.

Ahrons, C. (1981). The continuing coparental relationship between divorced spouses. *American Journal of Orthopsychiatry, 51*(3), 415–428.

Ahrons, C. (1994). *The good divorce: Keeping your family together when your marriage falls apart.* New York: Harper Collins.

Amato, P. (2001). Children of divorce in the 1990's: An update of the Amato and Keith (1991) meta-analysis. *Journal of Family Psychology, 15,* 335–370.

Amato, P., & Booth, A. (2001). The legacy of parents' marital discord: Consequences for children's marital quality. *Journal of Personality and Social Psychology, 81*(4), 627–638.

Amato, P., & Gilbreth, J. (1999). Nonresident fathers and children's well-being: A meta-analysis. *Journal of Marriage and the Family, 61,* 557–573.

Amato, P., & Keith, B. (1991). Parental divorce and the well-being of children: A meta-analysis. *Psychological Bulletin, 110*(1), 26–46.

Amato, P., Loomis, L., & Booth, A. (1995). Parental divorce, marital conflict, and offspring well-being during early adulthood. *Social Forces, 73,* 895–915.

American Academy of Child and Adolescent Psychiatry. (1997a). *Practice parameters for child custody evaluation.* Retrieved February 10, 2009, from http://www.aacap.org/galleries/PracticeParameters/Custody.pdf

American Academy of Child and Adolescent Psychiatry. (1997b). *Practice parameters for forensic evaluation of children and adolescents who may have been sexually abused.* Retrieved February 24, 2010, from http://www.aacap.org/galleries/PracticeParameters/Forensic.pdf

American Academy of Psychiatry and the Law. (2005). *Ethics guidelines for the practice of forensic psychiatry.* Baltimore: American Academy of Psychiatry. Retrieved February 25, 2010, from www.aapl.org/ethics.htm

American Law Institute. (2000). *Principles of the law of family dissolution: Analysis and recommendations.* Washington, DC: American Law Institute.

American Professional Society on the Abuse of Children. (1997). *Practice guidelines: Investigative interviewing in cases of alleged child abuse.* Chicago: American Professional Society on the Abuse of Children.

American Psychiatric Association. (2009). *The principles of medical ethics with annotations especially applicable to psychiatry.* Washington, DC: American Psychiatric Association.

American Psychological Association. (1991–2007). Reports of the ethics committee. *American Psychologist, 48–63.*

American Psychological Association. (1994). Guidelines for child custody evaluations in divorce proceedings. *American Psychologist, 54,* 677–680.

American Psychological Association. (2002). Ethical principles of psychologists and code of conduct. *American Psychologist, 57,* 1060–1073.

American Psychological Association. (2009). *Guidelines for child custody evaluations in family law proceedings.* Washington, DC: American Psychological Association. Retrieved April 14, 2010, from http://www.apa.org/practice/guidelines/child-custody.pdf

American Psychology-Law Society. (1991). Specialty guidelines for forensic psychologists. *Law and Human Behavior, 15*(6), 655–665.

Appel, A., & Holden, G. (1998). The co-occurrence of spouse and physical child abuse: A review and appraisal. *Journal of Family Psychology, 12*(4), 578–599.

Archer, R., Buffington-Vollum, J., Stredny, R., & Handel, R. (2006). A survey of psychological test use patterns among forensic psychologists. *Journal of Personality Assessment, 87,* 84–94.

Ash, P., & Guyer, M. (1986). The functions of psychiatric evaluation in contested child custody and visitation cases. *Journal of the American Academy of Child Psychiatry, 25,* 554–561.

Association of Family and Conciliation Courts. (1994). Model standards of practice for child custody evaluation. *Family and Conciliation Courts Review, 32,* 504–513.

Association of Family and Conciliation Courts. (2007). Model standards of practice for child custody evaluation. *Family Court Review, 45*(1), 70–91.

Association of Family and Conciliation Courts. (2009). *Guidelines for brief focused assessment.* Retrieved February 18, 2010, from http://afccnet.org/pdfs/BFA%20TF%202009%20final.pdf

Austin, W. (2000). Assessing credibility in allegations of marital violence in the high-conflict child custody case. *Family and Conciliation Courts Review, 38*(4), 462–477.

Austin, W. (2002). Guidelines for utilizing collateral sources of information in child custody evaluations. *Family Court Review, 40*(2), 177–184.

Austin, W. (2008a). Relocation, research and forensic evaluation, Part I: Effects of residential mobility on children. *Family Court Review, 46*(1), 137–150.

Austin, W. (2008b). Relocation, research, and forensic evaluation, Part II: Research in support of the relocation risk assessment model. *Family Court Review, 46* (2), 347–365.

Austin, W., Kirkpatrick, H., & Flens, J. (2010). Gatekeeping and child custody evaluation: Theory, measurement and applications. Association of Family and Conciliation Courts, 47th Annual Conference. Denver, Colorado, June 3, 2010.

Ayoub, C., Deutsch, R., & Maranganore, A. (1999). Emotional distress in children of high conflict divorce. *Family and Conciliation Courts Review, 37*(3), 297–314.

Baker, A. (2007). Adult children of parental alienation syndrome: Breaking the ties that bind. New York: Norton.

Bala, N., Hunt, S., & McCarney, C. (2010). Parental alienation: Canadian court cases 1989–2008. *Family Court Review, 48*(1), 164–179.

Bala, N., Mitnick, M., Trocmé, N., & Houston, C. (2007). Sexual abuse allegations and parental separation: Smokescreen or fire? *Journal of Family Studies, 13*(1), 26–56.

Bala, N., & Schuman, J. (1999). Allegations of sexual abuse when parents have separated. *Canadian Family Law Quarterly, 17,* 191–243.

Baris, M., & Garrity, C. (1994). *Caught in the middle: Protecting the children of high conflict divorce.* New York: Lexington Books.

Bathurst, K., Gottfried, A., & Gottfried, A. (1997). Normative data for the MMPI-2 in child custody litigation. *Psychological Assessment, 9*(3), 205–211.

Baumrind, D. (1967). Child care practices anteceding three patterns of preschool behavior. *Genetic Psychology Monographs, 75,* 43–88.

Bauserman, R. (2002). Child adjustment in joint-custody versus sole-custody arrangements: A meta-analysis. *Journal of Family Psychology, 16*(1), 91–102.

Beardslee, W., Versage, E., & Gladstone, T. (1998). Children of affectively ill parents: A review of the past 10 years. *Journal of the American Academy of Child & Adolescent Psychiatry, 37,* 1134–1141.

Benjamin, G., & Gollan, J. (2003). *Family evaluation in custody litigation: Reducing the risks of ethical infractions and malpractice.* Washington, DC: American Psychological Association.

Ben-Porath, Y. and Flens, J. (October 2010) *Using the MMPI-2-RF (Restructured Form) in child custody evaluations.* Institute at AFCC Regional Conference, Cambridge, MA.

Benjet, C., Azar, S., & Kuersten-Hogan, R. (2003). Evaluating the parental fitness of psychiatrically-diagnosed individuals: Advocating a functional-contextual analysis of parenting. *Journal of Family Psychology, 17*(2), 238–251.

Bernstein, D. (2002). Disinterested in *Daubert*: State courts lag behind in opposing "junk" science. Washington Legal Foundation, 12(14). Retrieved February 17, 2009, from http://www.wlf.org/upload/6-21-02Bernstein.pdf

Block, J., Block, J., & Gjerde, P. (1988). Parental functioning and the home environment of families of divorce: Prospective and concurrent analyses. *Journal of the American Academy of Child & Adolescent Psychiatry, 27*(2), 207–213.

Bow, J., Gould, J., Flens. J., & Greenhut, D. (2006). Testing in child custody evaluations: Selection, usage, and Daubert admissibility: A survey of psychologists. *Journal of Forensic Psychology Practice, 6*(2), 17–38.

Bow, J., Gottlieb, M., & Gould-Saltman, D. (2011). Attorneys' beliefs and opinions about child custody evaluations. *Family Court Review, 49* (2), 301–312.

Bow, J., & Quinnell, F. (2001). Psychologists current practices and procedures in child custody evaluations: Five years after American Psychological Association guidelines. *Professional Psychology: Research and Practice, 32,* 261–268.

Bow, J., & Quinnell, F. (2002). A critical review of child custody evaluation reports. *Family Court Review, 40,* 164–176.

Bow, J., & Quinnell, F. (2004). Critique of child custody evaluations by the legal profession. *Family Court Review, 40*(2), 164–176.

Bramlett, M., & Mosher, W. (2002). *Cohabitation, marriage, divorce, and remarriage in the United States (Vital and Health Statistics, Series 23, No. 22).* Hyattsville, MD: National Center for Health Statistics.

Braver, S., Ellman, I., & Fabricius, W. (2003). Relocation of children after divorce and children's best interests: New evidence and legal considerations. *Journal of Family Psychology, 17*(2), 206–219.

Bray, J. (1991). Psychosocial factors affecting custodial and visitation arrangements. *Behavioral Sciences and the Law, 9,* 419–437.

Bricklin, B. (1989). *Perception of Relationships Test manual.* Furlong, PA: Village Publishing.

Bricklin, B. (1990a). *Bricklin Perceptual Scales manual.* Furlong, PA: Village Publishing.

Bricklin, B. (1990b). *Parent Awareness Skills Survey manual.* Furlong, PA: Village Publishing.

Bricklin, B. (1995). *The Custody Evaluation Handbook: Research-Based Solutions and Applications.* New York: Bruner-Mazel.

Brodsky, S. (1999). *The expert expert witness: More maxims and guidelines for testifying in court.* Washington, DC: American Psychological Association.

Brodsky, S. (2004). *Coping with cross-examination and other pathways to effective testimony.* Washington, DC: American Psychological Association.

Brown, T. (2003). Fathers and child abuse allegations in the context of parental separation and divorce. *Family Court Review, 41,* 367–380.

Bruch, C. (2006). Sound research or wishful thinking in child custody cases: Lessons from relocation law. *Family Law Quarterly, 40*(2), 281–314.

Bruck, M., & Ceci, S. (2009). Reliability of child witnesses' reports. In J. Skeem, K. Douglas, & S. Lilienfield (Eds.), *Psychological science in the courtroom: Consensus and controversy* (pp. 149–171). New York: Guilford.

Budd, K. (2005). Assessing parenting competence in child protection cases: A clinical practice model. *Children and Youth Services Review, 27,* 429–444.

Budd, K., Clark, J., & Connell, M. (2011). *Evaluation of Parenting Capacity in Child Protection.* New York: Oxford University Press.

Byrne, J., O'Connor, T., Marvin, R., & Whelan, W. (2005). Practitioner review: The contribution of attachment theory to child custody assessments. *Journal of Child Psychology and Psychiatry, 46*(2), 115–127.

Caldwell, A. (2005). How can the MMPI-2 help child custody examiners? *Journal of Child Custody, 2*(1/2), 83–117.

California rules of court. Retrieved February 18, 2010, from http://www.courtinfo.ca.gov/rules/index.cfm?title=five& linkid= rule5_220

Calloway, G. (2005). The Rorschach: Its use in child custody evaluations. *Journal of Child Custody, 2*(1/2), 143–157.

Calloway, G., & Erard, R. (2009). Introduction to the special issue on attachment and child custody. *Journal of Child Custody, 6*(1/2), 1–7.

Capaldi, J., & Crosby, L. (1997). Observed and reported physical aggression in young, at-risk couples. *Social Development, 6,* 184–206.

Carlson, M., & Mclanahan, S. (2006). Strengthening unmarried families: Could enhancing couple relationships improve parenting? *Social Service Review, 80*(2), 297–321.

Carnes, C. (2000). *Forensic evaluation of children when sexual abuse is suspected* (Third Edition). National Children's Advocacy Center: Huntsville, AL.

Caspi, A., Henry, B., McGee, R., Moffitt, T., & Silva, P. (1995). Temperamental origins of child and adolescent behavior problems: From age 3 to age 15. *Child Development, 66,* 55–68.

Cavallero, L. (2010). UMASS Family Court Clinic: Brief, focused assessment model. In C. Erickson (Ed.), *Innovations in court services* (pp. 95–136). Madison, WI: Association of Family and Conciliation Courts.

Ceci, S., & Bruck, M. (1993). Suggestibility of the child witness: A historical review and synthesis. *Psychological Bulletin, 113*(3), 403–439.

Ceci, S., Kulkofsky, S., Klemfuss, J., Sweeney, C., & Bruck, M. (2007). Unwarranted assumptions about children's testimonial accuracy. *Annual Review of Clinical Psychology, 3,* 311–328.

Chassin, L., Curran, P., Hussong, A., & Colder, C. (1996). The relation of parent alcoholism to adolescent substance abuse: A longitudinal follow-up study. *Journal of Abnormal Psychology, 105,* 70–80.

Chemtob, C., & Carlson, J. (2004). Psychological effects of domestic violence on children and their mothers. *International Journal of Stress Management, 11*(3), 209–226.

Cherlin, A., Furstenburg, F., Chase-Lansdale, L., Kiernan, K., Morrison, D., & Teitler, J. (1991). Longitudinal studies of the effects of divorce on children in Great Britain and the United States. *Science, 252,* 1386–1389.

Cicirelli, V. (1991). Sibling relationships in adulthood. *Marriage and Family Review, 16,* 291–310.

Clark, C. (2008). Psychological testing in child and adolescent forensic evaluations. In E. Benedek & D. Schetky (Eds.), *Child and adolescent forensic psychiatry* (pp. 67–81). Washington, DC: American Psychiatric Publishing.

Clark, D., Moss, H., Kirisci, L., Mezzich, A., Miles, R., & Ott, P. C. (1997). Psychopathology in preadolescent sons of fathers with substance use disorders. *Journal of the American Academy of Child & Adolescent Psychiatry, 36,* 495–502.

Clark, H., Jr., & Estin, A. (2005). *Cases and problems on domestic relations* (7th ed.). St. Paul, MN: Thompson/West.

Clawar, S., & Rivlin, B. (1991). *Children held hostage: Dealing with programmed and brainwashed children.* Chicago: American Bar Association Press.

Cochran, R. (1991). Reconciling the primary caretaker preference, the joint custody preference, and the case-by-case rule. In J. Folberg (Ed.), *Joint custody and shared parenting* (pp. 218–240). New York: Guilford.

Coffman, J., Guerin, D., & Gottfried, A. (2006). Reliability and validity of the Parent-Child Relationship Inventory (PCRI): Evidence from a longitudinal cross-informant investigation. *Psychological Assessment, 18*(2), 209–214.

Collins, W., Maccoby, E., Steinberg, L., Hetherington, E., & Bornstein, M. (2000). Contemporary research on parenting: The case for nature and nurture. *American Psychologist, 55*(2), 218–232.

Condie, L. (2003). The psychology of parenting. In *Parenting evaluations for the court: Care and protection matters* (pp. 85–131). New York: Plenum.

Condie, L., & Koocher, G. (2008). Clinical management of children's incomplete comprehension of confidentiality limits. *Journal of Child Custody, 5*(3/4), 161–191.

Connell, M. (2005). Review of the "Ackerman-Schoendorf Scales for Parent Evaluation of Custody" (ASPECT). *Journal of Child Custody, 2*(1/2), 195–209.

Conners, K. C. (1997). *Conners' Rating Scales-Revised.* New York: Multi-Health Systems.

Coolahan, K., Fantuzzo, J., Mendez, J., & McDermott, P. (2000). Preschool peer interaction and readiness to learn: Relationships between classroom peer play and learning behaviors and conduct. *Journal of Educational Psychology, 92*(3), 458–465.

Cordell, C. (2005). Psychological assessment of children. In W. Klykylo & J. Kay (Eds.), *Clinical child psychiatry* (pp. 21–47). New York: Wiley.

Courtwright, D. (1982). *Dark paradise.* Cambridge, MA: Harvard University Press.

Cox, A., Thorpe, G., & Dawson, R. (2007). Review of the Personality Assessment Inventory (2nd ed.),Retrieved November 7, 2010 from *Buros Mental Measurement Yearbook* database.

Cui, M., Durtschi, J., Donnellan, M., Lorenz, F., & Conger, C. (2011). Intergenerational transmission of relationship aggression: A longitudinal study. *Journal of Family Psychology, 24* (6), 688–697.

Cummings, E., Davies, P., & Campbell, S. (2002). Developmental psychopathology and family process: Theory, research, and clinical implications. *Journal of the American Academy of Child & Adolescent Psychiatry, 41*(7), 886.

Cummings, E., Schermerhorn, A., Davies, P., Goeke-Morey, M., & Cummings, J. (2006). Interparental discord and child adjustment: Investigations of emotional security as an explanatory mechanism. *Child Development, 77*(1), 132–152.

Darnall, D. (1998). *Divorce casualties: Protecting your children from parental alienation.* New York: Taylor Publishing.

Davies, P., & Cummings, E. (1994). Marital conflict and child adjustment: An emotional security hypothesis. *Psychological Bulletin, 16*(3), 387–411.

Davis, S., & Bottoms, B. (2002). Effects of social support on children's eyewitness reports: A test of the underlying mechanism. *Law and Human Behavior, 26*(2), 185–215.

Deering's California codes annotated, (2010). Albany, NY: Lexis Nexis.

Depner, C., Leino, E., & Chun, A. (1992). Interparental conflict and child adjustment: A decade review and meta-analysis. *Family and Conciliation Courts Review, 30*(3), 323–341.

Dessau, L. (2005). A short commentary on Timothy M. Tippins and Jeffrey P. Wittman's "Empirical and ethical problems with custody recommendations: A call for clinical humility and judicial vigilance." *Family Court Review, 43*(2), 266–269.

DiClemente, C. (2006). Natural change and the troublesome use of substances. In W. Miller & K. Carroll (Eds.), *Rethinking substance abuse: What the science shows, and what we should do about it* (pp. 81–96). New York: Guilford.

Dishion, T., & Patterson, G. (2006). The development and ecology of antisocial behavior in children and adolescents. In D. Cicchetti & D. Cohen (Eds.), *Developmental psychopathology: Vol 3. Risk, disorder, and adaptation* (2nd ed., pp. 503–541). Hoboken, NJ: Wiley.

Donovan, D. (1999). Efficacy and effectiveness: Complementary findings from two multisite trials evaluating outcomes of alcohol treatments in theoretical orientations. *Alcoholism: Clinical and Experimental Research, 23*(3), 564–572.

Douglas, K., & Skeem, J. (2005). Violence risk assessment: Getting specific about being dynamic. *Psychology, Public Policy, and the Law, 11*(3), 347–383.

Drach, K., Wientzen, J., & Ricci, L. (2001). The diagnostic utility of sexual behavior problems in diagnosing sexual abuse in forensic child abuse evaluation clinic. *Child Abuse and Neglect, 25,* 489–503.

Drozd, L., Kuehnle, K., & Walker, L. (2004). Safety first: A model for understanding violence in child custody and access disputes. *Journal of Child Custody, 1*(2), 75–104.

Drozd, L., & Oleson, N. (2004). Is it abuse, alienation, and/or estrangement? A decision tree. *Journal of Child Custody, 1*(3), 65–106.

Duncan, G. J., & Hoffman, S. D. (1985). Economic consequences of marital instability. In M. David & T. Smeeding (Eds.), *Horizontal equity, uncertainty, and well-being* (pp. 427–469). Chicago: University of Chicago Press.

Dunne, J., & Hedrick, M. (1994). The parental alienation syndrome: An analysis of sixteen cases. *Journal of Divorce & Remarriage, 21*(3/4), 21–38.

Dutton, D. (2005). Domestic abuse assessment in child custody disputes: Beware the domestic violence research paradigm. *Journal of Child Custody, 2*(4), 23–42.

Dutton, D., Hamel, J., & Aaronson, J. (2010). The gender paradigm in family court process: Rebalancing the scales of justice from biased social science. *Journal of Child Custody, 7*(1), 1–33.

Ellis, D., & Stuckless, N. (1996). *Mediating and negotiating marital conflicts.* Thousand Oaks, CA: Sage.

Ellis, E. (2007). A stepwise approach to evaluating children for parental alienation syndrome. *Journal of Child Custody, 4*(1/2), 55–78.

El-Sheikh, M., & Buckhalt, J. (2003). Parental problem drinking and children's adjustment: Attachment and family functioning as moderators and mediators of risk. *Journal of Family Psychology, 17*(4), 510–520.

Elwyn, T., Tseng, W., & Matthews, D. (2010). Cultural competence in child and adolescent mental health. In E. Benedek, P. Ash, & C. Scott (Eds.), *Principles and practice of child and adolescent forensic mental health* (pp. 91–106). Arlington, VA: American Psychiatric Publishing, Inc.

Emery, R. E. (2004). *The truth about children and divorce: Dealing with the emotions so your children can thrive.* New York: Viking Penguin.

Emery, R. E. (2007). Rule or Rorschach? Approximating children's best interests. *Child Development Perspectives, 1*(2), 132–134.

Emery, R. E., & Laumann-Billings, L. (1998). An overview of the nature, causes, and consequences of abusive family relationships: Toward differentiating maltreatment and violence. *American Psychologist, 53*(2), 121–135.

Emery, R. E., Otto, R., & O'Donahue, W. (2005). A critical assessment of child custody evaluations: Limited science and a flawed system. *Psychological Science in the Public Interest, 6*(1), 1–29.

Encarta world English dictionary (North American ed.). (2009). Retrieved April 12, 2010, from http://encarta.msn.com/encnet/features/dictionary/DictionaryResults.aspx

Erard, R. (2005). What the Rorschach can contribute to child custody and parenting time evaluations. *Journal of Child Custody, 2*(1/2), 119–142.

Erickson, M., & Egeland, B. (1987). A developmental view of the psychological consequences of maltreatment. *School Psychology Review, 16,* 156–168.

Erickson, M., & Egeland, B. (1996). Child neglect. In J. Briere, L. Berliner, J. Bulkley, C. Jenny, & T. Reid (Eds.), *The APSAC handbook on child maltreatment* (pp. 4–20). Thousand Oaks, CA: Sage.

Erickson, S., Lilienfield, S., & Vitacco, M. (2007). A critical examination of the suitability and limitations of psychological tests in family court. *Family Court Review, 45*(2), 157–174.

Ewing, C. (2003). Expert testimony: Law and practice. In A. Goldstein & I. Weiner (Eds.), *Handbook of psychology: Vol. 11. Forensic psychology* (pp. 55–68). Hoboken, NJ: Wiley.

Fabricius, W., & Luecken, L. (2007). Postdivorce living arrangements, parent conflict, and long-term physical health correlates for children of divorce. *Journal of Family Psychology, 21*(2), 195–205.

Faller, K. C. (2007) *Interviewing children about sexual abuse: Controversies and best practice*, NY: Oxford.

Famularo, R., Fenton, T., Kinscherff, R., & Ayoub, C. (1994). Maternal and child posttraumatic stress disorder in cases of child maltreatment. *Child Abuse & Neglect, 18*(1), 27–36.

Fantuzzo, J., & Mohr, W. (1999). Prevalence and effects of child exposure to domestic violence. *Future of Children, 9*(3), 21–32.

Felner, D., Rowlison, R., Farber, S., Primavera, J., & Bishop, T. (1987). Child custody resolution: A study of social science involvement and impact. *Professional Psychology: Research and Practice, 18*(5), 468–474

Fisher, S., & Fisher, R. (1986). *What we really know about parenting.* Northvale, NJ: Jason Aronson.

Federal Rules of Evidence for the United Stated Courts and Magistrates (1975–2000). St. Paul, MN: West Publishing Co.

Flens, J. (2005). The responsible use of psychological testing in child custody evaluations: Selection of tests. *Journal of Child Custody, 2*(1/2), 3–29.

Flens, J., & Drozd, L. (Eds.). (2005). *Psychological testing in child custody evaluations.* New York: Haworth Press.

Fridhandler, B. (2007). Science and child custody evaluations: What qualifies as "scientific?" *Journal of Child Custody, 5*(3/4), 256–275.

Friedlander, S., & Walters, M. (2010). When a child rejects a parent: Tailoring the intervention to fit the problem. *Family Court Review, 48*(1), 98–111.

Friedrich, W. (2002). Child sexual behavior inventory: Normative, psychiatric, and sexual abuse comparisons. *Child Maltreatment, 6*(1), 37–49.

Friedrich, W. (2005). Correlates of sexual behavior in young children. *Journal of Child Custody, 2*(3), 41–55.

Friedrich, W., Fisher, J., Broughton, D., Houston, M., & Shafran, C. (1998). Normative sexual behavior in children: A contemporary sample. *Pediatrics, 101*(4), E9.

Friedrich, W., Fisher, J., Dittner, C., Acton, R., Berliner, L., & Butler, J. (2001). Child sexual behavior inventory: Normative, psychiatric, and sexual abuse comparisons. *Child Maltreatment, 6,* 37–49.

Frye, N., & Karney, B. (2006). The context of aggressive behavior in marriage: A longitudinal study of newlyweds. *Journal of Family Psychology, 20*(1), 12–20.

Furstenberg, F. (1990). Divorce and the American family. *Annual Review of Sociology, 16,* 379–403.

Furstenberg, F., Peterson, J., Nord, C., & Zill, N. (1983). The life course of children of divorce. *American Sociological Review, 48,* 656–668.

Garber, B. (2004). Parental alienation in the light of attachment theory: Consideration of the broader implications for child development, clinical practice, and forensic process. *Journal of Child Custody, 1*(4), 49–76.

Gardner, R. (1992). *The parental alienation syndrome: A guide for mental health and legal professionals.* Creskill, NJ: Creative Therapeutics.

Gardner, R. (2001). Should courts order PAS children to visit/reside with the alienated parent? A follow-up study. *American Journal of Forensic Psychology, 19,* 61–106.

Gerard, A. (1994). *Parent-Child Relationship Inventory (PCRI) manual.* Los Angeles: Western Psychological Services.

Giglio, J., & Kaufman, E. (1990). The relationship between child and adult psychopathology in children of alcoholics. *International Journal of the Addictions, 25,* 263–290.

Goldstein, J., Freud, A., & Solnit, A. (1973). *Beyond the best interests of the child.* New York: Free Press.

Goldstein, M. (2003). Parenting and substance abuse: A longitudinal analysis. *Dissertation Abstracts International: Section B: The Sciences and Engineering, 63*(11-B), 5515.

Goodman, G., Hirschman, J., Hepps, D., & Rudy, L. (1991). Children's memory for stressful events. *Merrill-Palmer Quarterly, 37,* 109–158.

Goodman, M., Bonds, D., Sandler, I., & Braver, S. (2004). Parent psychoeducational programs and reducing the negative effects of interparental conflict following divorce. *Family Court Review, 42*(2), 263–279.

Goodman, S., & Gotlib, I. (1999). Risk for psychopathology in the children of depressed mothers: A developmental model for understanding mechanisms of transmission. *Psychological Review, 106*(3), 458–490.

Gould, J. (2004). Evaluating the probative value of child custody evaluations: A guide for forensic mental health professionals. *Journal of Child Custody, 1*(1), 77–96.

Gould, J. (2005). Use of psychological tests in child custody evaluations. *Journal of Child Custody, 2*(1/2), 49–69.

Gould, J., & Martindale, D. (2007). *The art and science of child custody evaluations.* New York: Guilford Press.

Gould, J., & Stahl, P. (2000). The art and science of child custody evaluations: Integrating clinical and forensic mental health models. *Family and Conciliation Courts Review, 38*(3), 392–314.

Grandin, E., & Lupri, E. (1997). Intimate violence in the United States and Canada: A cross-national comparison. *Journal of Family Violence, 12*(4), 417–443.

Greenspan, S., & Greenspan, N. (2003) *The clinical interview of the child.* Washington, DC: American Psychiatric Publishing.

Grisso, T. (2003) *Evaluating competencies: Forensic assessments and instruments* (2nd ed.). New York: Springer.

Grisso, T. (2005). Commentary on "Empirical and ethical problems with custody recommendations": What now? *Family Court Review, 43*(2), 223–228.

Grossberg, M. (1985). *Governing the hearth: Law and the family in nineteenth-century America.* Chapel Hill: The University of North Carolina Press.

Gutheil, T., & Dattilio, F. (2008) *Practical approaches to forensic mental health testimony*. Philadelphia: Lippincott, Williams & Wilkins.

Hagan, M., & Castagna, N. (2001). The real numbers: Psychological testing in custody evaluations. *Professional Psychology: Research and Practice, 32*(3), 269–271.

Harden, P., & Pihl, R. (1995). Cognitive functioning, cardiovascular activity, and behavior of boys at high risk for alcoholism. *Journal of Abnormal Psychology, 104*, 94–103.

Harter, S. (2000). Psychosocial adjustment of adult children of alcoholics: A review of the recent literature. *Clinical Psychology Review, 20*, 311–337.

Harvey, V. (1997). Improving readability of psychological reports. *Professional Psychology: Research and Practice, 28*(3), 271–274.

Hearle, J., Plant, K., Jenner, L., Barkla, J., & McGrath, J. (1999). A survey of contact with offspring and assistance with child care among parents with psychotic disorders. *Psychiatric Services, 50*(10), 1354–1356.

Heilbrun, K. (2001). *Principles of forensic mental health assessment*. New York: Kluwer.

Heilbrun, K., Grisso, T., & Goldstein, A. (2009). *Foundations of forensic mental health assessment*. New York: Oxford University Press.

Hess, A. (1988). Accepting forensic case referrals: Ethical and professional considerations. *Professional Psychology: Research and Practice, 29*, 109–114.

Hesselbrock, V., & Hesselbrock, M. (2006). Developmental perspectives on the risk for developing substance abuse problems. In W. Miller & K. Carroll (Eds.), *Rethinking substance abuse: What the science shows, and what we should do about it* (pp. 97–114). New York: Guilford.

Hetherington, E. (Ed.). (1999). *Coping with divorce, single parenting, and remarriage: A risk and resiliency perspective*. Mahwah, NJ: Erlbaum.

Hetherington, E., Cox, M., & Cox, R. (1982). Effects of divorce on parents and children. In M. Lamb (Ed.), *Non-traditional families* (pp. 223–288). Hillsdale, NJ: Erlbaum.

Hetherington, E., & Kelly, J. (2002). *For better or worse: Divorce reconsidered*. New York: W.W. Norton.

Hetherington, E., & Stanley-Hagan, M. (1999). The adjustment of children: A risk and resiliency perspective. *Journal of Child Psychology and Psychiatry, 40*(1), 29–140.

Hewitt, S. (1999). *Assessing allegations of sexual abuse in preschool children: Understanding small voices*. Thousand Oaks, CA: Sage.

Hill, S., Shen, S., Lowers, L., & Locke, J. (2000). Factors predicting the onset of adolescent drinking in families at high risk for developing alcoholism. *Biological Psychiatry, 48*(4), 265–275.

Hodges, W. (1991). *Interventions for children of divorce: Custody, access, and psychotherapy*. New York: Wiley-Interscience.

Horvath, L., Logan, T., & Walker, R. (2002). Child custody cases: A content analysis of evaluations in practice. *Professional Psychology: Research and Practice, 33,* 557–565.

Hughes, P. (2006). The neglect of children and culture: Responding to child maltreatment with cultural competence and a review of *Child abuse and culture: Working with diverse families. Family Court Review, 44*(3), 501–510.

Hunsley, J., Lee, C., & Wood, J. (2003). Controversial and questionable assessment techniques. In S. Lilienfeld, S. Lynn, & J. Lohr (Eds.), *Science and pseudoscience in clinical psychology* (pp. 39–76). New York: Guilford.

Hynan, D. (2003). Parent-child observations in custody evaluations. *Family Court Review, 41*(2), 214–223.

Insabella, G., Williams, T., & Pruett, M. K. (2003). Individual and co-parenting differences between divorcing and unmarried fathers: Implications for court services. *Family Court Review, 41*(3), 290–306.

Isaacs, M. (1988). The visitation schedule and child adjustment: A three-year study. *Family Process, 27*(2), 251–256.

Jaffe, P., Baker, L., & Cunningham, A. (Eds.). (2004) *Protecting children from domestic violence: Strategies for community intervention.* New York: Guilford

Jenuwine, M., & Cohler, B. (1999) Major parental psychopathology and child custody. In R. Galatzer-Levy & L. Kraus (Eds.), *The scientific basis of child custody decisions* (pp. 285–318). New York: Wiley.

Johnson, M. (1995). Patriarchal terrorism and common couple violence: Two forms of violence against women in U.S. families. *Journal of Marriage and the Family, 57,* 283–294.

Johnson, M., & Leone, J. (2005). The differential effects of intimate terrorism and situational couple violence: Findings from the national violence against women survey. *Journal of Family Issues, 26*(3), 322–349.

Johnson, T. (2005). Young children's problematic sexual behaviors, unsubstantiated allegations of sexual abuse, and family boundaries in child custody disputes. *Journal of Child Custody, 2*(4), 111–126.

Johnston, J. (2003). Parental alignments and rejection: An empirical study of alienation in children of divorce. *Journal of the American Academy of Psychiatry and Law, 31,* 158–170.

Johnston, J., & Campbell, L. (1988). *Impasses of divorce: The dynamics and resolution of family conflict.* New York: Simon and Schuster.

Johnston, J., & Goldman, J. (2010). Outcomes of family counseling intervention with children who resist visitation: An addendum to Friedlander and Walters (2010). *Family Court Review, 48*(1), 112–115.

Johnston, J., & Kelly, J. (2004). Commentary on Walker, Brantley, and Rigsbee's (2004) "A critical analysis of parental alienation syndrome and its admissibility in family court." *Journal of Child Custody, 1*(4), 77–90.

Johnston, J., Kline, M., & Tschann, J. (1991). Ongoing post-divorce conflict in families contesting custody: Do joint custody and frequent access help? In J. Folberg (Ed.), *Joint custody and shared parenting* (2nd ed., pp. 177–184). New York: Guilford Press.

Johnston, J., Lee, S., Oleson, N., & Walters, M. (2005). Allegations and substantiations of abuse in custody-disputing families. *Family Court Review, 43,* 283–294.

Johnston, J., & Roseby, V. (1997). *In the name of the child: A developmental approach to understanding and helping children of conflicted and violent divorce.* New York: The Free Press.

Johnston, J., Walters, M., & Friedlander, S. (2001). Therapeutic work with alienated children and their families. *Family Court Review, 39,* 316–332.

Johnston, J., Walters, M., & Oleson, N. (2005). Is it alienating parenting, role reversal, or child abuse? A study of children's rejection of a parent in child custody disputes. *Journal of Emotional Abuse, 4*(4), 191–218.

Jones, E. (2001). Review of the stress index for parents of adolescents. Retrieved April 20, 2010 from *Mental Measurements Yearbook* database.

Joseph, J., Joshi, S., Lewin, A., & Abrams, M. (1999). Characteristics and perceived needs of mothers with serious mental illness. *Psychiatric Services, 50*(10), 1357–1359.

Kahng, S., Oyserman, D., Bybee, D., & Mowbray, C. (2008). Mothers with serious mental illness: When symptoms decline, does parenting improve? *Journal of Family Psychology, 22*(1), 162–166.

Kaufman, J., & Zigler, E. (1987). Do abused children become abusive parents? *American Journal of Orthopsychiatry, 57*(2), 186–192.

Keilin, W., & Bloom, L. (1986). Child custody evaluation practices: A survey of experienced professionals. *Professional Psychology: Research and Practice, 17,* 338–346.

Kelly, J. (2000). Children's adjustment in conflicted marriage and divorce. *Journal of the American Academy of Child & Adolescent Psychiatry, 39*(8), 963–973.

Kelly, J., & Emery, R. (2003). Children's adjustment following divorce: Risk and resilience perspectives. *Family Relations, 52*(4), 352–362.

Kelly, J., & Johnson, M. (2008). Differentiation among types of intimate partner violence: Research update and implications for interventions. *Family Court Review, 46*(3), 476–499.

Kelly, J., & Johnston, J. (2001). The alienated child: A reformulation of parental alienation syndrome. *Family Courts Review, 39,* 249–266.

Kelly, J., & Johnston, J. (2005). Commentary on Tippins and Wittman's "Empirical and ethical problems with custody recommendations: A call for clinical humility and judicial vigilance." *Family Court Review, 42*(2), 233–241.

Kelly, R., & Ward, S. (2002). Allocating custodial responsibilities at divorce. *Family Court Review, 40*(3), 350–370.

Kendall-Tackett, K., Williams, L., & Finklehor, D. (1993). Impact of sexual abuse on children: A review and synthesis of recent empirical studies. *Psychological Bulletin, 113,* 164–180.

Kessler, R., Chiu, W., Demler, O., & Walters, E. (2005). Prevalence, severity, and comorbidity of twelve-month DSM-IV disorders in the National Comorbidity Survey Replication (NCS-R). *Archives of General Psychiatry, 62*(6), 617–627.

Kirkland, K., Kirkland, K., King, G., & Renfro, G. (2006). Quasi-judicial immunity for forensic professionals in court-appointed roles. *Journal of Child Custody, 3*(1), 1–22.

Kirkland, K., McMillan, E., & Kirkland, K. (2005). Use of collateral contacts in child custody evaluations. *Journal of Child Custody, 2*(4), 95–109.

Kirkpatrick, H. D. (2004). A floor not a ceiling: Beyond guidelines—an argument for minimum standards of practice in conducting child custody and visitation evaluations. *Journal of Child Custody, 1*(1), 61–76.

Klykylo, W. (2005). The initial psychiatric evaluation. In W. Klykylo & J. Kay (Eds.), *Clinical child psychiatry* (pp. 3–19). New York: Wiley.

Kohm, L. (2008). Tracing the foundations of the best interests of the child standard in American jurisprudence. *Journal of Law & Family Studies, 10*(2), 337–376.

Kopetski, L. (1998). Identifying cases of parent alienation syndrome— Part I. *The Colorado Lawyer, 27*(2), 65–68. Retrieved September 3, 2008, from http://www.fact.on.ca/Info/pas/kopet98a.htm

Kovacs, M. (1992). *Manual for the Children's Depression Inventory.* New York: Mental Health Systems.

Kraus, L. (1999). Understanding the relationship between children and their caregivers. In R. Galatzer-Levy and L. Kraus (Eds.), *The scientific basis of child custody decisions* (pp. 58–73). New York: Wiley.

Kruh, I., & Grisso, T. (2009). *Evaluation of juveniles' competence to stand trial.* New York: Oxford University Press.

Kuehnle, K. (1996). *Assessing allegation of child sexual abuse.* Sarasota, FL: Professional Resource Press.

Kuehnle, K., & Connell, M. (Eds.). (2009). *The evaluation of child sexual abuse allegations: A comprehensive guide to assessment and testimony.* Hoboken, NJ: Wiley

Kuehnle, K., & Drozd, L. (2005) *Child custody litigation: Allegations of child sexual abuse.* New York: Haworth Press.

Kuenhle, K., & Kirkpatrick, H. (2005). Evaluating allegations of child sexual abuse within complex child custody cases. *Journal of Child Custody, 2*(3), 3–39.

Kulkofsky, S., & London, K. (2010). Reliability and suggestibility of children's statements: From science to practice. In E. Benedek, P. Ash, & C. Scott (Eds.), *Principles and practice of child and adolescent forensic mental health* (pp. 217–227). Washington, DC: American Psychiatric Publishing.

Lachar, D., & Gruber, C. (2001). Personality Inventory for Children (2nd ed.). Los Angeles: Western Psychological Services.

LaFortune, K., & Carpenter, B. (1998). Custody evaluations: A survey of mental health professionals. *Behavioral Sciences and the Law, 16,* 207–224.

Lamb, M. (Ed.) (1976) *The role of the father in child development.* New York: Wiley.

Lamb, M., & Kelly, J. (2001). Using the empirical literature to guide the development of parenting plans for young children: A rejoinder to Solomon and Biringen. *Family Court Review, 39*(4), 365–371.

Lamb, M., Orbach, Y., Sternberg, K., Hershkowitz, I., & Horowitz, D. (2000). Accuracy of investigators' verbatim notes of their forensic interviews with alleged child abuse victims. *Law and Human Behavior, 24*(6), 699–708.

Lamb, M., Sternberg, K., & Esplin, P. (1998). Conducting investigative interviews of alleged sexual abuse victims. *Child Abuse and Neglect, 22,* 813–823.

Lamb, M., Sternberg, K., Esplin, P., Herskowitz, I., & Orbach, Y. (1999). *The NICHD protocol for investigative interviews of alleged sex abuse victims.* Unpublished manuscript, National Institute of Child Health & Human Development, Bethesda, MD.

Lamb, M., Sternberg, K., Orbach, Y., Esplin, P., Stewart, H., & Mitchell, S. (2003). Age differences in young children's responses to open-ended invitations in the course of forensic interviews. *Journal of Consulting and Clinical Psychology, 71*(5), 926–934.

Lampel, A. (1986). Post-divorce therapy with highly conflicted families. *The Independent Practitioner, 6,* 2225.

Lampel, A. (1996). Children's alignments with parents in highly contested custody cases. *Family and Conciliation Courts Review, 34,* 229–239.

Larson, K., & McGill, J. (2010). Adolescent input into custody decisions: Evaluating decision-making capacities. *Journal of Forensic Psychology Practice, 10,* 133–144.

Laumann-Billings, L., & Emery, R. (2000). Distress among young adults from divorced families. *Journal of Family Psychology, 14,* 671–687.

Lawrence, E., & Bradbury, T. (2001). Physical aggression and marital dysfunction: A longitudinal analysis. *Journal of Family Psychology, 15*(1), 135–154.

Lee, C., & Bates, J. (1985). Mother-child interaction at age two years and perceived difficult temperament. *Child Development, 56*(5), 1314–1325.

Lee, S., & Oleson, N. (2001). Assessing for alienation in child custody and access evaluations. *Family Courts Review, 39,* 282–298.

Lehmann, P., & Ellison, E. (2001). Traumatic responding in children exposed to domestic violence: A cross-cultural study. *Journal of Ethnic and Cutlural Diversity in Social Work, 10*(4), 81–102.

Lewis, C. C. (1981). The effects of parental firm control: A reinterpretation of the findings. *Psychological Bulletin, 90,* 547–563.

Lieberman, A., & Van Horn, P. (1998). Attachment, trauma, and domestic violence: Implications for child custody. *Child and Adolescent Psychiatric Clinics of North America, 7*(2), 423–443.

Loftus, E., & Palmer, J. (1974). Reconstruction of automobile destruction: An example of the interaction between language and memory. *Journal of Verbal Learning and Verbal Behavior, 13,* 585–589.

Lubet, S. (1998). *Expert testimony: A guide for expert witnesses and the lawyers who examine them.* Louisville, CO: National Institute for Trial Advocacy.

Ludolph, P. (2009). Answered and unanswered questions in attachment theory with implications for children of divorce. *Journal of Child Custody, 6*(1/2), 8–24.

Luthar, S., & Suchman, N. (2000). Relational psychotherapy mothers' group: A developmentally informed intervention for at-risk mothers. *Development and Psychopathology, 12*(2), 235–253.

Maccoby, E., & Mnookin, R. (1992). *Dividing the child: The social and legal dilemmas of custody.* Cambridge, MA: Harvard University Press.

Main, M. (1996). Introduction to the special section on attachment and psychopathology: 2. Overview of the field of attachment. *Journal of Consulting and Clinical Psychology, 64*(2), 237–243.

Marafiote, R. (1985). *The custody of children: A behavioral assessment model.* New York: Plenum Press.

Marquardt, E. (2006). *Between two worlds: The inner lives of children of divorce.* New York: Three Rivers Press.

Martindale, D. (2004). Integrity and transparency: A commentary on record keeping in child custody evaluations. *Journal of Child Custody, 1*(1), 31–40.

Mason, M. (1994). *From father's property to children's rights: The history of child custody in the United States.* New York: Columbia University Press.

Massachusetts Probate and Family Court. (2008). *Standing Order 1–08. Standards for guardians ad litems/evaluators.* Retrieved February 18, 2010, from http://www.mass.gov/courts/courtsandjudges/courts/probateandfamilycourt/documents/standingorder1–08galevaluationsstandards.pdf

Masten, A., & Coatsworth, D. (1998). The development of competence in favorable and unfavorable environments: Lessons from research on successful children. *American Psychologist, 53*(2), 205–220.

Masten, A., Coatsworth, D., Neeman, J., Gest, S., Tellegen, A., & Garmezy, N. (1995). The structure and coherence of competence from childhood through adolescence. *Child Development, 66,* 1635–1659.

Matter of W. v. J., 233 N.Y.L.J. 111 (2005).

Mayes, L., & Truman, S. (2002). Substance abuse and parenting. In M. Bornstein (Ed.), *Handbook of parenting* (2nd ed., pp. 329–360). Mahweh, NJ: Erlbaum.

McCann, J. (2006). Measuring adolescent personality and psychopathology with the Millon Adolescent Clinical Inventory (MACI). In G. Koocher & S. Sparta (Eds.), *Forensic mental health assessment of children and adolescents* (pp. 424–439). New York: Oxford University Press.

McCann, J., Flens, J., Campagna, V., Collman, P., Lazzaro, T., & Connor, C. (2001). The MCMI-III in child custody evaluations: A normative study. *Journal of Forensic Psychology Practice, 1*(2), 27–44.

McCrady, B. (2008). Alcohol use disorders. In D. Barlow (Ed), *Clinical handbook of psychological disorders: A step-by-step treatment manual* (4th ed., pp. 492–546). New York: Guilford.

McGleughlin, J., Meyer, S., and Baker, J. (1999). Assessing child abuse allegations in divorce custody and visitation disputes. In R. Galatzer-Levy & L. Kraus (Eds.), *The scientific basis of child custody decisions* (pp. 357–388). New York: Wiley.

McGoldrick, M., Giordano, J., & Garcia-Preto, N. (Eds.). (2005). *Ethnicity and family therapy* (3rd ed.). New York: Guilford Press.

McIntosh, J., Smyth, B., Kelaher, M., Wells, Y., & Long, C. (2010). Three reports prepared for the Australian government (pp. 85–152). Available at http://www.ag.gov.au/www/agd/agd.nsf/Page/Families_FamilyRelationshipServicesOverviewofPrograms_ResearchProjectsonSharedCareParentingandFamilyViolence

McLanahan, S., & Sandefur, G. (1994). *Growing up with a single-parent: What hurts, what helps.* Cambridge, MA: Harvard University Press.

McLellan, J., McCurry, C., Ronnei, M., Adams, J., Eisner, A., and Storck, M. (1996). Age of onset of sexual abuse: Relationship to sexually inappropriate behaviors. *Journal of the American Academy of Child & Adolescent Psychiatry, 35,* 1375–1383.

McMahon, T., & Giannini, F. (2003). Substance abusing fathers in family court: Moving from popular stereotypes to therapeutic jurisprudence. *Family Court Review, 41*(3), 337–353.

Medoff, D. (2003). The scientific basis of psychological testing: Considerations following *Daubert, Kumho,* and *Joiner. Family Court Review, 41*(2), 199–213.

Meloy, J. (2007). The authority of the Rorschach: An update. In C. Gacono, B. Evans, N. Kaiser-Boyd, & L. Gacono (Eds.), *Handbook of Rorschach forensic psychology* (pp. 62–69). New York: Routledge.

Melton, G., Petrila, J., Poythress, N., & Slobogin, C. (2007). *Psychological evaluations for the courts: A handbook for mental health professionals and lawyers* (3rd ed.). New York: Guilford.

Mercer, D., & Pruett, M. (2001). *Your divorce advisor.* New York: Simon and Schuster.

Meyer, G., & Archer, R. (2001). The hard science of Rorschach research: What do we know and where do we go? *Psychological Assessment, 13*(4), 486–502.

Meyer, J., & Erickson, R. (1999). Legal and ethical issues in child custody litigation. In R. Galatzer-Levy & L. Kraus (Eds.), *The scientific basis of child custody decisions* (pp. 12–31). New York: Wiley.

Miller, S. (2005). *Victims as offenders: The paradox of women's violence in relationships.* Piscataway, NJ: Rutgers University Press.

Millon, T. (1987). *Millon Clinical Multi-Axial Personality Inventory – II.* Minneapolis, MN: National Computer Systems.

Millon, T., Millon, C., & Davis. R. (1997). *Millon Clinical Multi-Axial Personality Inventory – III.* Minneapolis, MN: National Computer Systems.

Millon, T., Millon, C., Davis, R, & Grossman, S. (2007). *Millon Adolescent Clinical Inventory* Minneapolis, MN: NCS/Pearson Assessments.

Minuchin, S. (1974). *Families and family therapy.* Cambridge, MA: Harvard University Press.

Mnookin, R. (1975). Child custody adjudication and judicial function in the face of indeterminacy. *Law and Contemporary Problems, 39,* 26–293.

Moore, T., & Stuart, G. (2004). Illicit substance use and intimate partner violence among men in batterers' intervention. *Psychology of Addictive Behaviors, 18,* 385–389.

Morey, L. (1991a). *The Personality Assessment Inventory: Professional manual* (2nd ed.). Odessa, FL: Psychological Assessment Resources.

Morey, L. (1991b). *Personality Assessment Inventory* Retrieved February 10, 2010 from *Mental Measurements Yearbook* database.

Mullen, K., & Edens, J. (2008). A case law survey of the Personality Assessment Inventory: Examining its role in civil and criminal trials. *Journal of Personality Assessment, 90*(3), 300–303.

Murphy, C., & Cascardi, M. (1999). Psychological abuse in marriage and dating relationships. In R. L. Hampton (Ed.), *Family violence prevention and treatment* (2nd ed., pp. 198–226). Beverly Hills, CA: Sage.

Murray, T. (1973). Thematic Apperception Test. Minneapolis, MN: Pearson/PsyCorp.

National Association of Social Workers. (1997). *Code of ethics of the National Association of Social Workers.* Washington, DC: National Association of Social Workers. Retrieved February 25, 2009, from http://www.socialworkers.org/pubs/code/code.asp

National Center for State Courts. (2008). *Custody decisions in cases with domestic violence allegations.* Chicago: American Bar Association. Retrieved March 3, 2009, from http://www.abanet.org/legalservices/probono/childcustody/domestic_violence_chart1.pdf

National Institute on Alcohol Abuse and Alcoholism. (2009). *Percent who drink beverage alcohol, by gender, 1939–2008.* Retrieved August 17, 2009, from http://www.niaaa.nih.gov/Resources/Database Resources/QuickFacts/AlcoholConsumption/dkpat25.htm

Nichols, A., & Maner, J. (2008). The good subject effect: Investigating participant demand characteristics. *Journal of General Psychology, 35*(2), 151–165.

Nichols, M. (2010) *Family therapy: Concepts and methods* 9th edition, Boston, MA: Pearson.

Nichols, W. (1986). Sibling subsystem therapy in family system re-organization. *Journal of Divorce, 9*(3), 13–31.

Nicholson, J., Biebel, K., Hinden, B., Henry, A., & Stier, L. (2001). *Critical issues for parents with mental illness and their families.* Rockville, MD: Center for Mental Health Services, Substance Abuse and Mental Health Services Administration Office of Policy, Planning and Administration. Retrieved May 3, 2009, from http://mentalhealth.samhsa.gov/publications/allpubs/ken-01-0109/default.asp

Nicholson, J., Sweeney, E., & Geller, J. (1998). Mothers with mental illness: I. The competing demands of parenting and living with mental illness. *Psychiatric Services, 49*(5), 635–642.

Nord, C. W., Brimhall, D., & West, J. (1997). *Fathers' involvement in their children's schools.* Washington, DC: National Center for Education Statistics.

O'Connell, M. (2009). Mandated custody evaluations and the limits of judicial power. *Family Court Review, 47*(2), 304–320.

O'Donahue, W., & Bradley, A. (1999). Conceptual and empirical issues in child custody evaluations. *Clinical Psychology: Science and Practice, 6,* 310–322.

O'Leary, K., & Mauiro, R. (2001). *Psychological abuse in violent relations.* New York: Springer.

O'Leary, S., & Slep, A. (2006). Precipitants of partner aggression. *Journal of Family Psychology, 20*(2), 344–347.

Otto, R. (2000). Use of the MMPI-2 in forensic settings. *Journal of Forensic Psychology Practice, 1,* 27–44.

Otto, R., Buffington-Vollum, J., & Edens, J. (2003). Child custody evaluation. In I. Goldstein & I. Weiner (Eds), *Handbook of psychology, Vol. 11. Forensic psychology* (pp. 179–207). New York: Wiley.

Otto, R., & Collins, R. (1995). Use of the MMPI-2/MMPI-A in child custody evaluations. In Y. Ben-Porath, J. Graham, G. Hall, & M. Zaragoza (Eds.), *Forensic applications of the MMPI-2* (pp. 222–252). Thousand Oaks, CA: Sage.

Otto, R., & Edens, J. (2003). Parenting capacity. In T. Grisso (Ed.), *Evaluating competencies: Forensic assessments and instruments* (2nd ed., pp. 229–307). New York: Springer.

Oyserman, D., Mowbray, C., & Zemenchuk, J. (1994). Resources and support for mothers with severe mental illness. *Health and Social Work, 19,* 132–142.

Patterson, C. (2006). Children of gay and lesbian parents. *Current Directions in Psychological Science, 15*(5), 241–244.

Pearson, J., & Thoennes, N. (2000). Supervised visitation. *Family Court Review, 38*(1), 123–142.

Poole, D., & Lamb, M. (1998). *Investigative interviews of children* (2nd ed.). Washington, DC: American Psychological Association.

Pruett, M., Ebling, R. & Insabella, G. (2004). Critical aspects of parenting plans for young children. *Family Court Review, 42*(1), 39–59.

Quinnell, F., & Bow, J. (2001). Psychological tests used in child custody evaluations. *Behavioral Sciences & the Law, 19*(4), 491–501.

Radke-Yarrow, M. (1991). Attachment patterns in children of depressed mothers. In C. Parkes, J. Stevenson-Hinde, & P. Marris (Eds), *Attachment across the life cycle* (pp. 115–126). New York: Tavistock/Routledge.

Redding, R., Floyd, M., & Hawk, G. (2001). What judges and lawyers think about mental health testimony: A survey of the courts and bar. *Behavioral Sciences and the Law, 19,* 583–594.

Reed, L. (1996). Findings from research on children's suggestibility and implications for conducting child interviews. *Child Maltreatment, 1*(2), 105–120.

Regier, D., Narrow, W., Rae, D., Manderscheid, R., Locke, B., & Goodwin, F. (1993). The de facto mental and addictive disorders service system. Epidemiologic Catchment Area prospective 1-year prevalence rates of disorders and services. *Archives of General Psychiatry, 50*(2), 85–94.

Reich, W., Earls, F., Frankel, O., & Shayka, J. (1993). Psychopathology in children of alcoholics. *Journal of the American Academy of Child & Adolescent Psychiatry, 32*(5), 995–1002.

Resetar, B., & Emery, R. (2008). Children's rights and European legal proceedings: Why are family practices different from legal theories? *Family Court Review, 46*(1), 65–77.

Reynolds, C., & Kamphaus, R. (2004). *BASC-2: Behavior Assessment System for Children, Second Edition Manual.* Minneapolis, MN: NCS Pearson, Inc.

Richman, K. (2009). *Courting change: Queer parents, judges, and the transformation of American law.* New York: New York University Press.

Riggs, S. (2005). Is the approximation rule in the child's best interest? *Family Court Review, 43*(3), 481–493.

Roberts, K. (2003). State supreme court applications of Troxel v. Granville and the courts' reluctance to declare grandparent visitation rights unconstitutional. *Family Court Review, 41*(1), 14–38.

Rohman, L., Sales, B., & Lou, M. (1987). The best interests of the child in custody disputes. In L. Weithorn (Ed.), *Psychology and child custody determinations: Knowledge, roles, and expertise* (pp. 59–105). Lincoln: University of Nebraska Press.

Rohrbaugh, J. (2008). *A comprehensive guide to child custody evaluations: Mental health and legal perspectives*. New York: Springer.

Rothbart, M., & Bates, J. (1998). Temperament. In N. Eisenberg (Ed.), *Handbook of child psychology: Vol. 3. Social, emotional, and personality development* (5th ed., pp. 105–117). New York: Wiley.

Sattler, J. (1998). *Clinical and forensic interviewing of children and families*. La Mesa, CA: Jerome Sattler, Inc.

Saywitz, K. (1995). Improving children's testimony: The question, the answer, and the environment. In M. Zaragoza, J. Graham, G. Hall, R. Hirschman, & Y. Ben-Porath (Eds.), *Memory and testimony in the child witness* (pp. 113–140). Thousand Oaks, CA: Sage.

Schepard, A. (2004). *Children, courts, and custody: Interdisciplinary models for divorcing families*. New York: Cambridge University Press.

Schermerhorn, A., Cummings, E., DeCarlo, C., & Davies, P. (2007). Children's influence in the marital relationship. *Journal of Family Psychology, 21*(2), 259–269.

Schuckit, M., Smith, T., Danko, G., Bucholz, K., Reich, T., & Bierut, L. (2001). Five-year clinical course associated with DSM-IV alcohol abuse or dependence in a large group of men and women. *American Journal of Psychiatry, 158,* 1084–1090.

Schutz, B., Dixon, E., Lindenberger, J., & Ruther, N. (1989). *Solomon's sword: A practical guide to conducting child custody evaluations*. San Francisco: Jossey Bass.

Sheras, P., Abidin, R., & Konold, T. (1998). *Stress Index for Parents of Adolescents*. Odessa, FL: Psychological Assessment Resources.

Silovsky, J., & Nice, L. (2002). Characteristics of young children with sexual behavior problems: A pilot study. *Child Maltreatment, 7*(3), 187–197.

Simons, R. (Ed.) (1996). *Understanding differences between divorced and intact families: Stress, interaction, and child outcome*. Thousand Oaks, CA: Sage

Smith-Slep, A., and O'Leary, S. (2005). Parent and partner violence in families with young children: Rates, patterns, and connections. *Journal of Consulting and Clinical Psychology, 73*(3), 435–444.

S.M. v. G.M., 233 N.Y. L.J. 64 (2005).

Solomon, J., & Biringen, Z. (2001). Another look at the developmental research: Commentary on Kelly and Lamb's "Using child development research to make appropriate custody and access decisions for young children." *Family Court Review, 39,* 355–364.

Solomon, J., & George, C. (1999). The effects of overnight visitation in divorced and separated families: A longitudinal follow-up. In J. Solomon & C. George (Eds.), *Attachment disorganization* (pp. 243–264). New York: Guilford

Sparta, S., & Stahl, P. (2006). Psychological evaluation for child custody. In G. Koocher & S. Sparta (Eds.), *Forensic mental health assessment of children and adolescents* (pp. 203–229). New York: Oxford University Press.

Stahl, P. (2004). Conducting child custody evaluations: A comprehensive guide. Thousand Oaks, CA: Sage.

Stahl, P. (2005). The benefits and risks of child custody evaluators making recommendations to the court. *Family Court Review, 43*(2), 260–265.

Stimmel, B. (2009). From addiction to abstinence: Maximizing the chances of success. *Family Court Review, 47*(2), 265–273.

Straus, M., & Gelles, R. (1988). *Intimate violence in families.* New York: Simon and Schuster.

Stuart, G., Meehan, J., Moore, T., Morean, M., Hellmuth, J., & Follansbee, K. (2006). Examining a conceptual framework of intimate partner violence in men and women arrested for domestic violence. *Journal of Studies on Alcohol, 67,* 102–112.

Stuart, R. (2004). Twelve practical suggestions for achieving cultural competence. *Professional Psychology: Research and Practice, 35*(1), 3–9.

Styron, T., Pruitt, M., McMahon, T., & Davidson, L. (2002). Fathers with mental illness: A neglected group. *Psychiatric Rehabilitation Journal, 25*(1), 215–222.

Substance Abuse and Mental Health Services Administration, Office of Applied Studies. (2006). *National survey on drug use and health, 2002, 2003, 2004, 2005, and 2006.* Rockville, MD: Substance Abuse and Mental Health Services Administration.

Substance Abuse and Mental Health Services Administration, Office of Applied Studies. (2009). *The NSDUH report: Children living with substance-dependent or substance-abusing parents: 2002 to 200.* Available at http://www.samhsa.gov/newsroom/advisories/ 0904294333.aspx

Suchman, N., & Luthar, S. (2000). Maternal addiction, child maladjustment, and sociodemographic context: Implications for parenting behaviors. *Addiction, 95,* 1417–1428.

Suchman, N., & Luthar, S. (2001). The mediating role of stress in methadone-maintained mothers' parenting. *Parenting: Science and Practice, 1,* 285–315.

Sullivan, M., Ward, P., & Deutsch, R. (2010). Overcoming Barriers Family Camp: A program for high conflict divorced families where a child is resisting contact with a parent. *Family Court Review, 48*(1), 116–135.

Swearer, S. (2001). Review of the stress index for parents of adolescents. Retrieved February 10, 2010 from *Mental Measurements Yearbook* database.

Teicher, M., Samson, J., Polcari, A., & McGreenery, C. (2006). Sticks, stones and hurtful words: Relative effects of various forms of childhood maltreatment. *American Journal of Psychiatry, 163*(6), 993–1000.

Tellegen, A., Ben Porath, Y., McNulty, J., Arbisi, P., Graham, J., & Kaeminer, B. (2003). *MMPI-2 restructured clinical (RC) scales: Development, validation, and interpretation.* Minneapolis: University of Minnesota Press.

Thoennes, N., & Tjaden, P. (1990). The extent, nature, and validity of sexual abuse allegations in child custody/visitation disputes. *Child Abuse and Neglect, 14,* 151–163.

Thomas, A., & Chess, S. (1977). *Temperament and development.* New York: Bruner/Mazel.

Thompson, R., Scalora, M., Limber, S., & Castrianno, L. (1991). Grandparent visitation rights. *Family Court Review, 29*(1), 9–25.

Tippins, T., & Wittman, J. (2005). Empirical and ethical problems with custody recommendations: A call for clinical humility and judicial vigilance. *Family Court Review, 43*(2), 266–269.

Tsushima, W., & Anderson, R. (1996). *Mastering expert testimony: A courtroom handbook for mental health professionals.* Mahwah, NJ: Erlbaum.

Uniform Marriage and Divorce Act. National Conference of Commissioners on Uniform State Laws (1970). Chicago, Ill.

U.S. Census Bureau. (2007). *Statistical abstract of the United States* (126th ed.). Washington, DC: U.S. Census Bureau.

U.S. Department of Health & Human Services, Administration for Children, Youth, and Families, (2009). *Child Maltreatment 2009.* Retrieved April 17, 2010 at http://www.acf.hhs.gov/programs/cb/pubs/cm09/cm09.pdf

U.S. National Center for Health Statistics. (2004). *National vital statistics reports.* Hyattsville, MD: National Center for Health Statistics.

Vaillant, G. *The natural history of alcoholism revisited.* Cambridge, MA: Harvard University Press.

Walker, J., Brantley, K., & Rigsbee, J. (2004). A critical analysis of parental alienation syndrome and its admissibility in family court. *Journal of Child Custody, 1*(2), 47–74.

Wallerstein, J., & Blakeslee, S. (1996). *Second chances: Men, women and children a decade after divorce.* New York: Houghton Mifflin.

Wallerstein, J., & Blakeslee, S. (2003). *What about the kids? Raising your children before, during, and after divorce.* New York: Hyperion.

Wallerstein, J., Corbin, S., & Lewis, J. (1988). Children of divorce: A ten-year study. In M. Hetherington & J. Arasteh (Eds.), *Impact of divorce, single parenting, and stepparenting on children* (pp. 197–214). Hillsdale, NJ: Erlbaum.

Wallerstein, J., & Kelly, J. (1980). *Surviving the breakup.* New York: Basic Books.

Walsh, C., MacMillan, H., & Jamieson, E. (2003). The relationship between parental substance abuse and child maltreatment: Findings from the Ontario Health Supplement. *Child Abuse & Neglect, 27,* 1409–1425.

Warner, L., Kessler, R., Hughes, M., Anthony, J., & Nelson, C. (1994). Prevalence and correlates of drug use and dependency in the United States: Results from the National Comorbidity Study. *Archives of General Psychiatry, 52*(3), 219–229.

Warrier, S. (2008). "It's in their culture": Fairness and cultural considerations in domestic violence. *Family Court Review, 46*(3), 537–542.

Warshak, R. (2000). Blanket restrictions: Overnight contact between parents and young children. *Family & Conciliation Courts Review, 38*(4), 422–445.

Warshak, R. (2001). Current controversies regarding parental alienation syndrome. *American Journal of Forensic Psychology, 19*(3), 29–57.

Warshak, R. (2003). Bringing sense to parental alienation: A look at the disputes and the evidence. *Family Law Quarterly, 37*(2), 273–301.

Warshak, R. (2007). Punching the parenting time clock: The approximation rule, social science, and the baseball bat kids. *Family Court Review, 45*(4), 600–619.

Warshak, R. (2010). Family bridges: Using insights from social science to reconnect parents and alienated children. *Family Court Review, 48*(1), 48–80.

Warshak, R. (2011). *Parental alienation: Not just another custody case.* Presentation at annual conference of Massachusetts Association of Guardian's ad Litem, Inc., Weston, MA., April 15, 2011.

Wasserman, D., & Leventhal, J. (1998). Maltreatment of children born to cocaine-abusing mothers. *American Journal of Diseases of Children, 147,* 1324–1328.

Wechsler, D. (2008). *Wechsler Adult Intelligence Scale, Fourth edition.* San Antonio, TX: Pearson/PsychCorp.

Weinberg, M., & Tronick, E. (1998). The impact of maternal psychiatric illness on infant development. *Journal of Clinical Psychiatry, 59,* 53–61.

Weissman, H., & DeBow, D. (2003). Ethical principles and professional competencies. In A. Goldstein & I. Weiner (Eds.), *Handbook of psychology: Vol. 11. Forensic psychology* (pp. 33–54). Hoboken, NJ: Wiley.

White, C., Nicholson, J., Fisher, W., & Geller, J. (1995). Mothers with severe mental illness caring for children. *The Journal of Nervous and Mental Disease, 183*(6), 398–403.

Whiteside, M. F. (1998). The parental alliance following divorce: An overview. *Journal of Marital and Family Therapy, 24*(1), 3–24.

Whittaker, D., Haileyesus, T., Swahn, M., & Saltzman, L. (2007). Differences in frequency of violence and reported injury between relationships with reciprocal and non-reciprocal intimate partner violence. *American Journal of Public Health, 97*(5), 941–947.

Widiger, T. (2001). Review of the Millon Clinical Multiaxial Inventory – III [Manual Third Edition]. *Buros Fourteenth Mental Measurement Yearbook.* Lincoln, NB: University of Nebraska.

Widom, C. (1989). Does violence beget violence? A critical examination of the literature. *Psychological Bulletin, 106*(1), 3–28.

Wolman, R., & Taylor, K. (1991). Psychological effects of custody disputes on children. *Behavioral Science and the Law, 9,* 399–341.

Zelechoski, A. (2009). *The content of child custody evaluation reports: A forensic assessment principles-based analysis.* Unpublished doctoral dissertation, Drexel University, Philadelphia, PA.

Zemenchuk, J., Rogosh, F., & Mowbray, C. (1995). The seriously mentally ill woman in the role of parent: Characteristics, parenting, sensitivity, and needs. *Psychosocial Rehabilitation Journal, 15,* 95–99.

Zibbell, R. (2005). Common couple aggression: Frequency and implications for child custody and access evaluations. *Family Court Review, 43*(3), 454–465.

Zill, N., Morrison, D., & Coiro, M. (1993). Long-term effects of parental divorce on parent-child relationship, adjustment, and achievement in young adulthood. *Journal of Family Psychology, 7,* 91–103.

Tests and Specialized Tools

ASEBA: Achenbach System of Empirically Based Assessment, formerly CBCL (Child Behavior Check List) (Achenbach, 2010).

ASPECT: Ackerman-Schoendorf Scales for Parent Evaluation of Custody (Ackerman, M., & Schoendorf, K., 1992).

BASC-2: Behavior Assessment Scales for Children, Second Edition (Reynolds, C., & Kamphaus, R., 2004).

BPS: Bricklin Perceptual Scales. (Bricklin, B., 1990a). Bricklin, B. (1990a).

PORT: Bricklin Perception of Relations Test (Bricklin, 1989).

CAT: Children's Apperception Test (Bellak, L. & Bellak, S, 1974).

CDI-2: Children's Depression Inventory (Kovacs, 1982).

Connors CBRS: Connors Comprehensive Behavior Rating Scales (Conners, 1997).

MACI: Millon Adolescent Clinical Inventory (Millon, T., Millon, C., & Davis, R., 1993).

MCMI-III: Millon Clinical Multiaxial Inventory-III (Millon, T., Davis, R., & Millon, C., 1997).

MMPI-A: Minnesota Multiphasic Personality Inventory–Adolescent (Butcher, J., Williams, C., Graham, J., Kaemmer, B., Archer, R., Tellegen, A., Ben Porath, Y., Hathaway, D., & McKinley, J., 1992).

MMPI-2: Minnesota Multiphasic Personality Inventory-2 (Hathaway, S., McKinley, J., & Butcher, J., 1942–1990).

MMPI-2-RF: Minnesota Multiphasic Personality Inventory-2-Restructured Form (Ben-Porath, Y. & Auke Tellegen, A., 2008).

PAI: Personality Assessment Inventory (Morey, L. 1991a).

PASS: Bricklin Parent Awareness Skills Survey (Bricklin, 1990b).

PCRI: Parent-Child Relationship Inventory (Gerard, A. 1994).

PIC-2: Personality Inventory for Children, Second Edition. (Lachar, D. & Gruber, C., 2001).

PSI: Parenting Stress Inventory (Abidin, R., 1995).

Roberts-2: Roberts Apperception Test for Children: 2 (Roberts, G, & McArthur, D, undated).

Rorschach Inkblot Method. (Exner, J., 2003).

TAT: Thematic Apperception Test (Murray, T., 1973).

Wechsler Adult Intelligence Scale IV (Wechsler, D. (1939-2008).

References for Tests and Specialized Tools

Abidin, R. (1995). *Parenting stress index* (3rd ed.) Odessa, FL: Psychological Assessment Resources.

Achenbach, T. (2010) *Achenbach system of empirically-based assessments.* Burlington, VT: Research Center for Children, Youth, & Families.

Ackerman-Schoendorf Scales for Parent Evaluation of Custody–Manual. (Ackerman, M. & Schoendorf, K., 1992). Los Angeles: Western Psychological Services.

Bellak, L. & Bellak, S. (1974). *Children's Apperception Test.* San Antonio, TX: Pearson/PsychCorp.

Ben-Porath, Y. & Auke Tellegen, A. (2008). *Minnesota Multiphasic Personality Inventory-2-Restructured Form.* San Antonio, TX: Pearson/PsychCorp.

Bricklin, B. (1989). *Perception of Relationships Test manual.* Furlong, PA: Village Publishing.

Bricklin, B. (1990a). *Bricklin Perceptual Scales manual.* Furlong, PA: Village Publishing.

Bricklin, B. (1990b). *Parent Awareness Skills Survey manual.* Furlong, PA: Village Publishing.Bricklin Perceptual Scales (Bricklin, 1990a).

Butcher, J., Williams, C., Graham, J., Kaemmer, B., Archer, R., Tellegen, A., Ben Porath, Y., Hathaway, D., & McKinley, J. (1992). *Minnesota Multiphasic Personality Inventory–Adolescent.* Minneapolis, MN: NCS Assessments.

Conners, K. C. (1997). *Conners' Rating Scales-Revised.* New York: Multi-Health Systems.

Exner, J. (2003). *The Rorschach: A comprehensive system: Basic foundations and principles of interpretation.* Vol. 1 (4th ed.) Hoboken, NJ: Wiley.

Gerard, A. (1994). *Parent-Child Relationship Inventory.* Los Angeles: Western Psychological Services.

Hathaway, S., McKinley, J., & Butcher, J. (1942–1990). *Minnesota Multiphasic Personality Inventory-2.* Minneapolis, MN.: NCS Assessments.

Kovacs, M. (1982). *The children's depression inventory: A self-rated depression scale for school-aged youngsters.* Unpublished manuscript, University of Pittsburgh.

Lachar, D. & Gruber, C. (2001). *Personality Inventory for Children – 2nd Edition.* Losa Angeles: Western Psychological Services.

Millon, T., Davis, R., & Millon, C. (1997). *Millon multiaxial personality inventory – III*. Manual (2nd ed.), Minneapolis, MN: NCS Assessments.

Millon, T., Millon, C., & Davis, R. (1993). *Millon Adolescent Clinical Inventory*. Minneapolis, MN: NCS Assessments.

Morey, L. (1991a). *The Personality Assessment Inventory: Professional manual* (2nd ed.). Odessa, FL: Psychological Assessment Resources.

Murray, T. (1973). Thematic Apperception Test. Minneapolis, MN. Pearson/PsychCorp.

Reynolds, C., & Kamphaus, R. (2004). *BASC-2: Behavior Assessment System for Children, Second Edition Manual*. Minneapolis, MN: NCS Assessments.

Roberts, G. *Roberts Apperception Test for Children*. Beverly Hills: Western Psychological Services.

Wechsler, D. (1939–2008). *Wechsler Adult Intelligence Scale*-IV. San Antonio, TX: Pearson/PsychCorp.

Case Law and Statutes

California Code of Civil Procedure §5.220–5.235.

Commonwealth v. Addicks, 5 Binn. 520 (Pa. 1815).

Daubert v. Dow Chemical Pharmaceuticals, 113 S. Ct. 2786 (1993).

Frye v. United States, 293 F. 1013 (D.C. Cir 1923).

Margo M. v. Martin S., Neb. App. LEXIS 98 (2006).

Mass. Probate and Family Court Standing Order 1-08.

Mercein v. People ex rel. Barry, 25 Wend 64, 101, (NY 1840).

Michigan's Child Custody Act, M. C. L. §722.23 (1970).

People v. Mercein, 3 Hill 399, 418 (NY 1842).

Prather v. Prather, 4 Desau. 33 (S.C. 1809).

Robb v. Robb, 268 Neb. 694 (2004).

Smith v. Tierney, 906 So. 2d 586 (La. 2005).

Uniform Marriage and Divorce Act (1970).

Watts v. Watts, 350 N.Y.S.2d 285 (1973).

W. Va. Code §48-9-206.

Key Terms

AFCC: The Association of Family and Conciliation Courts is an international, interdisciplinary professional organization (i.e., mental health, law, and the judiciary) concerned with issues in juvenile and family law.

Affidavit: A written declaration or statement of facts, often made under oath (e.g., "pains and penalties of perjury."). These documents often accompany the pleadings or motions that attorneys send to forensic evaluators at the start of an assessment.

A.L.I. "Principles": refers to the American Law Institute's *Principles of the Law of Family Dissolution* (ALI, 2000). Undertaken during the 1990's, this work of legal experts from around the country discusses the legal consequences of marital dissolution, but it also includes topics related to never-married parents and to others who have assumed caretaking roles in a child's life.

Alienated child: "one who expresses, freely and persistently, unreasonable negative feelings and beliefs (such as anger, hatred, rejection, and/or fear) toward a parent that are significantly disproportionate to the child's actual experience with that parent" (Kelly & Johnston, 2001).

Allegations: accusations made about one party against the other that are relevant to the legal case.

APA: American Psychological Association or American Psychiatric Association (in this work, American Psychological Association).

Approximation rule: proposed by the ALI, the "approximation rule" recommends that the proportion of caretaking time following a divorce should be about the same as it was for each parent during the marriage.

Attachment theory: Based on the work of John Bowlby, this theory posits that parents who are available and responsive to their infant's needs establish a sense of security. The infant knows that the caregiver is dependable, which creates a secure base for the child to then explore the world. These bonds form the foundation for relationships throughout the person's life.

Best Interests of the Child (BIC) standard: A vaguely-defined legal standard for deciding child custody disputes that suggests that judicial decisions be based on what is optimal for the affected child.

Bio-psycho-social: refers to aspects of an individual's functioning related to that person's psychological makeup, social/learned experiences, and genetic/physical factors.

Case law: the reported decisions of selected appellate and other courts that make new interpretations of the law and which, therefore, can be cited as precedents.

Child custody evaluation: a forensic mental health evaluation that assesses issues relevant to the child's best interests.

Clinical mental health assessment: a psychological or psychiatric evaluation to aid in diagnosis and provide information for the treatment of an individual, couple, or family.

Coercive control: refers to physical and/or psychological abuse intended to intimidate and exert power and control in an intimate relationship.

Collateral sources: secondary sources of information, records, or people that provide information relevant to the issues in dispute.

Conflict-oriented abuse: a type of aggression that is reactive and related to conflict between the partners, but which is not motivated by the need to have power and control over the partner. Also called situational couple violence, it generally involves less severe forms of aggression than does coercive control.

Confidentiality: In a clinical context, "confidentiality" refers to the obligation of the mental health professional to keep a client's communications from being disclosed.

Construct: a concept.

Cross-examination: testimony provided in response to questioning by the attorney who did not call the witness; more likely to take on an adversarial tone.

De facto parent: a person who takes on the role of a parent despite not legally being the parent.

Deposition: a legal proceeding in which a witness is questioned by the counsel for one party outside of court, usually in an attorney's office. In a deposition, the witness provides out-of-court sworn and recorded testimony.

Direct examination: testimony provided in response to questioning by the attorney who called the witness; more likely to be conducted in a supportive tone.

Empirical: denotes information gained by scientific methods including systematic observation, experience, or experiment.

Ex-parte: Latin for: "by or for one party"; refers to an action taken in the absence of one of the parties. For example, a court may make an ex parte order without hearing from one party. An ex-parte communication is one that is made without both parties present or represented.

Expert witness: a witness, who, by virtue of specialized knowledge or skill, can provide the court with facts and inferences drawn from those facts that will assist the court in reaching a conclusion on the issue addressed by the witness.

Fit: refers to the congruence between the parents' functional capacities and the children's needs and abilities.

Forensic mental health assessment: A multi-source, multi-modal psychological or psychiatric evaluation intended to produce relevant information for legal cases.

Functional analysis: A process whereby one reduces a psycho-legal concept or construct to its behavioral referents, those being the particular behaviors that logically relate to the concept. In the instance of this book, "parenting abilities" is a psycho-legal construct relevant to the legal standard of "best interests." A functional analysis of "parenting abilities" would deconstruct that into basic child caretaking behaviors, such as, feeding, bathing, helping with homework, reading to a child, etc.

Guidelines/standards: Guidelines are advisory statements of policies or procedures. Professional guidelines are not mandatory, and non-compliance does not result in disciplinary consequences. Standards most often refer to established norms or requirements usually accepted as an authority that, if not followed, might result in disciplinary consequences (e.g., from licensing boards).

Indeterminacy: a state of being unsettled or undecided; usually used in reference to descriptions of the Best Interests of the Child Standard.

Informed consent: In child custody, informed consent is a process that educates the parties to the litigation about the nature of the evaluation, the role of the examiner, the absence of confidentiality, the costs and time involved, and the work product created. Some believe that when parents are court-ordered to have a custody evaluation, the process should be labeled "informed assent," because the element of actual choice they have is limited.

Judicial discretion: the freedom for a judge to make decisions within the bounds of law and fact. In child custody cases, judges are afforded considerable judicial discretion to decide cases.

Jurisdiction: the state, or the location of the relevant court within a state, that has responsibility for a legal dispute.

Legal custody: the right and responsibility to make decisions relating to the health, education, and welfare of the child.

  A. Joint legal custody: both parents have equal rights to make major decisions about their child.

  B. Sole legal custody: Only one parent has the right to make major decisions about their child.

Physical custody: the right and obligation of a parent to have his child live with him.

  A. Joint physical custody: the child spends a significant amount of time with both parents.

  B. Sole physical custody: the child lives primarily with one parent and might have parenting time with the other.

Mandated reporter: a professional who is statutorily required to make a report to the appropriate state agency if she suspects that a child, elder, or handicapped person is being maltreated or neglected.

Modification: a petition or request by one party to the court to change an existing order or judgment of the court.

Parallel parenting: describes relationships between separated parents characterized by detachment. Each parent makes parenting decisions for the child during her respective parenting time without the expectation of cooperation or communication with the other parent.

Parens patriae: a legal philosophy that affords courts the discretion of a benevolent parent and allows decisions to be based on the "best interests of the child."

Parent attributes: the functional abilities or deficits of a parent.

Parenting capacity/ability: a psycho-legal construct that represents the set of skills and knowledge possessed by a parent that is (a) relevant to the age and developmental level of his child(ren), (b) appropriate within the cultural context of that subsystem of the family, and (c) necessary to provide adequate care of the child(ren).

Parenting plan: a family's custodial arrangements and the schedule of parenting times.

Primary caretaker standard: a legal/judicial philosophy in which custody is granted to the parent who had been historically "responsible for the care and nurturance of a child."

Privilege: also know as testimonial privilege; refers to the right to prevent the disclosure of confidential communications (e.g., between doctor and patient) in legal proceedings.

Pro-se: Latin for "for one's self"; representing one's self before the court without benefit of counsel. Also known as pro per.

Psycho-legal concept: the conceptual link between legal standards and behavioral or psychological constructs. It guides the evaluator in selecting issues to address relevant to the legal standard—for example, assessing parenting attributes to address best interest.

Psychological aggression: refers to verbal or other behavioral acts that cause emotional pain or which are used to control, intimidate, or coerce one's partner. This might exist independent of physical violence, or it could co-occur with it. Also called psychological or mental abuse.

Removal/relocation/move-away case: a legal action in which the parent with primary physical custody of a child petitions the court for permission to move with the child a distance that would interfere with the other parent's access to the child. The move may be within a state or across state lines.

Resilience: the ability of a person to adapt to or overcome adverse circumstances.

Retainer: money received by an evaluator toward the costs of performing an assessment. Retainers are the preferred method of payment in private-pay child custody cases.

Special master: a judicial officer appointed by the court for a specific task, such as to oversee discovery of relevant information in a legal dispute.

Statute: a law passed by the legislature of a state.

Stipulation: an agreement made by the parties in a legal proceeding.

Testimony: information offered under oath either in a court of law or in a recorded deposition.

Tender years doctrine: a legal/judicial principle that held that it was preferable for children, usually under the age of 7, to be primarily raised by their mothers, as mothers were endowed by nature to be superior caretakers.

Index

Abidin, R., 105
Achenbach Child Behavior Checklist
    (CBCL), 100
Achenbach System of Empirically
    Based Assessment (ASEBA), 156
Ackerman, M., 92, 97, 98–9t, 107t
Ackerman–Schoendorf Scales for Parent
    Evaluation of Custody (ASPECT),
    102–3, 107–8
acute stress disorder, 74
administrative assistants, 126
AFCC. See Association of Family and
    Conciliation Courts (AFCC)
affidavits, 134, 263
alienated child, 86, 263. See also under
    parents and parental issues
A.L.I. Principles, 19, 263
allegations, definition of, 263
alternative dispute resolution, 21
Amato, P., 63
American Academy of Child and
    Adolescent Psychiatry (AACAP)
    components of reports, 191
    Practice Parameters for Child Custody
        Evaluations, 35, 36t, 38–40, 53
    religion, impact of on family, 61–2
    use of recommendations, 186
American Academy of Psychiatry and the
    Law (AAPL)
    Ethics Guidelines for the Practice of
        Forensic Psychiatry, 115
American Law Institute (ALI), 19, 263
American Psychiatric Association
    Principles of Medical Ethics with
        Annotations Especially Applicable
        to Psychiatry, 115
American Psychological Association (APA)
    assessment practices, 94–5
    components of reports, 191
    cultural sensitivity, 61
    Ethical Principles of Psychologists and
        Code of Conduct, 115, 176
    Guidelines for Child Custody Evaluations
        in Family Law Proceedings, 34, 35,
        37–40, 53
    parent-child observations, 157–8
    use of recommendations, 186–7

American Psychology-Law Society
    (APLS)
    Specialty Guidelines for Forensic
        Psychologists, 115, 190
appointments, refusal of, 119–20
approximation rule, 19–20, 263
ASPECT (Ackerman–Schoendorf Scales
    for Parent Evaluation of Custody),
    102–3, 107–8
assessment research, 91–108
    child custody assessment instruments,
        102–5
    collateral sources, 96
    document review, 96–7
    examiners' reports, 93–4
    home visits, 95–6, 158
    parent-child observations, 95
    Parent-Child Relationship Inventory
        (PCRI), 106–8, 107t
    Parenting Stress Index (PSI), 105–6
    psychological testing, 97–102
    self-report surveys, 92–3
Association of Family and Conciliation
    Courts (AFCC)
    assessment practices, 94
    BFAs, use of, 123
    components of reports, 191
    contacting attorneys, 125
    cultural sensitivity, 61
    definition of, 125
    ex parte communications, 198
    informed consent agreements, 131
    Model Standards of Practice for Child
        Custody Evaluations, 34–5, 36t, 37,
        39–40, 118, 133, 263
    parent-child observations, 157–8
    recommendations, use of, 186
attachment theory
    and alienation, 86, 263
    and approximation rule, 19
    definition of, 263–64
    and parenting plans, 90
attorneys, contacting of, 124–5
Ayoub, C., 69–70, 73, 77, 81–2

batterers, 138
Bauserman, R., 89

Behavioral Assessment System for Children
(BASC), 156
Best Interests of the Child (BIC) Standard.
See also Appendix A
and assessment process. *See* forensic
mental health assessment
definition of, 264
and domestic violence, 69
friendly parent doctrine, 170–1
and interviews of children, 147
legal context of, 14–20
Addicks case, 7–8
and decline of maternal
preference, 10
vagueness of statutes, 15
BFAs (brief, focused assessments), 120–1,
122–3
bias, appearance of, 26–7, 120
bio-psycho-social, definition of, 264
Bloom, L., 92, 96, 97, 98–9*t*
boundary violations, 75–6
Bow, J., 92–4, 95, 96, 97, 98–9*t*, 100,
107, 190–1
Bricklin, B., 104, 190
Bricklin Perceptual Scales (BPS), 103,
104–5, 107
brief, focused assessments (BFAs), 120–1,
122–3
Brodsky, S., 194, 206

Campbell, L., 69, 171
Canadian Incidence Study, on sexual abuse
allegations, 74
Carpenter, B., 92
case law, definition of, 264. *See also*
specific cases
cautionary language, 188
child abuse/neglect. *See* children
Child Custody Act of 1970 (Michigan), 16–7
child custody evaluation, definition of,
21–2, 25
child protection evaluations, 54–5, 55*t*
children. *See also* parents and parental
issues; *specific aspects of custody
evaluation process*
alienated child, 86, 263
developmental competence in, 43
divorce, impact on, 63–8
distress/disorder, 64–6, 75
and parental alienation, 86–7
parental conflict, 67
parenting time, 67–8

risk/resilience, 66–8
inappropriate sexual behaviors by, 75–6
interviews of, 127–8, 149–53, 150–1*t*,
154–5*t*
maltreatment of, 70, 72–7
post-traumatic stress disorder in, 69, 74
psychological testing of, 153–6
and sexual abuse, 72–6, 130
sociolegal history of, 3–5, 9
Children's Apperception Test (CAT), 155
Children's Depression Inventory
(CDI), 156
child support, sociolegal history of, 9
Clark, C., 153
clinical evaluations, 54–5, 56–7*t*
clinical mental health assessment, 264
coercive control, 70–1, 264
Coffman, J., 106
collaborative law, 21
collateral sources
assessment research on, 96
data collection, 133, 159–60
definition of, 264
in psycho-legal reports, 185
common couple violence, 71–2, 264
Commonwealth v. Addicks (1815), 7–8
competence, in child development, 43
confidentiality, 54, 126, 270
conflict-oriented abuse, 71–2, 264
conflicts of interest, 119–20
Connell, M., 102–3
Conners Behavior Rating Scales (CBRS),
100, 156
construct, definition of, 264
consultants, as examiners, 28
co-parenting relationships, 40, 137, 170–1
court-appointed evaluator, 26, 54
courts. *See also* judicial discretion;
specific cases
juvenile courts, 9
knowledge of process of proceedings,
114–5
psycho-legal reports, 180–1
psychological information in, 49–53
descriptive approach, 50–2
interpretive approach, 50, 52–3
credibility, in reports, 192–3
cross-examination, 264
culture, influence of, 61–3, 171

data collection, 129–61
children, 146–56

informed consent agreements, 147–9
interview topics, 149–53
psychological testing, 153–6
sample questions, 154–5*t*
collateral sources, 133, 159–60
document review, 160–1
parent-child interaction, 156–9
parents, 130–46
informed consent agreements, 131–4
interview topics, 134–43
psychological testing, 143–6
Daubert v. Dow Chemical Pharmaceuticals (1993), 98, 201–3
DeBow, D., 37
de facto parent, definition of, 265
depositions, 124, 195, 196–7, 265
Deutsch, R., 69–70
developmental delays, 69, 78–9
direct examination, 204, 265
divorce
demographics, 59–61
geographic stability during, 91
impact on children, 63–8
distress/disorder, 64–6, 75
and parental alienation, 86–7
parental conflict, 67
parenting time, 67–8
risk/resilience, 66–8
interparental relationships during, 46–7
legal process of, 20–3
mediation, 21
and psychological aggression, 72
sociolegal history of, 4, 5, 9, 11–4
document review, 96–7, 160–1
domestic abuse/violence
and data collection, 138–9
impact on children, 68–9
report rates, 61
types of, 69–72
coercive control, 70–1
conflict-oriented abuse, 71–2, 264
psychological abuse/aggression, 70, 71–2
separation-instigated violence, 71
violent resistance, 71
dual roles, 119

Edens, J., 102–3, 104–5, 106
electronic recordings of evaluations, 130
emotional abuse, 70–2
empirical, definition of, 265
empirical foundations/limits, 59–108

alienation/estrangement of parents, 84–8
and attachment, 86
definition of, 84–6
prevalence of, 86–7
remedial challenges, 87–8
assessment practices, 91–108
child custody assessment instruments, 102–5
collateral sources, 96
document review, 96–7
examiners' reports, 93–4
home visits, 95–6
parent-child observations, 95
Parent-Child Relationship Inventory (PCRI), 106–8, 107*t*
Parenting Stress Index (PSI), 105–6
psychological testing, 97–102
self-report surveys, 92–3
child maltreatment, 72–7
impact on children, 70, 74–7
prevalence of, 72, 73–4
culture, influence of, 61–3
divorce, impact on children, 63–8
distress/disorder, 64–6
risk/resilience, 66–8
domestic abuse/violence, 61, 68–72
ethnicity, influence of, 61–3
parent demographics, 59–61
parenting plans, 88–91
psychiatric disorders of parents
impact on children, 78–80
impact on parenting, 78
prevalence of, 77–8
substance abuse of parents, 80–4
impact on children, 74, 82–3
treatment issues, 83–4
Equal Rights Amendment, 14
Erard, R., 153
estrangement. *See under* parents and parental issues
ethical issues. *See also specific ethics codes and guidelines*
dual roles, 119
evaluator knowledge of, 115–6
ex parte communications, 118, 198, 265
parental permission, 26–7
for state of the science experts, 28
Ethical Principles of Psychologists and Code of Conduct (APA), 115
Ethics Guidelines for the Practice of Forensic Psychiatry (AAPL), 115

ethnicity, influence of, 61–3, 171
evaluation preparation, 111–28
  child-related logistics, 127–8
  clarification of referral questions, 116–8
  contacting attorneys, 124–5
  defining scope of evaluation
    complexity of case, 121
    evaluator's capabilities, 122
    expectations of court/attorneys/
      parties, 122
    financial resources, 121–2
    local practices, 122–3
    referral questions, 120
    time demands, 121
  qualifications
    clinical knowledge/skills, 111–3
    knowledge of ethical issues, 115–6
    knowledge of law/legal process, 113–5
    knowledge of practice standards, 113–5
  refusal of appointments, 119–20
  scheduling initial appointments, 125–7
examiners/evaluators
  as consultant, 28
  as hired by attorney, 26–8
  qualifications
    clinical knowledge/skills, 111–3
    knowledge of ethical issues, 115–6
    knowledge of law/legal process, 113–5
    knowledge of practice standards, 113–5
  role of, 24–8
  as science expert, 27–8
ex parte communications, 118, 198, 265
expert witnesses, 194, 199–200, 265

fact witnesses, 199
faked good responses, 94, 144
family structure and changing laws.
      See legal context of custody
family therapy, 87
fathers. *See* men/fathers
fear-generating intimidation. *See* domestic
      abuse/violence
Federal Rules of Evidence (FRE), 200–1
fee agreements, 117, 118, 131, 134
feminism and decline of maternal
      preference, 10
fit concept
  definition of, 265
  in forensic mental health assessment,
    39–40, 45–6
  and interpretation, 168–9
  in interpretation of data, 185

forensic mental health assessment, 31–57
  classes of information
    and BIC Standard, 32–3
    psycho-legal concepts, 33–7
  comparisons
    to child clinical evaluations, 54–5,
      56–7*t*
    to child protection evaluations, 54, 55*t*
  definition of, 271
  parent attributes, 37–40
    and child's psychological needs, 38–9
    co-parenting relationships, 40
    definition of, 37–8, 267
    and resulting fit, 39–40
  parenting capacity/ability
    and assessment, 41–9
    and child's needs, 43–5
    and interparental relationships, 46–7
    and resulting fit, 45–6
  psychological information in courts,
    49–53
    descriptive approach, 50–2
    interpretive approach, 50, 52–3
forensic mental health assessment (FMHA)
      model. *See* data collection
forensic mental health professionals, 112
friendly parent doctrine, 170–1
Frye v. United States (1923), 199–201
functional analysis, definition of, 265

Garber, B., 86
Gardner, R., 84–5, 87–8
gender. *See also* men/fathers; women/
      mothers
  bias due to approximation rule, 19–20
  and domestic violence, 70–1
  nongendered test norms, 146
genetic inheritance and psychiatric
      disorders, 78–9
Goldman, J., 88
Gould, J., 41–4, 175, 201–2
Grant, Robert, 6
Grisso, T., 33, 37, 39–40
guardians *ad litem* (GALs), 21, 26, 198
*Guidelines for Child Custody Evaluations in
      Family Law Proceedings* (APA), 34,
      35, 36*t*, 37–40, 53
guidelines/standards, definition of, 265

Harvey, V., 191
Health Insurance Portability and
      Accountability Act (HIPAA), 133

Heilbrun, K., 93–4, 177, 187, 188
home visits, 95–6, 127, 158–9, 192
Horvath, L., 69, 73, 77, 82, 93, 95–6, 100
House-Tree- Person (HTP)/Kinetic Family
 Drawing (KFD), 98, 99*t*
hypotheses and interpretation, 165–7

inappropriate sexual behaviors by children,
 75–6
indeterminacy, definition of, 266
inferential data, 51–2
informed consent, definition of, 266
informed consent agreements. *See also*
 Appendices B/C
 in child data collection, 147–9
 function of, 118, 125
 in parental data collection, 131–4
interparental relationships during divorce/
 separation, 46–7
interpretation, 163–73
 and child's special needs, 167–8
 conservative approach to, 172–3, 185–6
 co-parenting relationships, 170–1
 hypotheses
  alternative, 166–7
  analysis of, 165–6
  generation of, 165–6
 impact on parenting, 167
 model for interpretation, 163–5, 164*t*
 parent-child fit, 168–9
 special issues, 171
 structured approach to, 163–5
interviews
 of children
  about parents, 152–3
  age appropriate, 148–9, 152
  circumstances of, 127–8
  listing of topics, 150–1*t*
  sample questions, 154–5*t*
 of collateral contacts, 160
 of parents
  background information, 136–7
  BIC Standard, 147
  desired outcomes, 142–3
  identification of concerns/wishes, 141–2
  listing of topics, 134–5
  parenting activities/abilities, 141
  postseparation relationships, 139–40
  reports on children, 140–1
  spousal/couple relationships, 137–9
intimate partner aggression. *See* domestic
 abuse/violence

intimate terrorism. *See* coercive control
intimidation. *See* domestic abuse/violence
irrational alienation, 84–5

Johnston, J., 69, 73, 85–6, 88, 171
joint custody, 17, 18*t*, 89
journals, 202
judicial discretion. *See also* courts
 definition of, 266
 in family law cases, 5–6
 and maternal preference doctrine, 9
 variability of, 14, 19
jurisdiction, definition of, 266
juvenile courts, 9

Keilin, W., 92, 96, 97, 98–9*t*
Kelly, J., 63, 84, 85–6
KFD (House-Tree- Person/Kinetic Family
 Drawing), 98, 99*t*
Kirkland, K., 96
Kramer v. Kramer (1979), 10

LaFortune, K., 92
Lee, S., 73
legal context of custody, 3–29
 Best Interests of the Child (BIC)
  Standard, 14–20. *See also* Appendix A
 Addicks case, 7–8
 and decline of maternal preference, 10
 legal process, 20–3
 role of child custody examiner, 24–8
  as consultant, 28
  court-appointed evaluator, 26, 54
  as hired by attorney, 26–8
  as science expert, 27–8
 sociolegal history
  child support, 9
  maternal preference doctrine, 8–14
  modern divorce, 4, 5, 9, 11–4
  paternal dominance doctrine, 3–5, 6
  tender years doctrine, 5–8, 10–1
legal custody, definition of, 18*t*, 266
legal process, 20–3
Logan, T., 69
Lubet, S., 194

Maccoby, E., 195
maltreatment of children. *See* children
mandated reporter, 266
Maranganore, A., 69–70
Margo M. v. Martin S. (2006), 202
Martindale, D., 41–4, 175

Mason, M., 5–6
maternal preference doctrine, 6–7, 8–14
McCann, J., 101, 146
MCMI. *See* Millon Clinical Multiaxial
  Inventory (MCMI–II/III)
mediation, 21
Melton, G., 103, 187, 190
men/fathers. *See also* parents and parental
  issues
  alcohol use, 81
  child maltreatment allegations by, 73
  custody in never-married cases, 23
  postdivorce contact with children, 68
  sociolegal history of
  child support, 9
  paternal dominance doctrine, 3–5, 6
mental abuse, 70–2
mental health assessment. *See* forensic
  mental health assessment
Mercein v. People (1840), 8
Millon Clinical Multiaxial Inventory
  (MCMI–II/III), 98–9, 101, 144,
  145–6
Millon Adolescent Clinical Inventory
  (MACI), 99
mini-evaluations, 120
Minnesota Multiphasic Personality
  Inventory (MMPI and MMPI-2), 97,
  98*t*, 101–2, 143, 144, 145
Minnesota Multiphasic Personality
  Inventory for Adolescents (MMPI-A),
  99, 99*t*, 155
Minnesota Multiphasic Personality
  Inventory-2, Restructured Form
  (MMPI-2-RF), 101–2
Mnookin, R., 195
model agreements, 118. *See also*
  Appendices B/C
*Model Standards of Practice for Child
  Custody Evaluations* (AFCC), 34–5,
  36*t*, 37, 39–40, 118, 133, 263
modification requests, 23, 267
mothers. *See* women/mothers

National Association of Social Workers
  (NASW), 115
National Institute on Alcohol Abuse and
  Alcoholism (NIAAA), 80–1
neglect of children. *See* children
never-married parental circumstance,
  23, 60
nonmaleficence, 176

observational data, 51. *See also* data
  collection
Oleson, N., 73
Otto, R., 102–3, 104–5, 106

parallel parenting, 60, 267
parens patriae doctrine, 6, 13, 267
Parental Alienation Syndrome (PAS), 84–5
Parental Custody Index (PCI), 102–3
parent attributes
  definition of, 37–8, 267
  in forensic mental health assessment,
    37–40
  and child's psychological needs, 38–9
  co-parenting relationships, 40
  and resulting fit, 39–40
Parent Awareness Skills Survey (PASS),
  103–4, 107*t*
parent-child interaction
  assessment research on, 95
  observational data collection, 128
  evaluator role, 157
  home visits, 158–9
  in office setting, 157–8
  prior to child interviews, 149
  setting, 156–7
Parent-Child Relationship Inventory
  (PCRI), 106–8, 107*t*
Parenting Stress Index (PSI), 105–6, 107–8
parents and parental issues. *See also*
  children; men/fathers; women/
  mothers
  alienation/estrangement of, 84–8
  and attachment, 86
  definition of, 84–6, 263
  prevalence of, 86–7
  remedial challenges, 87–8
  de facto parent, 265
  divorce
    demographics of, 59–61
    geographic stability during, 91
    impact on children, 63–8, 75, 86–7
    interparental relationships during, 46–7
    legal process of, 20–3
    and psychological aggression, 72
  friendly parent doctrine, 26–7
  parallel parenting, 60, 267
  parent education, 20–1
  parenting capacity/ability
    definition of, 267
    in forensic mental health assessment,
      41–9

parenting plans
 and attachment theory, 90
 definition of, 267
 examples of, 21
 and outcomes for children, 88–91
 postdivorce, 68
 psychiatric disorders of
 impact on children, 78–80
 impact on parenting, 78
 prevalence of, 77–8
 psychological testing of, 143–6
 substance abuse of, 80–4
 impact on children, 74, 82–3
 treatment issues, 83–4
PAS (Parental Alienation Syndrome), 84–5
PASS (Parent Awareness Skills Survey),
 103–4, 107*t*
paternal dominance doctrine, 3–5, 6
paternity and custody in never-married
 cases, 23
pathological alienation, 84–5
PCI (Parental Custody Index), 102–3
PCRI (Parent-Child Relationship
 Inventory), 106–8, 107*t*
Perception of Relationships Test (PORT),
 104, 107*t*
Personality Assessment Inventory (PAI),
 99–100, 101, 144
Personality Inventory for Children
 (PIC), 156
personality tests, 97–100, 98–9*t*
physical custody, definition of, 18*t*, 266
PORT (Perception of Relationships Test),
 104, 107*t*
post-traumatic stress disorder in children,
 69, 74
poverty, 9, 13
*Practice Parameters for Child Custody
 Evaluations* (AACAP), 35, 36*t*,
 38–40, 53
practice standards, 113–5. *See also specific
 standards*
Prather v. Prather (1809), 6–7
preparation for evaluations. *See* evaluation
 preparation
primary caretaker standard, 18, 267
*Principles of Medical Ethics with
 Annotations Especially Applicable to
 Psychiatry*, 115
privilege, definition of, 267
professional guidelines chart, 33–7, 36–7*t*.
 See also specific guidelines

professionalism of reports, 193–4
projective drawing tasks, 98
pro-se litigants
 challenges of, 23
 contacting of, 124, 125
 definition of, 267
PSI (Parenting Stress Index), 105–6,
 107–8
psychiatric disorders. *See under* parents and
 parental issues
psycho-legal concepts
 definition of, 33, 267
 in forensic mental health assessment,
 33–7
psychological abuse, 70–2
psychological aggression, 70–2, 267
psychological needs of child, assessment of,
 38–9, 43–5
psychological testing
 of children, 153–6
 choice of instruments, 143–4
 of parents, 143–6
 in reports, 192
 research on, 97–102

qualifications of examiners. *See* examiners
Quinnell, F., 92–4, 95, 96, 97, 98–9*t*, 100,
 107, 190–1

readability of reports, 189–90
referral questions, 116–8, 120, 136
releases, required signatures, 133
religion and child custody evaluations, 61–2
removal/relocation/move-away cases, 123,
 140–1, 268
report writing and testimony, 175–208.
 See also Appendix D
 child custody testimony, 195–208
 absence of attorney collaboration, 198
 case law, 200–3
 credibility tips, 204–7
 depositions, 196–7
 evaluator neutrality, 198
 infrequency of, 195
 lack of feedback, 198–9
 qualifications of experts, 203–4
 timeframe of, 197
 types of witnesses, 199–200
 uniqueness of data, 197
 expert witness testimony, 194–5
 psycho-legal reports, 175
 audiences of, 180–2

report writing and testimony (*Continued*)
  psycho-legal reports (*Continued*)
    child data, 184
    collateral data, 185
    credibility, 192–3
    effects of, 178–80
    functions of, 177–8
    interpretation of data, 185–6
    orientation section, 183
    parent data, 183–4
    professionalism of, 193–4
    readability of, 189–90
    recommendations, 186–9
    transparency of process, 191–2
    user-friendliness of, 190–1
research literature. *See* empirical
  foundations/limits; *specific authors*
resilience, definition of, 268
restraining orders, 122, 124, 139–40
resulting fit. *See* fit
retainers, 118, 124, 125–6, 268
risk/resilience in children of divorce, 66–8
Robb v. Robb (2004), 202
Roberts Apperception Test, 99*t*, 155
Rohrbaugh, J., 105, 157–8, 176, 190
Rorschach Inkblot Test, 97–8, 99*t*, 101,
  146, 155

safety concerns, 124, 126–7
Schutz, B., 190
separation-instigated violence, 71
sexual abuse of children, 72–6, 130
situational couple violence, 71–2, 264
Smith v. Tierney (2005), 202
S.M. v. G.M. (2005), 201
social workers, 115
sociolegal history of child custody. *See* legal
  context of custody
sole physical custody, 17, 18*t*
special master, definition of, 268
Specialty Guidelines for Forensic Psychologists
  (APLS), 115, 190
state of the science experts, 27–8
states
  approximation rule, 20
  child support funding, 9
  disuse of tender years doctrine, 10–1
  domestic violence as best interest factor, 69
  friendly parent doctrine, 170–1
  joint custody, 16–8
  laws on batterers and custody, 138
  model parenting plans, 89

  and UMDA provisions, 15–6, 114
  use of attorney GALs, 21
stipulation, definition of, 268
Stress Index for Parents of Adolescents
  (SIPA), 106
Stuart, R., 62–3
substance abuse. *See under* parents and
  parental issues

tender years doctrine, 5–8, 10–1, 268
testimonial privilege, definition of, 267
testimony, 134, 268. *See also* report writing
  and testimony
Thematic Apperception Test (TAT), 98,
  99*t*, 155
Tilghman, William, 7
time demands, 121
Tippins, T. M., 51
transparency of process, in reports, 191–2
trials, 195, 198–9
tribal warfare, use of term, 171

understandability of reports, 191
Uniform Marriage and Divorce Act of
  1970 (UMDA), 15, 114
user-friendliness of reports, 190–1

validity in testing, 144–5
violent resistance to domestic abuse, 71
voir dire process, 202
volunteer lawyers, 23

Walker, R., 69, 86
Wallerstein, J., 63, 84
Walters, M., 73
Warshak, R., 85
Watts v. Watts (1973), 10
Weissman, H., 37
witnesses, 194–5, 199–200, 265
Wittman, J., 51
women/mothers. *See also* parents and
  parental issues
  alcohol use, 81
  child maltreatment allegations by, 73
  custody in never-married cases, 23
  and domestic violence, 70–1
  sociolegal history of
    absence of legal rights, 3–5
    maternal preference doctrine, 6–7, 8–14
W. v. J., Matter of (2005), 202

Zelechoski, A., 93–4, 100

About the Authors

Geri S. W. Fuhrmann, PsyD, is Associate Professor of Psychiatry and Pediatrics, Director of Child and Family Forensic Center, at the University of Massachusetts Medical School. Child and Family Forensic Center is a clinical and teaching center within the Department of Psychiatry and provides evaluations for courts when legal decisions affect the lives of children. Dr. Fuhrmann co-authored *Parents Apart*®, a parent education program for separating parents, which has been nationally recognized for its sensitivity to issues of domestic violence. She received the Manual Carballo Governor's Award for Excellence in Public Service (2001), the highest award bestowed by the governor. Her clinical interests and areas of practice focus on child forensic psychology—particularly parenting after separation, domestic violence, and the impact of parental separation on children (especially those with special needs)—and pediatric psychology. She conducts and supervises forensic evaluations pertaining to child custody, consults, and works as a parenting coordinator for separated parents. In addition to training and consulting locally, Dr. Fuhrmann is a frequent presenter on issues relevant to child custody at regional and national conferences.

Robert A. Zibbell, PhD, is a psychologist in independent practice with Tananbaum & Zibbell, P.C., in Framingham, MA. He performs evaluations of families who litigate disputes over their children in family court. He also works as a parenting coordinator with divorced or non-marital parents, assisting them to resolve ongoing child-related disputes. He has authored publications about issues relevant to these areas of professional practice. In different venues over the past 20 years, he has presented on assessment and practice issues in local and national conferences and has provided training to family court probation officers, mental health professionals, family law attorneys, and judicial officers.